PROPERTY RIGHTS AND POVERTY

THOMAS A. HORNE

Property Rights and Poverty

Political Argument in Britain,

1605–1834

The University of North Carolina Press

Chapel Hill and London

©1990 The University of North Carolina Press

All rights reserved

Manufactured in the United States of America

The paper in this book meets the guidelines for permanence and
durability of the Committee on Production Guidelines for Book
Longevity of the Council on Library Resources.

Library of Congress Cataloging-in-Publication Data

94 93 92 91 90   5 4 3 2 1

Horne, Thomas A. (Thomas Allen), 1947–
    Property rights and poverty : political argument in Britain,
1605–1834 / by Thomas A. Horne.
        p. cm.
    Includes bibliographical references.
    ISBN 0-8078-1912-3 (alk. paper)
    1. Right of property—Great Britain—History.   2. Welfare rights
movement—Great Britain—History.   3. Political science—Great
Britain—History.   I. Title.
JC605.H67   1990
330.1'7—dc20
                                                    89-77791
                                                        CIP

Portions of this work appeared earlier, in somewhat different form, as
"Economic and Moral Improvement: Francis Hutcheson on
Property," *History of Political Thought* 8, no. 1 (1987), reprinted by
permission of the publisher; "Welfare Rights as Property Rights: An
Historical Perspective," in *Responsibility, Rights, and Welfare*, ed.
J. Donald Moon (Boulder, Colo., 1988), reprinted by permission of
Westview Press; and "The Poor Have a Claim Founded on the Law of
Nature: William Paley and the Rights of the Poor," *Journal of the
History of Philosophy* 23, no. 1 (Jan. 1985), copyright 1985 by the
Journal of the History of Philosophy, reprinted by permission of
the journal.

TO

Emily and Abigail

CONTENTS

ACKNOWLEDGMENTS

A number of scholars have read this manuscript and made suggestions for its improvement. Eldon Eisenach, Julian Franklin, Richard Teichgraeber, and Cheryl Welch were kind enough to read it in its entirety. The attention they paid to the manuscript and the invaluable criticisms they made have put me deeply in their debt. I also want to thank Joseph Kestner, Michael Mosher, and Paul Rahe, colleagues of mine at the University of Tulsa, for reading parts of the manuscript and for their lively and learned conversation. Leann Anderson typed the manuscript and for that I am most grateful. Without the support and patience of my wife, Kathryn, I would never have been able to finish this project.

Fellowship support from the National Endowment for the Humanities enabled me to spend the academic year 1986–87 working full time on the manuscript. Summer stipends from the University of Tulsa provided support in 1984 and 1985.

Some of the arguments presented here first appeared in essay form. "The Poor Have a Claim Founded on the Law of Nature: William Paley and the Rights of the Poor" was published by the *Journal of the History of Philosophy* 23, no. 1 (1985); "Economic and Moral Improvement: Francis Hutcheson on Property" was published by the *History of Political Thought* 8, no. 1 (1987); and "Welfare Rights as Property Rights" was included in J. Donald Moon, ed., *Responsibility, Rights, and Welfare* (Boulder, Colo.: 1988). I thank publishers and editors for permission to reprint.

PROPERTY RIGHTS AND POVERTY

Genesis 1:26   And God said, Let us make man in our image, after our likeness; and let them have dominion over the fish of the sea, and over the fowl of the air, and over the cattle, and over all the earth, and over every creeping thing that creepeth upon the earth.

27   So God created man in his own image, in the image of God created he him; male and female created he them.

28   And God blessed them, and God said unto them, Be fruitful, and multiply, and fill the earth, and subdue it; and have dominion over the fish of the sea, and the fowl of the air, and over every living thing that moveth over the earth.

29   And God said, Behold, I have given you every herb bearing seed, which is upon the face of all the earth, and every tree, in which is the fruit of a tree yielding seed; to you it shall be for food.

30   And to every beast of the earth, and to every fowl of the air, and to every thing that creepeth upon the earth, wherein there is life, I have given every green herb for food: and it was so.

31   And God saw everything that he had made, and, behold, it was very good. And the evening and the morning were the sixth day.

B etween 1605, when Hugo Grotius first wrote to defend common access to the open seas, and 1834, when the English Parliament passed the New Poor Law to limit access to public assistance, property rights were at the center of political debates over who should be included and who should be excluded from the benefits of political and economic life. Because these disputes concerned situations in which the legal rights of municipal law were absent, under attack, or in need of moral justification, they took place within the language of natural law or natural rights. To think of people as the possessors of rights, especially to think of them as holding property rights before the establishment of government, is a characteristic of liberal political thought. Thus the focus of this study will be on the nature of that broad and diverse tradition.

I begin with Grotius because he was thought, at least by his British readers, to have virtually created the modern natural law vocabulary through which natural rights and duties, especially those concerning property, became central to political argument. By 1834 the argument over property rights had taken on a form recognizably contemporary, and it is for that reason that I will end with the debates over the changes in the English Poor Law that were enacted that year. Demands that public assistance be abolished, limited, or expanded as well as more radical demands that workers own the factories in which they labored anticipate the politics of liberal welfare states in the late twentieth century.

This study is not a history of the way property rights were widely understood among the various groups in British society, nor is it a legal history of property rights in common or statute law, nor is it concerned with the relationship between property and the development of a civic personality that was at the heart of the civic humanist tradition. Its focus is on the books and essays published mostly in Britain during this period that attempted to analyze property rights, usually in an effort to contribute to political argument. Both the particular historical contexts that prompted authors to write about property rights in the language of natural law and the more general, transhistorical, and common features that came with thinking about property in this way are considered. Just as authors were shaped by the language of natural law they used, they reshaped it to accomplish their ends before passing it on to others. But it was a relatively coherent tradition that continued to be passed on, one capable of shaping and constraining argument, even of those (such as Jeremy Bentham and his followers) who sought to free themselves from it.

To grasp the nature, strength, and breadth of this tradition, it is necessary to consider many more theorists than the few who normally make up the canon in the history of liberal political thought. The meaning of property rights emerged from a discussion that included essayists, philosophers, economists, paternalists, and radicals, as well as liberal political theorists. John Locke, Thomas Paine, and Jeremy Bentham appear, to be sure, but so do Richard Cumberland, Thomas Reid, William Paley, John Thelwall, Jane Marcet, Mountifort Longfield, and many more. The disadvantage of this approach is that it makes it difficult to look at the complex ideas of the few most significant theorists with all the detail that might be desired. On the other hand, it provides an opportunity to see how the seminal theorists (such as Locke) were read and interpreted, sometimes in surprising ways, by others writing about property rights. Even more important, this approach is the only way to appreciate the diversity of interpretation within the modern natural law tradition and to gain a more solid basis for generalizing about the meaning of natural property rights in English-speaking political thought.

The intellectual history of property rights that was embedded within the political thought of this period passed through several stages. That this should have occurred is not surprising considering the changes that took place between 1605 and 1834 in the issues and groups that dominated political discussion. In particular, I note the way the analysis of property rights was tied to the needs of mercantilist economic policy, the requirements of peace and political order, the struggles over representative institutions, the attempts to spur economic growth in Scotland and England, the desire to protect those who were hurt by or left out of that growth, and the more radical demands that wage earners share equitably in the growing wealth they created. Each of these contexts called forth a particular interpretation of what it meant to have a property right.

But though there is a great deal of diversity in the way property rights were understood and used throughout this period, there is continuity in the way these discussions revolved around the same conceptual difficulty.

They all had to find some way to express the two necessarily intertwined aspects of property rights in the natural law tradition—the right under some circumstances to exclude others from the control and use of resources and the right under other conditions to be included in the use of resources necessary for life or livelihood. Though these rights are now separated into those to property and those to welfare, in the tradition of analysis presented here both were property rights, one exclusive and the other inclusive or common.

Discussions about the correct meaning of property rights—the balance that should exist between the exclusive and inclusive aspects of property—continue to play a central role in the political arguments of contemporary liberal welfare states. Not surprisingly, this has meant that historical reconstructions of the place of property rights in a liberal tradition that is more or less our own often have been taken to have consequences for current debates. However much this may be objected to as violating the distinction between history and philosophy, it seems to me to be an inevitable part of our political debate, indeed, of the debates of any people who think of themselves as part of a historical community, and better faced squarely than ignored. Let me, then, briefly set out the relationship between current and historical understanding and the way the history of property rights presented in this book might bear on our understanding of a liberal tradition.

As the intellectual history of this period has often been written, political theorists in the seventeenth century came to stress, to a new and unprecedented degree, the legitimate ability of owners to do what they wanted with their property and to exclude others from its use. As a result, the idea of rights to common property or resources owned by all became less important. This new attitude toward property rights has been taken to mark the beginning of liberal political thought and to have continued as the center of liberalism through the nineteenth century. Only if an owner had the ability to act freely from the interference of others could the historic goals of liberalism—limited government and unfettered economic activity—be accomplished.

Many liberals have continued to argue that for the values of freedom and individualism to be realized, people must be understood to have property in themselves, which enables them to exclude others from the use of their talents, abilities, and labor, as well as in the goods they acquire in a free economic market. "The defence of private property," John Gray has written, "is one that connects it with the autonomy of the individual—his ability to effectively implement his life plans—and not just with negative liberty. One may even say that, whereas the constitutional framework of a liberal order protects the basic liberties in their formal or negative form, it is private property that embodies them in their material or positive form."[1] On this view, the liberal welfare state seems without intellectual coherence and, perhaps worse, a step down the road to socialism. For at the same time that it protects private property, it limits the exercise of property rights. Or, put another way, it enforces the welfare claims of some to use resources it otherwise defends as privately owned. The view that the welfare state was without coherent foundations was behind the development of the distinction between classical and modern or welfare liberalism. The purpose of such a distinction has always been to deny a continuity between the foundations of liberalism as they were established in the seventeenth, eighteenth, and nineteenth centuries and the interventionist and redistributivist policies of the welfare states in the twentieth century.

In response to these criticisms, defenders of the welfare state, eager to maintain its continuity with a long-standing liberal tradition, deny that exclusive property rights have ever been constitutive of liberal freedom. If "life, liberty, and property" has been the rallying cry of liberal politics, it may be important that property was mentioned last. In conflicts between these values, then, there would be nothing illiberal about a representative government overriding individual property rights for the better realization of life and liberty. Property rights take on even less importance if equality is added to the list of values traditionally at the center of liberal concerns. As L. T. Hobhouse wrote early in the century, "To maintain individual freedom and equality we have to extend the sphere of social control. . . . We must not assume any of the rights of property as axiomatic. We must look at their actual working and consider how they affect the life of society."[2] The argument that rights to property can be balanced against other rights, however, assumes an understanding of property rights that allows them to be balanced. That is, it denies exclusive property rights a special status among the rights liberals want to protect and as a result begins with assumptions libertarian liberals would reject.

The libertarian insistence that strong individual rights to property have been at the historical center of a liberal tradition has been seconded by many of liberalism's critics. They have always argued that because liberalism was devoted to individual property rights it was incapable of understanding and expressing the opportunities of a life lived with others in a community. Of course, the individualism that property rights make possible for the libertarian is characterized by the communitarian or socialist critic as atomistic or possessive individualism. Karl Marx summarized the way liberalism's critics have understood the liberal attitude toward private property rights when he wrote in the 1840s, "The right of property is the right to enjoy one's fortune and to dispose of it as one will, without regard for other men and independently of society. It is the right of self interest. . . . None of the supposed rights of man, therefore, go beyond the egoistic man, man as he is, as a member of civil society: that is, an individual separated from the community, withdrawn into himself, wholly preoccupied with his private interest and acting in accordance with his private caprice."[3]

The argument of this book is that both the libertarian defense and the communitarian criticism of a liberal theory of property rights miss the mark. And that is not just because property is only one of the values that liberalism has defended, though that is certainly true. Rather, it is because the liberal understanding of property, especially during the classic period of liberal theorizing covered in this book, always contained both inclusive and exclusive (or common and individual) elements. The limitation of exclusive individual rights in the name of claims to be included in the use of resources occurred, then, within the logic of a liberal property right and not only through the sacrifice of property to democracy, liberty, the common good, or some other values. Virtually every defense of the right to exclude written during this period carried with it a self-limiting feature under which exclusion could no longer legitimately occur. Thus, though the tradition under consideration here defended individual rights to property as consistent with, even required by, natural law, it also insisted that all individuals had a right, at least under some circumstances, to the use of the resources that were necessary to their welfare. The right to exclude and the right to be included were not understood to be necessarily contradictory or antagonistic interpretations of a just property arrangement. The problem of liberal property rights was and is to find ways to recognize both aspects of the right to property. How to include as many as possible in property ownership, the conditions under which people in need could legitimately invoke their inclusive or welfare rights, and the level of welfare their rights entailed are the issues posed by this way of thinking. The inclusive right to property has a history, then, just as the right to exclude does. In fact, they are equally part of a continuous liberal history—a history within which we still live—which cannot be understood if either is ignored. The intellectual history presented in this book suggests that the liberal welfare state's legal recognition of rights to welfare is the realization of aspirations long held and of moral values deeply ingrained and that so far from being at odds with the liberal tradition of private property rights, it is instead the fulfillment of that tradition.

ONE

The Natural Right to Property
Grotius to Pufendorf

In the sixteenth and seventeenth centuries two great social movements occurred that made the philosophical analysis of property a political necessity. The first, European exploration and discovery, brought with it an expansion in international trade that engendered conflicts over colonies and trade routes. The issues raised by this expansion included the extent to which the ocean could be claimed as a nation's property, how the more advanced nations could come to own land inhabited by less developed people, and how these people could become the property (slaves) of Europeans. The theories of legitimate and illegitimate acquisition that were developed to answer these questions also played a role in the discussions of just war that were part of the attempt to bring order to a period of considerable upheaval. The second movement that brought importance to the concept of property was the struggle between absolutist rulers and representative institutions. Since this conflict almost always took as one of its forms an argument over taxation, interpretations of the natural right to property became central to political debate.

The initial arguments over the legitimacy of the European conquests took place in Spain. Francisco de Vitoria asked in a lecture he gave in 1537 "by what right the barbarians [American Indians] had come under the rule of the Spaniards."[1] His answer to this question was noteworthy because he relied on neither papal jurisdiction nor Roman law but on natural rights, especially those to property. Vitoria was followed in this line of argument most importantly by two Jesuits, Luis de Molina and Francisco Suarez. But though the intellectual achievement of these Spanish jurists was considerable, their works were not part of the British discussion on natural law and natural property rights. The analysis of natural law upon which they drew began with the Dutch lawyer Hugo Grotius, whose work was largely uninformed by the insights of the Spanish school. Adam Smith's opinion, that "Grotius seems to have been the first who attempted to give the world any thing like a regular system of natural jurisprudence," was widely shared.[2]

In the half-century after Grotius published his masterpiece, *The Rights of War and Peace* (1625), John Selden, Thomas Hobbes, Richard Cumberland, and Samuel Pufendorf all published their classic texts on the laws and rights of nature. Although there were important political and philosophical differences between these writers, their enterprise with regard to property was much more unified. Not only did it seek to answer the same theoretical question—how could God's grant of the earth to all mankind be consistent with exclusive private rights to property—but it also shared a common orientation. That is, all of these philosophers accepted the legitimacy of private property in general and, more specifically, the distribution of property that existed in their society. Their task was to demonstrate the consistency between the property rights of their society and the principles of natural law. Their disagreements typically took the form of pointing out the possible weaknesses in their opponents' defense of the status quo and the way their own formulations provided even stronger bulwarks to the social edifice. Only a deeply felt sense of the fragility of the social system, not surprising in the seventeenth century, explains the importance these writers attached to even the most technical issues in the philosophical analysis of property. Leonard Krieger's comment that Pufendorf's "whole purpose was to represent existing institutions as logical deductions from the moral and political theory that validated social life in general" is appropriately applied to all of the writers considered in this chapter, at least with regard to the institution of property.[3] To accomplish their purpose, they all made the preservation of human life central to their moral and political theory.

Grotius and Selden

Hugo Grotius (1583–1645) was born in Delft and educated at universities in Leiden and Paris. Among his contemporaries, he was most famous for having generated his rights theory almost entirely without theological assumptions. Neither God's will nor God's law was at the center of his understanding of natural law. Instead, he built upon the foundation of man's innate sociability and consequent desire for peace. Since God had created man, he could write that "the mother of natural law is human nature itself."[4] Thus he understood civil societies as created by individuals through the use of contracts for the purpose of protecting their rights and bringing peace to their communities. "For the design of society is that one should quietly enjoy his own, with the help and by the united force of the whole community" (pp. 25–26). That his rights theory ended in a defense of absolutism and slavery, as these situations were understood as legitimate resignations of individual rights, similarly led to controversy. The combination of rights theory and absolutism has led a number of recent commentators to refer to his work as "janus faced," a characterization also appropriate to parts of his property theory.[5]

The incident that occasioned Grotius's consideration of property is well known.[6] The Dutch and Portuguese were competing for trade in the Indian Ocean. The Portuguese claimed a monopoly in that trade. In 1603 a ship of the Dutch East India Company captured a Portuguese ship and its rich cargo. Against an outcry over that action, particularly by Mennonite shareholders in the Dutch East India Company, Grotius was hired by the directors to write a defense of the lawfulness of the seizure. The result was *De Jure Praedae* (*On the Law of Prize*), written in 1605 but not published until it was discovered by accident in 1864. Chapter 12 of that work, however, was published in 1609 under the title *Mare Liberum* (*Freedom of the Seas*). To argue that the Dutch captain's seizure was a just act in a just war, Grotius held that the monopoly claims of the Portuguese were illegitimate and that those claims and the actions based on them constituted an injury to Dutch traders. The basis of his position was that the open seas could not be made private property. His analysis, then, sought an understanding of the right to make property private as much to limit as to defend the use of that right. As we shall see, both Pufendorf and Jean Barbeyrac objected to Grotius's account of property on the grounds that it did not sufficiently stress the conceptual requirement that property entailed the right to exclude others. In most important respects Grotius's theory of property remained unchanged from his early concern with this incident to *De Jure Belli ac Pacis* (*The Rights of War and Peace*) and its more general concern for just war and international order.

In *The Rights of War and Peace* Grotius considered the origin of property rights as he explicated one of the causes of a just war, the recovery of property or a debt. Individuals, he argued, can have property rights in two different ways. In their capacity as individuals they can own private property, while as members of mankind they participate in common rights, which they share with others, to property that has not or cannot be legitimately made private (p. 141). A private or exclusive claim to some part of the open seas, Grotius tried to show, violated the common rights in which the Dutch shared. Such a claim literally took property that belonged to the Dutch and others. The clear implication was that war could be made justly upon a country that acted on these claims to punish it and to recover the property its citizens had taken.

Grotius began his analysis with God's grant to mankind of dominion over the earth and all it contained. The interpretation of this grant began most discussions of property in the natural law tradition and was the center of great controversy. Grotius interpreted this grant as making all mankind the inheritors of one general patrimony. In the earliest stages of human history, when people were few, friendly, and had a minimum of needs or wants, individuals simply took from this patrimony what they needed. And during the time they used or consumed what they had taken, they had a right that it was unjust for another to deprive them of: "Almighty God at the Creation, and again at the deluge, gave to mankind in general a dominion over things of this inferior world. . . . From thence it was, that every man converted what he would to his own use, and consumed whatever was to be consumed; and such a use of the right common to all men did at that time supply the place of property, for no man could justly take from another, what he had thus taken to himself" (pp. 142–43). Grotius likened this situation to that described by Cicero in his famous theater analogy. Cicero argued that though the seats of a public theater were common property, all theatergoers had a right to the seats they occupied during the performance. It is important for the history of property rights that Grotius thought that a right could be created simply by the individual's seizure. This was, however, only a use right, it could occur only in a situation of abundance, and it could last only as long as use lasted.

Complete property rights—ones that extended beyond use—became necessary as the original conditions of friendship, simplicity, and abundance gave way to discord, desire, and scarcity (p. 145). The psychological characteristics associated with the Fall and the rivalry between Cain and Abel—jealousy, murder, lust, and ambition—destroyed the original, spontaneous respect each had for the appropriation of others. Property rights were first required for movables. Later, an increase in both population and desires that prompted some to work hard and others to hope to consume without working required property rights in land. Without pushing the theater analogy too far, it is easy to see how unnecessary assigned seats would be if the theater were large, the spectators few, and their friendship (willingness to let others have the best seats) great. Some assignments would become necessary even if the spectators remained few but became ambitious or jealous, each satisfied only with the best seat. The necessity of assigned seats would become crucial as the number of theatergoers increased. Property rights were needed, according to Grotius, to moderate conflict between ambitious individuals over scarce resources. Thus Grotius argued that life could be preserved in a situation of abundance only if people could use the fruits of the earth undisturbed and in a situation of scarcity only if everyone respected established boundaries. Rights enabled people to live together in peace.

Rights could not be acquired in ways that were incapable of reducing conflict. For example, property rights had to be publicly known. Grotius emphasized that neither internal acts (because others cannot know them) nor simply seeing something (which can be done by many at once, among other problems) could convey to an individual a property right. Here he was challenging claims to owning islands that were merely sighted or on which only a little time was spent.

But though use rights were established by individual acts, property rights were based on a general agreement that divided what was already possessed among the parties (probably allowing all to keep what they had) and that stipulated that what was unoccupied at the time of the contract should become the property of the first person to seize it. In one of the most important passages in the intellectual history of property rights, Grotius wrote:

> Thus also we see what was the original of property, which was derived not from a mere internal act of the mind, since one could not possibly guess what others intended to appropriate to themselves, that he might abstain from it; and besides several might have a mind to the same thing, at the same time; but it resulted from a certain compact and agreement, either expressly, as by a division; or else tacitly, as by seizure. For as soon as living in common was no longer approved of, all men were supposed, and ought to be supposed to have consented, that each should appropriate to himself, by right of first possession, what could not have been divided. (Pp. 145–46)

Unfortunately, it is not easy to disentangle the relative importance of agreement and possession or occupation in this formulation. To what extent did agreement alone turn possessions into property? To what extent must possession or occupation bring forth agreement?[7] Since the rights to use that preceded property rights were based on individual seizures and the terms of the contract were that thereafter first possession would confer on individuals full property rights, no less an authority than Pufendorf virtually ignored the contractual element and saw this theory as based on possession.

Because individual property rights in goods and land promoted preservation and peace, the ability of people to live together as God intended, they were consistent with, indeed, demanded by, natural law. But having sketched the origin of a natural right, Grotius simultaneously set out the limits of that right. Things remained subject to common rights if their private appropriation was not possible (because a publicly recognizable possession was impossible) or was not required for peace (because they were not scarce and could be enjoyed by all without conflict). Grotius's point was to show that the open seas fell into that class of things that could not be privately appropriated and that the attempt to do so was an injury to others who had a common right not to be excluded from a resource that could be used by all without inconvenience. The private appropriation of the seas, he maintained, was not necessary for peace, nor was it possible to occupy an unconfined fluid in constant motion (pp. 147–48).

The Portuguese claims to monopolize the trade of the Indian Ocean were illegitimate. They were attempts to make private what was common. It is important that Grotius's argument worked best if the ocean were understood as owned by all, rather than as simply unowned. To use a distinction crucial to Pufendorf, and to all who wrote after him, Grotius probably should be understood as thinking of the ocean as a positive community rather than a negative community.[8] Thus the ocean was unaffected by the contract that divided goods already possessed and allowed first possession to make private the goods that remained. It continued in that state of common ownership that characterized the original grant from God. The just cause of war used by Grotius against the Portuguese was the recovery of property, which implied that the Dutch were part owners of the ocean which the Portuguese were trying to take.

Grotius's understanding that the world was once owned by everyone through their common rights helps to explain why he insisted on a presumption in favor of common property and equality. Every time something was individually appropriated, everyone else lost what was once theirs as well as the opportunity to appropriate what was unowned. Now this loss would be agreed to, presumably, because it was more than offset by the benefits of private property—peace and incentives to industry. But when these benefits did not accompany private possession, Grotius limited the right to exclude others even from property that had in other respects been made private. He referred to the original contract that established property to express this point and argued that it must have been the intention of those who first introduced property to deviate as little as possible from the rules of natural equity. Thus he thought difficulties in interpreting both customary and written laws ought to be settled by reference to mankind's original equality (p. 149).

One of the most important examples of the way this presumption worked in favor of common rights was the case of individual necessity or dire need. In these circumstances, "that ancient right of using things, as if they still remained common, must revive, and be in full force: for in all laws of human institutions, and consequently, in that of property too, such cases seem to be excepted" (p. 149). This right included the ability to demolish a neighbor's house to keep a fire from spreading, to cut the nets that entangled a ship, and to take property from another and not be guilty of theft in order to preserve oneself from starvation. It is important that this right was not derived by Grotius from an obligation to be charitable but from an interpretation of the logic of the original contract that established property rights. In the case of starvation, however, Grotius insisted that the magistrate must be asked for aid before a private owner was asked and that only if both refused assistance were the ancient common rights revived and the individual able to take whatever was necessary. He added that the owner must be repaid as soon as possible. But it remained important that for Grotius, one aspect of the right to property was the right to use what was necessary for self-preservation, a right to be included in the fruits of the earth given by God to everyone.

In the case of extreme necessity, the presumption in favor of common property completely elided the right to private property. In many other cases this presumption worked to limit individual rights. The principle Grotius seemed to use was that people had a right to use the property of another if that use caused no detriment to the owner. Grotius first considered situations in which scarcity did not exist. Individuals had a right to light their fires by using someone else's, they had a right to drink in someone's river, and in most cases they had a right to free passage through another's land. This last right was used to legitimate European incursions into the territory of less developed people. It also meant that nations could not rightfully impose a duty on goods that passed over their land, unless such passage caused expenses to be incurred. But in this case the duty ought only to raise enough money to compensate for the costs. Moreover, strangers expelled from their country had a right to settle in unoccupied parts of another country (pp. 149–58).

The length of the shadows cast by inclusive or common rights over private rights can be seen in two other questions of commerce. With regard to the selling of food, clothing, and medicine, goods clearly necessary for self-preservation, Grotius maintained that "everyone has a right of buying these at a reasonable rate" (p. 155). This injunction also came into play in the question of the legitimacy of monopolizing colonial trade, that is, of reaching an "agreement" whereby one country agreed to sell all of its products to a single foreign country. Such a monopoly was not unjust, Grotius argued, so long as the buying country was willing to sell the products of its colonial trade to all others at a reasonable price. The Portuguese complaint that competition would lower their profits showed that they were violating this rule and selling the goods they obtained from their colonies at exorbitant prices. "Monopolists of overseas trade," Grotius concluded in *Mare Liberum*, "are as criminal as monopolist speculators in grain."[9] But this limit seemed to apply only to necessities and to fall away when the product of the trade was a luxury, "a matter of mere profit" (pp. 158, 304).

The way Grotius's interpretation of natural law simultaneously defended and limited rights to property can be seen in his discussion of wills and testaments. It was in the "very nature of property," he wrote, to have the "power of disposing of, or transferring, all or any part of their effects to other persons" (p. 214). Last testaments were justified under this rule, for he understood them as transferring property to another while retaining until death the rights to possess and enjoy the property. The importance of the owner's intention meant that the property of those who died intestate should go to the persons to whom they would have most likely left it (p. 220). Yet natural law also limited wills. First, children had a right to inherit that part of their parent's estate that was equal to what was necessary for their "maintenance" (not the entire estate); and second, under natural law all the children, not just sons or the first son, should inherit (p. 225).

We can begin to understand the relationship between natural right and municipal law in Grotius by noting that after he set out the natural rules for the succession of property he added that they could all be set aside by civil law. Nor was this an isolated case. For example, though monopolies (of luxury goods) did not necessarily violate natural law, so that individuals had a natural right to enter into the agreements that created them, monopolies could be legitimately prohibited by civil law, if that served the public good. Similarly, though animals, fish, and birds were by natural law in common, so that each individual had a natural right to become their owner by catching them, civil law could restrain this liberty and enable only one person or a few people to catch and own them (p. 250). These three examples help make clear that Grotius did not think of natural rights as necessarily limiting the actions of a government toward its citizens. In fact, in the example of the right to wild animals, Grotius was explicitly arguing against those who maintained that civil laws limiting this right were illegitimate. Natural law, Grotius wrote in reply to this argument, applied only in cases when civil law was silent.

The relationship Grotius thought existed between natural law and civil law is easier to understand if we remember that his goal was to moderate international conflict by limiting both the frequency of war and its most barbaric acts. His problem was to find standards to apply to the international setting, which was defined by the absence of civil law, and his solution was to fill this absence with natural law. His method was based on accepting the legitimacy of civil codes, surveying them for similarities, and then applying the principles he found behind these similarities to international relations in the form of natural law. His identification of natural law with the law of nations was summarized in his quoting with approval the saying of Heraclitus, "That is certain, which universally appears to be so" (though Grotius added, "at least among very civilized nations") (p. 114).

It was not that natural law and natural rights did not apply to all people and all times—they did. But because of the importance of the obligation under natural law to obey one's contracts, natural law applied in civil society primarily to validate the contracts people had made with one another and with their sovereign. Thus the creation of a state required giving to the sovereign the right to raise taxes and regulate property in the public interest. The natural right to property, then, did not extend to granting the individual a right to exclude the public power of the community:

Right strictly taken is again of two sorts, either private and inferior, which tends to the particular advantage of each individual: or eminent and superior, such as a community has over the person and estates of all its members for the common benefit, and therefore it excels the former. Thus a regal power is above that of a father and master; a king has a greater right in the goods of his subjects for the public advantage, than the proprietors themselves. And when the exigencies of the state require a supply, every man is more obliged to contribute towards it, than to satisfy his creditors. (Pp. 4–5)

The enormous importance Grotius gave to contracts explains his tolerance for constitutional variety, the reason he could write that "a people may choose what form of government they please" (p. 64). The obligation to contracts was essential to his desire for peace. It stood behind every government's ability to bring order to its territory, and it legitimized international treaties, particularly those ending war. But it also led him in *The Rights of War and Peace* to argue that individuals could sell themselves into slavery, fathers could sell sons into slavery, and nations could give up all of their rights to a prince. But just as the agreement that created full property rights had to be understood as voided when starvation threatened, the consent of a people to obey a sovereign did not extend to situations of "the hard necessity of dying." According to "the intention of those who first entered civil society . . . it may be presumed they would have declared that one ought not to bear with everything" (p. 112).

In 1618 John Selden, who was to become a respected jurist, scholar, and member of Parliament was asked to defend British claims to the North Sea against Grotius's *Mare Liberum*. A dispute that arose in 1635 between England and Holland over fishing rights led him to revise and publish for the first time the manuscript he had written earlier. Selden's argument in *Mare Clausum* was simple. He adopted what he took to be the general principles of Grotius and rejected the specific points that led Grotius to see the land and the sea as different cases. Like Grotius, Selden traced the origin of property rights to "a consent of the whole body or universality of mankind (by the mediation of something like a compact, which might bind their posterity) for quitting of the common interest or ancient right in those things that were made over thus by distribution to particular proprietors; in the same manner as when partners or co-heirs do share between themselves any portions of those things which they hold in common."[10]

This contract not only divided the area occupied by individuals and conferred on them property rights, it also included a provision (more explicit in Selden than in Grotius) whereby individuals renounced their rights to that area of the earth not actually possessed by anyone. This renunciation was required for a positive community in which "all men were indifferently and without distinction lords of the whole" to be made private through individual occupation (p. 22). Thus, after the contract, those areas not possessed come to be the property of the first to "corporally seize them, with an intent of possessing, holding, using, and enjoying" (pp. 22–23). This model, in which a positive community was divided into private rights through a contract that also legitimated the first possession of goods not possessed at the time of the contract, Selden took to be not only his own opinion but also "to be the opinion of the most excellent Hugo Grotius" (p. 23). The Grotian recognition of use rights prior to a contract received only brief mention by Selden in this work, in part because he thought the period before discord would make a property agreement necessary was so short (p. 18).

Selden did, however, make two criticisms of Grotius. His first involved Grotius's argument that the sea could not be made private in the same way the land was. Selden denied that the sea was different because it was inexhaustible or because it could not be subjected to boundaries. To the question of whether the sea was inexhaustible he answered that many of the resources of the sea (pearls and fish, for example) were scarce. And as a solution to the problems of boundaries he suggested the use of latitude and longitude. He also thought that Grotius was inconsistent to write that the ocean near the shore could be owned but not the open seas (pp. 135–40).

Selden's second criticism concerned the existence or continuation of common rights into the modern world. The renunciation of common rights in the contract that Selden had imagined was so complete that common rights ceased to cast any shadows over private rights. He did not accept the right to free passage, the rights of harmless use, or the right to immigration (pp. 124–26). Selden argued that Grotius had confused right with charity in these cases, a point he extended to the situation of necessity.[11]

Selden distinguished between obligatory and permissive natural law to argue that though almost all agreements were permitted by natural law, it was obligatory that all parties to any agreement obeyed its provisions. As a result, Selden thought that all questions about the rights and duties of citizens depended for their answer on the historical contract that could be shown to have grown between a people and their government.[12] Even more than Grotius, Selden cautioned that respect must always be given "to local laws and customs which limit or restrain this [property] right" (p. 24). The renunciation of common rights explains why the right of necessity could not be invoked, but the ability of a people to make virtually any law they wanted opened the way for a nation to turn voluntary charity toward the poor into a system of poor relief financed by taxes. Thirty or so years later, when Pufendorf recommended state-financed poor relief, he cited the authority of Selden to help convince his readers.[13]

In the eighteenth century Selden was widely known through his *Table-Talk*, a collection that purported to be his conversational opinions. Here the central importance of keeping contracts was reiterated again and again. Can a people "labor to regain" their freedom? Selden answered, "We must look at the contract; if that be rightly made, we must stand to it."[14] Must a man pay his debts even if it will leave him with nothing? "Let them look to the making of the bargain" (p. 194). Should Nero be obeyed? Selden argued, "The people had made Nero emperor. They agree, he to command, they to obey: then God comes in, and casts a hook upon them, 'keep your faith': then comes in, 'all power is of God' " (p. 235). According to Selden, every law was a contract to which everyone had consented (p. 221). Thus theft and trespass were wrong only because they constituted breaches of a contract.

The broad outlines of the analysis of property rights found in Grotius and Selden characterized most of the more philosophic property discussions in the seventeenth and eighteenth centuries. This analysis typically proceeded through four levels, each one of which posed questions that a full theory had to answer. The first level concerned the nature of God's grant and the original community of goods. The second required the derivation of a use right. In the third the transformation of use rights into property rights had to be explained. And in the last level of analysis it was necessary to set out the property provisions in the contract that established civil government. As the analysis moved from level to level, the new right of the higher level built upon and preserved or made void the right it replaced. The nature of the original grant, the question of whether use and/or property rights in the state of nature came from consent or first possession, and the question of whether any natural property rights could be invoked against existing civil laws presumed to have been agreed to by the people were all particularly controversial. The way these questions were answered would determine the length of the shadows natural rights to property, particularly common or inclusive rights, would cast over a civil society.

Filmer, Ireton, and Hobbes

The difficulties that may exist in the Grotian account of the relationship between the law of nature, the laws of nations, and the municipal laws of a particular country were not lost on his contemporaries, especially under the circumstances created by the English Civil War and the importance that came to be attached to all discussions of political obligation. These problems were particularly evident in the discussion of property. To what purpose were all of the rules of natural property ownership, in what sense were they natural, if such rules could be set aside by civil law? Robert Filmer seized upon this uncertain relationship and used it to discredit all theories that had a natural rights foundation. In the essay he published on Grotius in 1652 (along with ones on Hobbes and John Milton) he tried to put Grotius in a dilemma.[15] Men, he wrote, could be obligated to the laws of nature and the rights they conferred only if they were God's laws. But if they were God's laws, Filmer asked, how could they be rightfully contravened by civil law? Or, if natural law and natural rights could be set aside by civil law, in what sense were they natural, and why was there an obligation to obey them when civil law was silent? He charged that no logical connection could be made between the equality and freedom that were the foundations of thinking of people having natural rights and the legitimate obligations of subjects in civil society. His defense of Charles I led him to insist that any rights theory was ultimately subversive of the obedience subjects had to give if political order were to be maintained.

Filmer used this perspective specifically to challenge the idea that there could have been a transition from a natural community of property to individual property. If property was given by God in the form of communal rights to use, he argued, individuals could not legitimately remove it and make it private, by seizure or by contract: "The common use of things was natural so long as dominion was not brought in: dominion, he saith, was brought in by the will of man, whom by this doctrine Grotius makes to be able to change the law which God himself cannot change, or so he saith. He gives a double ability to man; first to make that no law of nature, which God made to be the law of nature; and next, to make that a law of nature which God made not" (p. 266). To this general criticism Filmer added some others concerning the original contract that divided the land. He wanted to see a record of this contract, he wanted to know how it could have been possible to gather everyone together, and he wondered how that contract could bind the posterity of those who agreed to it. He also pointed out that such an agreement had to be unanimous (p. 273). Thus, like Selden, Filmer took Grotius to have worked with the idea of an original positive community, which could have led to private property only if everyone agreed to renounce their right.

Filmer's target was a way of thinking about government that imagined that it was created by people through the renouncing of their natural rights. He feared that individuals who thought government existed by their consent would also believe their consent could be withdrawn: "If it were a thing so voluntary, and at the pleasure of men when they were free to put themselves under subjection, why may they not as voluntarily leave subjection when they please, and be free again" (p. 273). His anxiety over the subversive consequences of the idea of a political contract was carried over to the idea of a contract creating property rights. Could individuals withdraw their consent from that contract and reinstitute a community of goods? Asserting that such a community was natural seemed to Filmer very dangerous indeed. Grotius's belief in the right of necessity (a right that did dissolve the agreement that instituted private property, at least for the individual in need) was evidence to Filmer that his fears were justified (pp. 66, 274). Thus Filmer adopted the position that God's grant of the earth was to Adam as his private property, which enabled him to deny that a community of any kind had ever existed.

The question of whether natural rights to property existed, which Filmer denied, and, if they did, whether they continued to have any moral importance once political communities were constituted, which Selden denied, arose during the Civil War in 1647. At Putney the dissatisfied soldiers of the parliamentary army, known as Levellers, invoked natural rights to argue for a wider franchise. Their antagonists in the debate, Oliver Cromwell and Henry Ireton, the leaders of the parliamentary forces, worried, no less than the monarchist Filmer, that people who thought they possessed natural rights would be ungovernable. Nor were they entirely wrong to be concerned. A year after the Putney debates, as the Levellers' agitation became more intense, one of their pamphlets ended with, "Oh dissolve not all government into the prime laws of nature, and compel us to take the natural remedy to preserve ourselves, which you have declared no people can be deprived of."[16]

The Leveller position was summarized by Colonel Thomas Rainborough when he said, "Every man that is to live under a government ought first by his own consent to put himself under that government." From this principle Rainborough argued that laws could be legitimate only if they were passed by representatives elected by (virtually) all adult males. Ireton objected that this meant that the laws respecting property would be made by people who were elected from a population that was largely propertyless and that they might try to use the law to take from the wealthy and give to themselves. When Rainborough replied that the Levellers respected God's injunction not to steal, Cromwell moved the argument away from the actual intentions of the Levellers to the consequences of using natural law and "birthright" arguments: "No man says that you have a mind to anarchy, but that the consequences of the rule tends to anarchy, must end in anarchy."[17]

Because of this criticism, the Levellers later included in many of their manifestoes the explicit rule that even representative assemblies had to be prohibited from passing legislation that would "levell mens estates, destroy propriety, or make all things common." The Levellers had no quarrel with the legitimacy of private property, even if it were unequally distributed. They wanted to increase the economic opportunities available to their largely urban, artisan following. They never missed a chance to attack monopolies or to criticize excise taxes. But they also consistently asked that measures be taken to keep people from misery and beggary "in so fruitful a nation as through Gods blessing this is," and they sometimes also demanded that recently enclosed fields be "laid open" so that the tenants could again enjoy common rights.[18] The justification for these last two demands, however, seems always to have been the ancient rights of Englishmen.

The moderate economic program of the Levellers did not impress Ireton. He saw natural rights arguments as an inevitable threat to constitutions and the distribution of property rights that existed under them. His fear was that the natural equality that lay behind the Levellers' claim for equal political rights might also apply to economic resources: "If you will hold forth that as your ground, then I think you must deny all property too, and this is my reason. For thus: by that same right of nature . . . that you pretend . . . one man hath an equal right with another to the choosing of him that shall govern him—by the same right of nature, he hath the same equal right in any goods he sees—meat, drink, clothes—to take them and use them for his sustenance." Ireton's argument was that the Grotian right of necessity, "the right of nature . . . to have sustenance rather than perish," as he put it later in the debate, was incompatible with anyone actually enjoying an exclusive property right. "I do not see where that man will stop, as to point of property, so that he shall not use against other property that right he hath claimed by the Law of Nature." Thus Ireton insisted that the right to property was most secure when it was based on historical constitutions and positive law. "The Law of God doth not give me property, nor the Law of Nature, but property is of human constitution. . . . Constitution founds property."[19] To Ireton, the Civil War was fought to defend the British constitution from the unjust acts of the king, and not in the name of natural equality or natural rights that could be turned against the constitution.

The idea that political and social order required denying the natural right to property was above all associated with the work of Thomas Hobbes. Though Hobbes was himself a natural rights philosopher, and for that reason was criticized by Filmer, he shared with Filmer and Ireton the belief that property rights were created by civil law and could not be said to exist before the sovereign declared them. Hobbes, we shall see, accepted a good deal of the Grotian model but argued that that model was unable to establish a natural right to property.[20]

Hobbes began with an original community of goods that can best be understood as a positive community. The idea that in the state of nature "all things belonged to all men" appeared in *Leviathan*, *De Cive*, and the *Elements of Law*.[21] But the result of everyone owning everything in the state of nature was that no one could own anything in particular, "that there be no propriety, no dominion, no mine and thine distinct; but onely that to be every mans that he can get; and for so long, as he can keep it" (*L*, p. 188). To make this argument work, Hobbes denied that either first possession or a division by contract could bring property rights to a prepolitical state. He tried to demonstrate that in the state of nature the right to preserve oneself would overwhelm all attempts to establish exclusive rights that others could recognize.

Hobbes's criticisms of the legitimacy of contracts in the state of nature are familiar. Since "the bonds of words are too weak to bridle men's ambition, avarice, anger, and other passions" (*L*, p. 196), it would have been impossible in the state of nature for contracts that required actions by others in the future to create order. Unable to count on the performance of others, and aware that performing first had risks, individuals rightfully seeking to preserve themselves would not enter into agreements. And because their desire for self-preservation was not unjust, they would commit no wrong by breaking any contract they might make. "If a covenant be made, wherein neither of the parties perform presently, but trust one another; in the condition of mere nature . . . upon any reasonable suspicion, it is void" (*L*, p. 196). Obedience to contracts was an important obligation under natural law, according to Hobbes, but it was secondary to self-preservation and in force only when it was consistent with that primary value.

Hobbes had no doubt that in the state of nature people would seize goods and use force to continue to possess them. Nor were these people committing a wrong. They were simply taking what was theirs from a community of goods of which they were co-owners. In fact, Hobbes included within natural law a rule of first possession (*L*, pp. 212–13, *DC*, pp. 50–51, *EL*, pp. 296–97). In the *Leviathan* natural laws nine and ten prohibited pridefulness and arrogance. In this spirit the eleventh law required that arbitrators deal equally with the parties to a controversy. Taken together, these laws were manifestations of a presumption in favor of equality; or, as Hobbes said, "equal distribution is the law of nature" (*L*, p. 213). Problems arose when that over which there was contention could not be divided equally. The twelfth law stated that things that could not be divided should be enjoyed in common. But how could equality be preserved when individuals contended for goods that could not be enjoyed in common or divided equally? This situation was the one both Grotius and Hobbes understood as making individual property necessary. A large population of avaricious individuals competing for scarce resources (not just land but the most desirable land, for example) would not be able to live together with common rights, nor would it be possible to bring peace to a situation of scarcity by dividing shares equally. Under these conditions the thirteenth law required division by lot, which Hobbes interpreted to mean that "those things which cannot be enjoyed in common, nor divided, ought to be adjudged to the first possessor" (*L*, p. 213). Not only "first seizure" but also primogeniture fell under this rule. Because being first in these cases was understood by Hobbes as winning a lottery in which all presumably had an equal chance, the presumption in favor of equality was not violated.

But though first possession, like the obligation to agreements, was sanctioned by natural law, it was also incapable of bringing property rights, the mutual recognition of ownership, to the state of nature. The right of self-preservation, which each individual properly interpreted for himself, overwhelmed both contracts and first possession and as a result made it impossible for rules of ownership to emerge. Individuals might reach agreements about property but would commit no wrong in the state of nature if they failed to live up to them. They could seize what they thought they needed, but another could try to seize it too. In the absence of a sovereign to enforce rules, individuals were bound to follow the laws of nature only *in foro interno*, not by their acts, *in foro externo*. "He that should be modest," Hobbes observed, "and performe all he promises . . . where no man else should do so, should best make himself a prey to others, and procure his own certain ruine, contrary to the ground of all Lawes of Nature, which tend to natures preservation" (*L*, p. 215).

Hobbes's analysis of property was meant to demonstrate the incoherence of the doctrine that property rights were natural or derived from a natural community of goods prior to the creation of a sovereign. Property rights could exist only under a sovereign power that was created when individuals renounced their right to all things and authorized the sovereign to define and enforce mine and thine. They were no longer joint owners who could take what was theirs when they thought necessary; their renunciation of rights meant they now confronted a world, in effect, owned by the sovereign, who decided what they and others had rights to against one another. "The distribution of the materials of this nourishment, is the constitution of mine, and thine, and his; that is to say, in one word propriety; and belongeth in all kinds of common-wealth to the sovereign power" (*L*, pp. 295–96). The purpose of Hobbes's argument is clear. By demonstrating that property rights could not have existed in a state of nature, he hoped his readers would understand that the rights they enjoyed to their goods were the result of civil laws, which deserved their deepest respect. As civil law was the command of the sovereign, it made no sense to claim that the property rights that were created by the sovereign could not be changed by the sovereign. The idea that a citizen could have an "absolute property in his goods" so that even the sovereign could be excluded, a right to one's goods so strong that its violation by the sovereign could justify resistance, simply made no sense to Hobbes (*L*, pp. 367, 373). Such "absolute" rights could not have come from agreements prior to the contract that created a sovereign, nor could they have arisen from first possession or seizure. And because transferring the right to govern required transferring the means to govern, the sovereign had to have the right to regulate and tax property (L, p. 197).

Though Hobbes's attack on a natural right to property that could exclude the sovereign was motivated by his political concerns, such a right was incompatible with his economic views. His generally mercantilist economic policy suggestions—that government control international trade, tax luxuries, provide employment for all, and encourage "navigation, agriculture, fishing, and all means of manufacture" (L, pp. 294–302; DC, pp. 150–51)—all point to a large and powerful government using the law to regulate and tax widely.

Hobbes, Filmer, and Ireton differed in their politics and philosophy, but they were all certain that property rights were better preserved through a theory that stressed their civil, rather than their natural, origins. Yet the central place Hobbes gave to self-preservation virtually required that individuals retain a shadow of their original right in the form of a right of necessity. The contract that established sovereignty and individual property did not create this right, but rather specifically exempted it from the general renunciation of rights required for a civil society. Though the holding of this right was usually discussed by Hobbes in the context of the breakdown of political power and resistance to government authority, it was also linked to the situation of dire economic need. Under these circumstances the individual was not bound to obey the civil laws that created property rights. Not only did Hobbes defend the right of necessity (perhaps against Selden's reduction of it to charity), but he interpreted it very broadly. The *Elements of Law* stated that individuals could not renounce their rights "to the use of fire, water, free air, and a place to live in, and to all things necessary for life" (EL, pp. 295–96). The right to fire and water I take to be Grotius's right of harmless use, and the right to a place to live was his right to emigrate and settle in the unoccupied lands of another country. Virtually the same list appeared in *De Cive* (DC, p. 51), and a somewhat expanded list appeared in *Leviathan*. Here the rights that could not be renounced included those to "enjoy air, water, motion, ways to go from place to place, and all things else without which a man cannot live, or not live well" (L, p. 212). The right to medicine was added later in the book (L, pp. 268–69). It also may be important that Hobbes did not rehearse the Grotian caveats regarding the duty, before these rights could be invoked, to ask the sovereign and private individuals for aid, and after the right of necessity had been used, to repay what was taken.

Hobbes recognized an absolute right to the necessities of life. In effect, he argued that a property right understood as the right to exclude was derived from civil law, whereas a right to be included in the blessings of nature required for self-preservation was a natural right that could never be renounced. In a proposal that reminds us of the existence of the Elizabethan Poor Law and the social policy of James I and Charles I, he suggested that the sovereign institute a program to provide for the needy. Those unable to maintain themselves "ought not to be left to the charity of private persons; but to be provided for . . . by the laws of the commonwealth" (L, pp. 387, 299). The obvious advantage of such a program, indeed the reason why no state with people who were very poor could afford to do without it, was that it rendered unnecessary the right of necessity and, therefore, contributed to public order.

Cumberland and Pufendorf

In the period between the English Civil War and the controversies that led to the Glorious Revolution, two important works appeared that used the idea that property rights were natural. Both *A Treatise of the Laws of Nature* (1672) by Richard Cumberland and *Of the Law of Nature and Nations* (1672) by Samuel Pufendorf relied on the natural right to property to defend moral and political order from what the authors thought were the insecure foundations upon which Hobbes had built.

Bishop Richard Cumberland, a strong defender of the restored monarchy in England, attacked Hobbes's ideas as tending to rebellion and tyranny, anarchy and arbitrary power. He did not understand how Hobbes could begin by affirming freedom and equality as natural without casting doubt on the legitimacy of the inequality that must characterize civil society. "It is . . . dangerous to teach, that an equal distribution is commanded by the laws of nature . . . although it [an unequal distribution] be absolutely necessary to a monarchical constitution."[22] At the same time, the absence in Hobbes of an obligation to contracts made in the state of nature suggested to Cumberland the destruction of moral constraint upon sovereigns in their relations with one another and with their subjects (p. 364). These constraints were particularly important to him because he thought of sovereigns as remaining in the state of nature with regard to their subjects (p. 351). If Hobbes were correct that "property may be arbitrarily settled and unsettled by the sole will of the supreme powers in every state . . . there is no law to restrain states from perpetual war; no law to oblige rulers of states to seek the public good of their subjects" (p. 326). Asserting equality and freedom while simultaneously denying an obligation to natural law must have seemed to Cumberland the worst possible combination of ideas. It was an invitation to moral and political chaos, an attack on the very idea of right and wrong, on religion, and on the sovereignty of God. Cumberland had to save the Restoration from the support of Thomas Hobbes.

In an important sense, the tendencies to both anarchy and tyranny that Cumberland saw in Hobbes's work stemmed directly from the absence of a property right in his understanding of the state of nature. The right of everyone to everything summarized for Cumberland the moral anarchy in Hobbes's thought, the way individual opinion came to replace natural law as the standard of right. The natural right to property, then, demonstrated to Cumberland far more than the way individuals came to have rights to particular goods. It affirmed the sovereignty of God, it brought order to natural man, and it explained the limited purpose for which sovereign power was created—to protect the property of its citizens.

To Cumberland natural law philosophy did not criticize the world by holding up to it a standard it could not meet; rather it legitimated the world as it existed by showing how it was in accord with the laws of nature. But whereas this task previously had been performed mainly by the idea of contract so that the major duty of man was to live up to the contracts he made, in Cumberland the concept of the common good took precedence. Cumberland's philosophical enterprise was to demonstrate that God had laid on all the obligation to promote the common good, that this obligation was as strong in the state of nature as in civil society, and that in pursuing the common good or the good of others people promoted their own good (p. 16). Cumberland concluded that both philosophy and experience proved that the inviolability of property rights was essential to the public good.

Experience, Cumberland maintained, taught that food, housing, and clothing were necessary to the common good, to the preservation and comfort of mankind. Those things that produced these benefits were, then, part of natural law. Since a coat, for example, could not be of use to two people at the same time, nor a piece of food nourish two at the same time, the products of the earth had to be limited to specific people at particular times if they were to serve the common good (pp. 55–56). Abstract reason reached the same conclusion. Thus Cumberland also deduced a property right from the self-evident maxim that "the same bodies cannot at the same time be in more places than one: that the same bodies cannot at the same time be moved toward several places (especially if contrary), so as to be subservient to the opposite wills of several men" (p. 62). Cumberland self-consciously employed the language of science here to confront Hobbes's use of geometry. He was also agreeing with Grotius (and, in fact, quoted him) to show that in a primitive community of goods natural law justified an individual use right. The necessary limitation of one thing to one person at a time justified "that primitive right to things by first occupancy" and, in an explicit disagreement with Hobbes, Cumberland referred to this primitive right in a precivil condition "as a kind of property" (pp. 64–65). The state of nature was not a war of all against all; Cumberland argued that even in its earliest stages it was given order by the rights and duties of use rights to property (p. 315).

But just as in Grotius, use rights were soon transformed. The obvious benefits of individual use led to a further division through an express agreement that established "a more complete dominion of property" (p. 65) by extending the area of private property and by making property rights perpetual rather than limited to use. For the inconveniences of common property Cumberland had recourse to the familiar arguments of Aristotle, though he did not push these points so far as to deny that some property (such as a field) could be jointly owned. But consent and contracts were for Cumberland clearly secondary justifications for property rights, not as important to him as the legitimacy conferred by the common good. The way the common good enveloped consent can be seen in his statement that "men, who are obliged to promote the common good, are likewise *necessarily obliged* to consent" (pp. 313–14, emphasis added) to respect the property rights of others. The common good, it seems, made consent an offer it could not refuse.

Although Cumberland had used the model of property rights with which we are familiar, it is important to note that he put rights on a somewhat different foundation and modified the vocabulary used to discuss them. Property rights were not derived directly from self-preservation and contracts but, like all other rights, were based on the public good. "No one," he declared, "has a right to violate the public good" (p.

317). In Cumberland, then, as in the work of the most famous defender of the ethics of the public good, Jeremy Bentham, the common good justified virtually any current distribution and set as the main task of sovereign power the protection of property rights that actually existed. Cumberland's desire to use property rights founded on the common good to deny Hobbes's argument that such rights were created by the sovereign was so strongly felt that it drove him to an extraordinarily conservative position. Even to think about the distribution of property was unnecessary, perhaps even wrong, to Cumberland. "We all find it readymade to our hands, in a manner plainly sufficient to procure the best end, the honor of God and the happiness of all mankind" (p. 322). He concluded that since the happiness that currently existed was "greater than any prudent man could hope to attain by . . . endeavoring to introduce a new division of all property. . . . A desire of innovation in things pertaining to property, is unjust" (pp. 322–23). Since the common good was better provided by the distribution of property and power that individuals found than by any distribution they could make, it was every-one's duty to preserve the government and property rights that charac-terized their society.

In Cumberland's work the agreements concerning property rights that people had made because of their benefits were acts that had occurred in the past, not invitations to contemporaries to divide property anew. Only war could result from such attempts. But if it became necessary to dis-pose of disputed property, Cumberland followed Hobbes in suggesting first the use of an impartial arbitrator, "an Umpire," and if that failed, the use of chance or lot. And like Hobbes he saw primogeniture as a form of casting lots (p. 322).

Cumberland's argument that any property system should be defended because of its contribution to the public good had nothing to do with avarice or commerce and everything to do with divine and temporal order. He constantly repeated the need for moderation in the pursuit of wealth and reminded his readers that they should acquire goods, at least in part, so they could be given away (pp. 337–38). He affirmed the moral duty of giving alms to the poor and interpreted the common good to require "that necessaries, at least, be allowed to all without violation" (p. 321), though whether this requirement was meant to give the poor a right or the wealthy a duty was unclear.

A set of ethics much like Cumberland's is found in the Cambridge Platonist Henry More. His *Enchiridion Ethicum* (1666) was the text used at Harvard College in the 1730s and 1740s and was an important vehicle for the transmission of seventeenth-century ideas into the eighteenth century. As much as Cumberland, More was at pains to emphasize how important it was to seek wealth moderately and how unimportant external goods were for happiness: "What is it that the high and mighty do more enjoy than others. . . ? Do the rich and powerful eat or drink with better relish, than even that man that labors the whole day, and mixes temperance with his sweat? Is their sleep more sound, or health of mind or body more robust? If this commonly be otherwise, why may we not suspect, that such potentates and men of wealth, are also as much troubled with vain imagination, as men that are devoted to virtue, and the sciences."[23] More explicitly included in his understanding of a property right the right to have necessities as well as the right not to have them taken: "The man, who falls into poverty, but yet is honest, has a sort of right or title to receive alms; and he, who has gotten anything by lawful industry, has a right to keep it" (p. 112). His concern that individuals have enough to live happily is evident in his aphoristic *Noema*.

—Tis good for a man to have wherewithal to live well and happily.
—If tis good for one man to have wherewithal to be happy; it evidently follows, tis twice as good for two men to be happy, thrice for three, a thousand time for a thousand; and so of the rest.
—Tis better that one man be disabled from living voluptuously, than that another should live in want and calamity. (P. 26)

A defense of the existing distribution of property, a concern that economic desires be moderate, and a recognition of the right of necessity were all characteristic of seventeenth-century attitudes toward property. We should not be surprised, then, to find that these attitudes were also at the center of the analysis that constituted the philosophical apogee of this period, *The Law of Nature and Nations* by Samuel Pufendorf. John Locke's opinion that Pufendorf's work was the "best book of its kind" was widely shared long into the eighteenth century.[24]

Pufendorf like Cumberland found it impossible to believe that God could have left people in the state of moral anarchy described by Hobbes. How could it be denied that people had an obligation to follow natural law if God was acknowledged as the author of nature and the laws it contained? Pufendorf described Hobbes's distinction between the laws found in Scripture, to which people were obligated, and the laws of nature found by reason, to which Hobbes said people owed no obligation, as "a useless piece of subtlety and niceness" (p. 47). Both laws were for Pufendorf "the will and command of God," laws to which people were obligated because He was their superior. In the second edition of *The Laws of Nature* Pufendorf cited Cumberland as "guide and master" on the question of how natural law could be apprehended through experience and sense, rather than through innate ideas, and maintained that Cumberland's view that natural law required benevolence was consistent with his own definition that it enjoined people "to promote and preserve a peaceful sociableness with others, agreeable to the main end and disposition of the human race in general" (p. 139). Neither prudence nor municipal law was strong enough a foundation for Cumberland and Pufendorf, as they had been for Hobbes. Instead, both wanted to link the principal institutions of society to natural law and its author.

Pufendorf recognized that Hobbes's description of the state of nature as a state of war depended on assumptions and arguments tied to property. Only in a state in which goods were scarce and everyone had a right to everything would relations between people inevitably become a war of all against all. But to Pufendorf, an insistence on scarcity was an affront to the benevolence of God, who could not have been "so unkind, or so sparing in His provision for the human race, that two persons must always lay claim to the same thing" (p. 117). Hobbes also was wrong to underestimate the power of people to reason, forgetting that man was "an animal whose noblest and chiefest part is reason" (p. 113). Reasonable people living together in conditions of relative plenty would not equate their opinion with right but would instead guide their actions by "a common, a firm, and a uniform measure," which was natural law (p. 113). Since natural law affirmed those rules that led to the preservation of mankind, an end that would be thwarted if it conferred rights that contradicted one another, Pufendorf argued that natural law could not have given to everyone a right to everything. Instead, natural law taught "that no man hurt another, who doth not assault and provoke him; that everyone allow others to enjoy their own goods and possessions; that he faithfully perform what he contracted for; and voluntarily promote the interest and happiness of others" (p. 114).

But though Pufendorf wanted to show that rights to property existed in the state of nature to buttress his view that the natural relations between people (and, just as important, between sovereigns) were ordered and peaceful, he did not think he could use the theory of Grotius without revision.[25] The problem was that though a natural right to property could help legitimate ordered relations between parties in a state of nature, the Grotian formulation of this right, with its presumptions in favor of common property, could also be used to undermine civil law and the property rights it protected. Pufendorf criticized Grotius, Thomas More, and Tommaso Campanella for suggesting that private property was morally only second best, a sign of decline, an institution that need not have supplanted a community of goods if only people had continued to live with friendship and charity as they did in the first stages of human history (p. 368).

Pufendorf also did not accept Filmer's belief that property was always private (p. 364). Pufendorf had to find a way to express the original relationship of people to the earth that avoided the creation of any moral norm, communal or private, lest it call into question some aspect of property in civil society. His solution was to claim that the original grant from God was "indefinite, general, and indifferent," one of "potential dominion" (p. 373). He expressed this conception by using the idea of a negative community, a situation in which no one owned anything and "things . . . lie free for any taker" (p. 362). Not only did a negative community describe the original grant from God so that it was impossible to argue that any actual distribution of property violated natural law or natural rights, it also escaped the problem of conflict or anarchy that Hobbes saw was engendered by the contradiction in a positive community of everyone having a right to everything.

To Pufendorf the Grotian theory of the origin of property rights had two distinctive elements. The first was the theory of a positive community; the second was that something like a property right could be created by first use, possession, or occupation. Since Pufendorf believed that the first possession argument depended at least in part on a positive community, his rejection of the right of everyone to everything also took the ground out from under first possession. According to Pufendorf, an individual in the Grotian model could be said to have a right to the fruit he picked in a state of abundance only because he already had a right to that fruit in common with others. His first possession of the fruit made private what had previously been owned in common, but it did not create ownership. For Grotius, then, the problem was how common rights could become private rights, whereas Pufendorf, beginning with the rightless world of a negative community, had to consider how there could be any property rights.

Pufendorf argued that the individual act of seizing something from a negative community did not carry with it the moral content that was necessary to create a right that others had to respect. He saw no difference between the seizure of food by people and the seizure of food by animals. Just as that act by an animal in no way prevented another animal from taking what the first had gathered, the seizing of something by one person created no moral presumption against a like seizure by another person. Pufendorf's argument was that a property right, recognized by the public and obliging others not to steal, could be created only from the propertyless world of a negative community by individuals consenting to respect what others possessed. "The grant of almighty God, by which he gave mankind the use of earthly possessions, was not the immediate cause of dominion; as this [dominion] is directed against other men, and with relation to these . . . necessarily presupposeth some human act, and some covenant either tacit or express" (p. 364). The moral content of a property right, he insisted, could be supplied only by agreements between individuals.

Pufendorf did not mean to say that before an isolated individual could pick berries from a bush, he had to seek someone's permission, only that the taking by itself should not be understood as creating a right. Similarly, when people lived more closely together, their property rights should not be traced to their acts of seizure but to the consent that could have been inferred from their leaving one another's goods alone. Only through an agreement could the physical act of taking become the moral act of owning. The centrality of contracts to moral relations in Pufendorf's understanding is illustrated by his argument that people can kill and eat animals because it was not possible to make contracts with them (p. 357). Pufendorf believed he had detected arguments in Grotius that weakened the case for property rights. In the idea of a positive community Pufendorf found a normative ideal that could be used to criticize private property, while in first possession he uncovered a morally problematic origin for the first rights to property.

Because property rights were legitimated by agreements, Pufendorf thought natural law approved any system of rights that grew from consent so long as it was not internally contradictory, tended to disturb society, or enabled one person to engross what God gave to preserve mankind (p. 365). He envisioned a wide variety of property systems, with many combinations of private and communal rights, as falling under the legitimacy conferred by natural law. It was not necessary for him to list the specific contracts that led to property because he understood property rights to have grown slowly, through successive stages and by many agreements.

That Pufendorf thought his theory was less ambiguous and more strongly conservative than that of Grotius is evident in his discussion of the right of necessity. The problem was whether anyone could ever have a right to the goods of another against the owner's consent. Pufendorf first remarked that the rich had an obligation to give to the poor and that one of the advantages of private property was that it made charity possible (p. 207). He added, citing the authority of Selden, that there was no reason why civil law could not turn the duty of charity into a "strict and perfect obligation," that is, a system of assistance financed through taxes (p. 207). In a society in which the poor received subsistence from magistrates, the right of necessity could not be invoked (p. 207). Thus Pufendorf had narrowed the question of a right of necessity to situations in which unemployed individuals could not get a job, or charity from the wealthy, or subsistence from the government. Under these circumstances individuals who through no fault of their own faced a dire emergency could legitimately take from another, though he insisted that they ought to do so with the intent of paying restitution when they were able. "We conceive, therefore, that such a person doth not contract the guilt of theft, who happening not through his own fault, to be in extreme want . . . shall either forcibly or privily relieve himself out of their abundance; especially if he do it with full intention to pay the value of them, when-ever his better fortune gives him ability" (p. 207).

Pufendorf and Grotius agreed that the right of necessity existed, but they disagreed on its foundations. To understand Pufendorf's point we must remember that he largely ignored Grotius's use of the contract. Pufendorf, then, tried to show that the proper understanding of such a right could not be derived from what he thought was the most distinctive feature of the Grotian model—the ability of people to have a right to what they took from the positive community. Instead, he linked the right of necessity to the contracts that created property rights, contracts that were necessary only because property rights had to be created from a negative community. To Pufendorf, the right to take from another in a dire emergency was based on the supposition that individuals would not consent to a system of rights that might require that they starve.

Pufendorf argued that working with the idea of an original positive community made it impossible to emphasize enough that the individual in need only temporarily had a legitimate reason to take what belonged to another. And if, in necessity, goods returned to universal or common ownership there would be no reason to insist upon restitution. Repaying another was consistent only with the idea that in necessity the rights of others were overridden, which was not expressed in the Grotian model, in which the reconstitution of a positive community in effect destroyed the rights of others. Pufendorf's fear that the assumption of a positive community could compromise the integrity of private property was even clearer in his next objection. He argued that because of that assumption Grotius enabled the right of necessity to be used by "knaves and drones" rather than just the unfortunate (p. 208). Thus Pufendorf suggested that neither limiting necessity to the deserving nor requiring restitution was compatible with an original positive community.

Pufendorf also upheld his views on the right of necessity against the theories of Lambert Velthuysen, which also were based on property rights originating in first possession (pp. 366–67). Pufendorf argued that since property rights derived from first possession arose independently of the actions or agreements of others, the situation of one person could not legitimately limit the holdings of another. The extreme autonomy implied in a right derived independently of anyone else's intention, concern, interest, or welfare so separated people that they could never be understood to have a right to take someone else's property. Only a theory in which property developed from a negative community through the mutual recognition of contracts could explain why property was subject to the right of necessity.

Pufendorf believed that a system of property rights was sanctioned by natural law because it moderated conflict and encouraged industriousness. Like all the natural law philosophers, he saw natural laws as providing the standards necessary for the creation and maintenance of peaceful communities in which human life would be preserved and allowed to flourish. But the particular system of law adopted by a society depended on the unique characteristics of that society. Although property rights in general were required by natural law, civil law legitimated the specific property owned by specific individuals. The recognition of diversity in property arrangements that this implied required an understanding of sovereign power as able to change and modify property rights. Thus Pufendorf had no sense that the natural right to property was violated by the need to give it up in order to create civil society (p. 626). He defended eminent domain (p. 262) and the moral superiority of the public over all private interests and enumerated specific powers that the state had to have over the wealth of individuals for it to perform its tasks. These powers included the creation of trading monopolies, sumptuary laws, wage and price controls, guilds, the regulation of inheritance and marriage, and the right to compel people to work. Pufendorf also believed, though less strongly than did Grotius, in the rights of harmless use.

In his discussion of the rights to fish and hunt, the case in which people might be understood to be in a natural state with regard to goods still in a primitive negative community, a number of these themes are brought together. His sense that there could be a variety of property arrangements and that it was the right of the sovereign to decide these questions was illustrated by his argument that the laws governing hunting and fishing "depend on the will of the sovereign, and not on any natural and necessary law, what the private members of the state shall enjoy" (p. 388). The prince did not own the animals, but he was "lord of the soil where they run" (p. 388) and could prohibit or allow anyone to use the land for whatever purpose he judged convenient. But though Pufendorf noted that the rules regulating hunting varied greatly, he suggested some good reasons why hunting should be limited. Laborers should not be allowed to quit their work and ramble about the woods, perhaps turning to robbery, and they certainly should not be trusted with arms. By contrast, hunting was good practice for the nobility and therefore could be restricted to them. The link between these conservative sentiments and his use of a negative community is evident. Since wild animals and fish are in a negative community, it could not be said that the prince or sovereign, in prohibiting the people from hunting and fishing, was taking away from them anything that was theirs or was violating their communal property rights (p. 389).

The indeterminacy of natural law with regard to property rules was also evident in his disagreement with Grotius over wills and testaments. Pufendorf denied that the right to make a will was implicit in the idea of a property right or was prescribed by the law of nature. Wills were the creation of civil law. Thus, though in the absence of law property should be split among all the children, he explicitly mentioned the legitimacy of civil law establishing primogeniture, among other possible rules of succession (pp. 420–31). His use of Selden's distinction between the obligatory and permissive law of nature should remind us how little any of the seventeenth-century natural law philosophers thought the natural right to property required or prohibited any particular property arrangement (pp. 389–90).

Only in his discussion of international competition, a situation obviously without civil law, did natural law guide and limit property rights. Because property was established to deal with the problems of scarcity, it had no role to play when a good was inexhaustible. The ocean could be enjoyed by all without harm to any and could not be possessed or defended, and therefore it could not be made private. Since attempts to do so could not be of benefit, there being more than anyone could use, only the desire to harm others could be the motive. "He is not to be endured who out of vain and senseless greediness should lay claim to more than he could ever spend," Pufendorf wrote in this regard (p. 383). Similarly, it would be an "intolerable arrogance" for a family to claim and attempt to keep others off an island that could sustain more people and was greater than their needs required (p. 486).

Pufendorf's overriding concern for order, a concern he shared with all of those philosophers considered so far, led him to an ethical ideal of moderation. He counseled his readers time and again to beware of great ambition, arrogance, vainglory, and avarice. His distance from the problems of a market society can be seen in the way his greatest concern was always with the desire for glory and praise, rather than with avarice and material goods. As with Hobbes, his descriptions of man's pridefulness, ambition, and covetousness were not meant to legitimate these characteristics but as cautions against them: "We must moderate our desire and our pursuit of those things. . . . We must not then on any account give loose reins to our desire of getting . . . or to be perpetually employed in the endless labor of increasing" (pp. 168–69).

The background of war and revolt that characterized the seventeenth century is evident on every page written by these natural law philosophers. If they began their analysis with individuals and rights, it was only the better to end with obligations to princes. They could not understand how order could be maintained among the ambitious in the absence of a strong state exercising control over both political and economic life. Thus, though the natural right to property as it was used from Grotius to Pufendorf played an important role in discussions of just war and colonial trade, in legitimating existing distributions of property, and in defending natural law and the benevolence of God, it was never thought to support individual rights against the requirements of the community. Only in the inclusive right of necessity did the right to property result in a defense of the individual against the weight of social institutions. The right of necessity was an exception to a general defense of exclusive property, but its existence attested to the fundamental status of the preservation of human life in these theories and the way that value could override all others. Moreover, the ideas out of which it was fashioned—natural equality, common rights, and consent—were passed on to later theorists who could use them to build even stronger protections against starvation and suffering.

TWO

The Right to Property
and the Right to Representation

Tyrrell, Locke, and Sidney

The intent of the natural law philosophers from Grotius to Pufendorf was to provide the firmest possible defense for the social institutions they thought were required to maintain peace. In England, however, in the last quarter of the seventeenth century, this vocabulary was turned against one of those institutions, the Stuart monarchy of Charles II and James II, in the name of two others, the Protestant establishment and the power of Parliament.

The most influential defense of the monarchy to be published in this period was Robert Filmer's *Patriarcha* (first published in 1679 but written in 1637–38). As we have already seen from his *Observations on Grotius*, Filmer subjected the idea of natural rights and social contract to powerful criticism. His use of biblical history and English historical precedent was certainly more persuasive than Hobbes's use of geometry and philosophy, and his popularity (especially among the clergy) illustrates the deeply conservative tenor of this period.[1]

Three important books against Filmer's defense of the monarchy were written between 1680 and 1683, all of which used at least to some extent the vocabulary of the natural law tradition. To counter the position that the king was the ultimate owner of the land in England, James Tyrrell in *Patriarcha Non Monarcha*, John Locke in *Two Treatises of Government*, and Algernon Sidney in *Discourses Concerning Government* had recourse to the idea that individuals had a natural right to property. They used this right to establish an original freedom and independence among men, to base government on consent, and, in their most important contribution, to interpret the terms under which that consent was given. No one, they argued, would have agreed to enter civil society and to give up property rightfully accumulated without insisting on certain limits to government power and on the right to rebel—to revoke their consent—if these limits were violated.

The consequence of using the natural law vocabulary, however, was to become open to the charge of wanting to "level" estates. However baseless these charges were (and as we have seen they were baseless even when applied to the Levellers) they forced the Whigs into an ideological competition with the defenders of the monarchy, each asserting that the other could not provide a coherent defense of property and inequality.[2] According to the Whigs, private property was in jeopardy from a powerful Catholic king who considered himself the ultimate owner of the land, while to Tories property was in jeopardy from Whigs who believed in an original common and natural equality. In this competition to prove one's conservative credentials with regard to ownership, the Whigs were not without weapons. For as we have seen, the vocabulary they used had as its primary purpose the defense of unequal property arrangements. As Tyrrell wrote against Filmer, "If there are any such desperate inconveniences . . . that attend this doctrine of natural freedom, and community of all things, it is more than I can find."[3]

In this chapter I will also consider the work of Jean Barbeyrac. Through his translations he more than anyone was responsible for transmitting the natural law treatises of Grotius and Pufendorf to the eighteenth century. The notes and citations he provided to his translations became the prisms through which these writers were viewed, almost as important to later generations as the texts themselves. Barbeyrac's interest in Locke and Sidney and the many references he made to their work also helped spread their influence.

Tyrrell

James Tyrrell was the author of an impressive work in British history, *Bibliotheca Politica* (1694), but he is probably more widely known because of his close association with John Locke. Tyrrell and Locke were often together in 1680–83 and no doubt talked of the best way to respond to the enormous popularity that greeted the publication of *Patriarcha*. Out of this collaboration came Tyrrell's *Patriarcha Non Monarcha* as well as Locke's *Two Treatises*. Tyrrell's work, then, reflects how an opponent of the king, under the influence of Locke, read the natural law discussion of property.[4]

Though Tyrrell was a strong supporter of the Whig position from the exclusion crisis to the Glorious Revolution, his political thought was always relatively moderate.[5] In this attitude he seems to be at one with most of those who opposed Charles II and then James II and who worked for the ascension to the throne of William and Mary. Thus he assured his readers that his attack on Filmer had not led him to embrace the commonwealth men, democracy, Milton, or rebellion. He averred that his friends were "moderate men" who believed a monarchy "tempered by known laws . . . to be the best in the world." And between the alternatives of democracy and arbitrary government, he said, "I know not which is worst, to be gnawn to death by rats, or devoured by lions" (Preface).

Tyrrell's attitude toward property was even more explicitly conservative than his political ideas.[6] Only by defending the existing distribution of property could he label the king's acts as "invasions" of the rights of others. He argued that it was Filmer's error to "render all things to be so much the Prince's right, that the subjects can claim a property in nothing which he shall please to take from them" (Preface). Tyrrell's devotion to the thought of Bishop Cumberland—he translated and abridged Cumberland's *Laws of Nature* to make it available to a wide audience—is a good indication of his moderation.[7]

To argue that individuals had rights to property that existed independently of the king, Tyrrell employed in *Patriarcha Non Monarcha* the natural law conventions of an original community and a right to use part of the common for self-preservation. He explicitly defended Grotius from Filmer's argument that a primitive community was inconsistent with the distinction of mine and thine.

> So likewise supposing the earth and the fruits thereof to have been at first bestowed in common on all its inhabitants; yet since God's first command to man was, increase and multiply, if he hath a right to perform the end, he hath certainly a right to the means of his preservation, and the propagation of his species, so that were all in common, yet when once any man had by his own labor acquired such a proportion of either as would serve the necessities of himself, and family, they became so much his own, as that no man could without manifest injustice rob him of the necessities of life. (Pp. 99–100, Sig. L2r–L3v; also p. 97, L1r)

To deny any individual the right to take what was required for preservation would be to give to someone who did have property a right of life and death over another. As Tyrrell pointed out against Filmer, the denial of this right would have given Adam the right to starve Eve (p. 102, L4v). That Adam could not have had such a right meant that all people must have been able to use from the common what was necessary for their preservation. Natural equality, natural freedom, and natural independence were, for Tyrrell, all expressed in this natural use right.

Tyrrell's mention of labor to describe the exercise of a use right probably reflected his collaboration with Locke. But Tyrrell was as likely to use occupation or possession as labor to describe the act of taking from the common, which suggests that he did not see labor as a particularly new or significant way to define the process by which the first property rights were established. Tyrrell's lack of precision here illustrates the sense in which the physical and public act of laboring was broadly understood as a way of occupying and possessing.

Tyrrell cautioned that a use right extended only to what could be actually used or possessed so that a man could claim only what he "can well manure for the necessities of himself and family" (p. 114, M2v). This limit on appropriation guaranteed that there would be enough for everyone to subsist in the state of nature without the conflict that would be engendered by scarcity. In Tyrrell's work the requirement of use for the establishment of a right led to prohibitions against individuals claiming for themselves or their country large, unoccupied islands merely by setting foot on them. It also served as a justification for European settlers claiming land in the New World on the grounds that native Indians could not claim more than they could use or needed to live (pp. 112–14, M1v–M2r).

But use rights established by individual acts of labor or occupation were sufficient for the survival of the human race only in the condition of abundance. When population grew to the point that there were more people "than the country can well maintain from its own products, there will presently arise a necessity of division of lands" (p. 113, M1r), which would probably occur through a "general agreement of many men in the division of a territory" (p. 116, M3v). Tyrrell's great admiration for Grotius is evident in his property theory. Although he began with a negative community, as Pufendorf did, and used Locke's labor formulation to help explain the origins of use rights, his general understanding of the way use rights were transformed into property rights through a general agreement was Grotian to the core. As Tyrrell wrote, "In most things Grotius may be very well defended" (p. 117, M3r).

Tyrrell used the fact that after land was divided there would be "a great many . . . without any share" to help explain the origin of government (p. 114, M2r). Because so many would be landless, laws had to be made and "punishments ordained" for those who violated the property rights settled by the original division and the agreements made subsequent to it. That government came after property in Tyrrell's discussion of natural law and was created to protect it was certainly meant to reassure the conservative English clergy: "I hope the great difficulty which hath puzzled some divines, which is prior in nature, propriety or civil government is now cleared, since it is apparent, propriety, understood either as the application of natural things to the uses of particular men, or else as the general agreement of many men in the division of a territory, or a kingdom, must be before government, one main end of which is to maintain the dominion or propriety before agreed on" (p. 116, M3v).

Tyrrell followed the "excellent Pufendorf" in maintaining that the original community was a negative community, and he too thought that natural law placed almost no constraints on the property arrangements a people might choose. Though he thought that common property became less appropriate with economic development, he insisted that the decision to choose between or mix private and public was given to "the discretions of those several parcels of mankind who agreed to live together . . . as it might conduce to . . . their common safety and interest" (p. 112, M1v). The existence of a negative community also suggested to Tyrrell that the state of nature would not contain rules of inheritance. His position, that such rules would emerge only from "compact in a commonwealth," was obviously designed to allow Parliament to exclude James II from the throne (p. 49). As in Pufendorf, the open-endedness implied in a negative original community and the ability of a people to decide on their property arrangements was not meant to invite innovation but rather to ensure that virtually any distribution (including and especially the present one) was consistent with natural law.

Tyrrell moved from a use right based on possession/occupation/labor through a division of lands by "general agreement" to a government created by consent. Through this progression Tyrrell contrasted the origins of private use in individuals acting alone for their own welfare with the origins of political power in mutual consent. Whereas the title to use was based on the good of the people who held it, the exercise of political power was justified by the good of the people who created it (pp. 64, 86). All human relations that involved power had to be understood as origi-

nating in contracts and limited by the intentions of the contractors that
their good be protected. In politics this meant that "no body is understood to have conferred more power by his will upon a monarch, than a
reasonable man can judge necessary to that end" (p. 257). A monarch
who, for example, used the prerogative power to pursue private ends
against his subjects violated the terms of the contract as it had grown in
England as well as the natural law injunction "to endeavor the common
good of mankind" (p. 17). And because individuals had the right to
punish violators of natural law (pp. 13, 115), kings could be actively
resisted. His specific use of a thief to illustrate that a violator of natural
law and "enemy of all mankind" could be killed had obvious importance
to a debate over nonparliamentary taxation (p. 64).

Filmer had argued that a derivation of property that began with a
primitive community and moved through a division by agreement was a
defective foundation for property rights because it seemed to imply that
property rights could be voided by the withdrawal of consent. Tyrrell
particularly had to respond to this charge, for he explicitly linked the
division of land to the creation of a group who would have ample reason
to desire the destruction of a property system—the landless. But so far
was Tyrrell from believing that the working poor were entitled to property that he specifically reminded them of their obligations to obey the
laws that legitimated their landless status. Tyrrell adopted Cumberland's
moral injunction to act for the good of the public as well as his identification of the status quo with public happiness to prohibit individuals
from changing the distribution of property into which they were born.

> Since the common good of mankind, is the highest end a man can
> propose to himself, and the common good of the city, or common-
> wealth where he lives, the greatest subordinate end next to that, and
> that both government and property were at first introduced by com-
> mon consent for the good of those humane societies that first agreed
> to it, every succeeding member of that commonwealth, or civil so-
> ciety, though born never so many ages after, is as much obliged to
> the observation thereof, as they that first instituted it; and though
> some men either by their own fault, and the carelessness, or prodi-
> gality of their ancestors, may perhaps be now under such circum-
> stances by reason of their poverty, as the civil government may ap-
> pear inconvenient to them, and the property now established
> contrary to their interests, as having perhaps little share either in
> lands, or goods, he is not therefore at liberty to resist the govern-

ment, and to change the course of his property already established: and this by the law of nature, without any divine revelation: since no man can disturb the general peace of humane society for his own private advantage, or security, without transgressing the natural laws of God, by bringing all things into as far as in him lies out of the settled course they now are in, into a state of anarchy and confusion. (Pp. 107–8, L6r–L7v)

Of course, this formulation of the natural law obligation to respect current holdings not only protected property from those without any but also defended it from the private and unlawful actions of the king.

Because the obligation to preserve oneself and others played such a vital role in Tyrrell's political arguments, it had to be made consistent with his strong defense of a property system that necessarily included propertyless individuals whose preservation could be threatened under certain economic circumstances. Tyrrell's defense of resistance required that the right of self-preservation could not be alienated, that none of the laws or agreements of civil society could override "that natural right every man hath to his own preservation" (pp. 110–11, L8v–L8r). Tyrrell had to acknowledge the right of necessity and argued that in this form the right of self-preservation continued to operate even in civil society. An individual "ready to perish . . . [can] make use of some of the superfluous necessaries of life which another man has laid by for the future uses of himself, and family, and that were without his consent, if it can by no other means be obtained" (p. 111, L8r). Although the relationship between the right of necessity and the injunction to respect current property holdings because of their contribution to the common good is unclear, it may be that Tyrrell assumed that there was little danger to the public good if an individual in dire circumstances simply took what self-preservation required. To accept the right to take from the rich if one was about to die, was unable to work, had begged magistrates and citizens to no avail, and was under an obligation to repay as soon as possible was to satisfy the right of self-preservation in the weakest way possible. It allowed Tyrrell to use self-preservation to generate rights that limited monarchs while escaping its potentially dangerous consequences for the distribution of land.

Locke

Though John Locke and James Tyrrell were close friends in the early 1680s, it would be a mistake simply to conflate their thought. It is probably accurate to place Tyrrell on the more moderate wing of the Whigs opposed to Charles II and James II and to see Locke on the more politically radical wing. Tyrrell's repeated dissociation of the "people" from the "rabble" may show a less democratic temperament than Locke's. They shared the desire to use natural law to defend the legitimacy of the property relations of their time. Only such a defense could help gather support from Whig landowners and convict the king of invading the property rights of legitimate property owners. But there are two important differences. In Locke's work there was an interest in economic growth and in the prevention of starvation that went far beyond what we have encountered so far.

In the *First Treatise* Locke wrote that the center of Filmer's system was that "men are not born free, and therefore could never have the liberty to choose either Governors, or Forms of Government. Princes have their Power Absolute, and by Divine Right, for Slaves could never have a Right to Compact or Consent. Adam was an absolute Monarch, and so are all Princes ever since."[8] The image behind Filmer's denial of natural freedom was the father's power over his children, a situation plausibly understood as given by God rather than chosen by the parties. He argued that the king's power over his subjects was a similar relationship because subjects were born under monarchs as children were born under fathers. Thus Locke saw Filmer defending "a Divine unalterable Right of Sovereignty, whereby a Father or Prince hath an Absolute, Arbitrary, Unlimited, and Unlimitable Power over the Lives, Liberties and Estates of his Children and Subjects" (1:9). As this quotation indicates, the power of the father over the children was based not only on his "begetting them" (which as Locke pointed out was strangely silent about the role of the mother) but also on the ownership he exercised over the property that nourished them. Perhaps because kings could not be said to "beget" their subjects, but could be thought to own the land that maintained them, Locke paid special attention to Filmer's statement that "the Grounds and Principles of Government necessarily depend upon the Original of Property" (1:73). Against the idea that Adam and rulers subsequent to him were the owners of the land in their kingdoms, Locke, like Tyrrell, deployed the natural law vocabulary of an original common which everyone had the right to use for self-preservation.

Locke's property theory can be summarized in the following way. Against Filmer he maintained that there was an original community of goods and not the private domain of Adam; against Hobbes he maintained that the original community could give way to private property rights peacefully; against Pufendorf he argued that these rights did not require consent; and in modification of Grotius he held that the original rights that people had to what they took from the common were more accurately understood through the idea of labor than through occupation or possession. That is, Locke used labor to help demonstrate the moral component of possession or occupation against Pufendorf's criticism that such acts were mere seizures. The specific intention of Locke's discussion of property was apparent in his summary of chapter 5. "I shall endeavor to shew, how Men might come to have a property in several parts of that which God gave to Mankind in common, and that without any express Compact of all the Commoners" (2:25). One of his purposes, then, was to show how natural law sanctioned the move from a common to the holdings that characterized English society so that a king who invaded those holdings could be seen as violating natural law.

The first question to consider about Locke's derivation of property in the *Second Treatise* is whether it developed from a negative or a positive community. That Locke did not use these distinctions to clarify his thought is odd indeed. He knew Pufendorf's work, and he must have known that Tyrrell used the distinction. Moreover, his correspondent and perhaps most important eighteenth-century interpreter, Jean Barbeyrac, relied on the idea of a negative community in his very Lockean analysis. Yet though this question will remain difficult to answer, perhaps we should begin by remembering how absorbed Locke was in Filmer's argument. This, in itself, suggests that Locke was working with the idea of a positive community. That was the way Filmer understood Grotius, and it is because he understood Grotius that way that he could first argue against Grotius that a primitive community could not give way to private rights without consent and then ridicule the possibility and legitimacy of consent. The absence of the distinction between a negative and a positive community in Locke can be understood as Locke's decision to accept Filmer's challenge to explain how a positive community could give way to private rights without consent, rather than reformulating it through the introduction of Pufendorf's distinctions.[9]

This reading is consistent with the language Locke used throughout chapter 5, a language that always described the common as owned by all rather than as unowned. He denied that it was robbery to take by labor

"what belonged to all in common" (2:28); he likened the common to a
fountain, the water of which "be every ones" (2:29); he described the
person who took more than he could use as taking what "belongs to
others" (2:31, 46), as having "invaded his neighbor's share" (2:37) and
as having "robbed others" (2:46). His argument that labor "overbal-
ance[s] the community of land" (2:40) clearly suggested that labor
overrode the rights that others had in the common and was incompatible
with the idea that labor for the first time established rights in what
before had been unowned. And insofar as he often seemed to think of the
state of nature as an English common (2:26) he was thinking of land
owned by many in common and not land common because it was unowned.

Locke traced the idea that common property should fall under the
control of private individuals first of all to God's intentions. As the earth
and all the people on it were the "workmanship" of God and, as a result,
His property, the uses to which His earth was put by His people were
governed by His purposes (1:39; 2:6). And since "the great design of
God" was for people to "increase and multiply" (1:41), Locke concluded that everyone was "bound to preserve himself and . . . as much as
he can, to preserve the rest of Mankind" (2:6). This injunction would be
disobeyed and His grant of the earth for mankind's subsistence would be
in vain if individuals were not able to take from the common and have
their appropriation respected by others. Thus, though the obligation to
preserve oneself prompted individuals to appropriate, the obligation to
preserve others required that appropriations be respected, understood as
a right, by others. Locke, then, rejected consent on the ground that some
might starve before it could be obtained (2:28, 32). His point was that
the right to use from the common and the obligation to respect what
others were using were based on our obligations to God and that these
obligations were in full force in the presence or absence of the approval
of others. "Reason, which was the voice of God in him, could not but
teach him . . . that pursuing that natural inclination he had to preserve
his Being, he followed the will of his Maker. . . . And thus Man's Property in the Creatures, was founded upon the right he had, to make use of
those things, that were necessary or useful to his Being" (1:86).

But Pufendorf's objection to these theories still had merit. Why should
the seizure of food by one person create an obligation not to seize in
another who was also under an obligation to use what was required to
stay alive? Pufendorf thought that because rights were built on mutual
recognition, were inevitably social, it was more accurate to think that as

individuals enjoyed their food undisturbed a web of tacit contracts was created and that to steal was wrong because it was a breach of those socially created contracts. There has persisted into the twentieth century a criticism of Locke, based on the idea that rights are social creations, which is summarized in the characterization of his theory as "the divine right of grab."[10]

Locke's response to Pufendorf's criticism of first possession arguments was to reinterpret possession as labor so as to give possession a moral content. Of course, as Locke found an alternative to consent he also escaped all the problems Filmer had insisted characterized the consent basis of property. Throughout the discussion of occupation or possession in the natural law tradition labor never seemed far from what was meant. Thus, after Pufendorf argued that people agreed to let unowned land become the property of the first occupant, he explained, "One man is adjudged to be the occupant of land, when he tills or manures it, or when he encloseth it with settled boundaries and limits."[11] Locke's acuteness was to take this implicit identification of occupation with labor and by making it explicit to draw arguments and conclusions that had escaped others.

The moral content of labor, the reason it created a right that others were obligated to respect, was explained by Locke in several ways. First, as we have seen, in laboring the individual was obeying a command of God and fulfilling an obligation to self-preservation. Second, in laboring the individual joined to the earth given in common a part of himself that was solely and legitimately his. In Locke's famous metaphor of "mixing" one's labor with nature, the right an individual had to his person was extended to include a right to that part of nature fashioned by the individual (2:27). An individual's right to exclude another from his person became a right to exclude another from that part of nature appropriated by the person's labor. Locke's third argument was that in laboring, the individual added a value to nature that "overbalances" the rights of the common (2:40). In some sense that part of nature that had been worked on and improved was a different object (at least 90 percent different, according to Locke) than the object to which the community had a claim. The relationship between property and preservation is evident in all these arguments. People would not mix their labor with nature and increase the value of nature's gifts, which was necessary if they were to preserve themselves and others, if they did not enjoy the security of knowing the product of their work was theirs.

Although it is logically possible to distinguish the mixing argument from the adding value argument or the individual act of laboring from its public benefit, Locke certainly never did. When he explained in paragraph 29 what he meant by the mixing metaphor, he moved immediately to the idea that labor mixed with nature increased its value: "Labour put a distinction between them and common. That added something to them more than nature, the common mother of all, had done; and so, they became his private right" (2:28). So important was the argument that labor added value that Locke devoted four paragraphs to its explanation, in effect making a traditional justification of property rights on the grounds that they increased prosperity (2:40–43).

Insofar as Locke could identify possession with labor, he could argue that it was not a mere seizure (or an occupation or a grab) but an action in accordance with God's will that increased the resources of the earth so that they could be better used to "support and comfort mankind." Moreover, Locke argued that labor alone could appropriate from a positive community only during abundance. Like the others in this tradition, he understood the first kind of right to emerge from the common to be a use right, which he described by the requirements that nothing taken could spoil and that enough and as good had to be left for others.[12] Given the plenty bestowed on man by God, and the moderate proportion taken by each under these limits, "he that leaves as much as another can make use of, *does as good as take nothing at all*" (2:33, emphasis added). Since no harm could come to anyone from the labor that an individual used to remove something from the common under these conditions, no theft could occur, no one's rights could be violated, and no one could be required to give or get permission or consent. Suppose even now, Locke wrote, an individual were planted in one of the "vacant places of America." Would such a person's appropriations harm the rest of mankind? Would anyone need to give consent before an individual in America picked some fruit (2:36)? Thus Locke could argue that a positive community characterized by abundance could give way to individual use rights based on labor.

Locke considered limits to appropriation in answer to the question of whether individuals could own as much as they were able to mix their labor with. The issue was whether individual appropriations would lead to "quarrels or contentions." Against Hobbes's charge that the common could not give way peacefully to private rights, Locke pointed out that with "the plenty of nature's provisions," "the few spenders," and the small "provision the industry of one man could extend itself [to]," arguments over the size of individual shares would not arise (2:31). Under these circumstances most individuals would lack a motive for violating the rights of others, and those few who did steal would be clearly wrong and easily punished. Limiting the first rights to emerge from the common to use maintained the abundance that allowed Locke to see rights others would respect developing peacefully and without consent. Locke's disagreement with Hobbes on this point was long-standing. In his eighth essay on the law of nature (written in 1660) Locke argued, "The duties of life are not at variance with one another, nor do they arm men against one another—a result which . . . follows . . . if men are . . . by the law of nature in a state of war . . . what else indeed can human intercourse be than fraud, violence, hatred, robbery, murder, and such like, when every man not only may, but must, snatch from another by any and every means what the other in his turn is obliged to keep safe."[13]

It was a common move in the natural law tradition to turn use rights into property rights through a contract that became necessary when abundance ceased, usually because of increases in population and the desires of people. To some extent Locke followed this path. But instead of having recourse to an express agreement that was historically suspect, Locke saw in the use of money a specific act that could be understood as giving consent to the transformation of use rights into more permanent property rights. Using money as the mechanism for giving consent to full property rights also had the advantage of linking consent to an ongoing process that continued to obligate through every transaction in a commercial economy.

Locke argued that with population increase came a complexity in economic organization that led to the use of money. Although money was, in part, responsible for increasing desires, it simultaneously increased the motivation to labor and facilitated commercial transactions. As a result, the goods available to people increased at a rate that far exceeded the pressure put on these goods by population.[14] Thus the agreements to use money continued abundance and as a result allowed labor to continue to confer rights. But because of the special qualities of money, the rights it conferred were full, permanent property rights, and these were to large and unequal landholdings. Seen from this perspective, Locke's first innovation in the derivation of property rights was to use labor to provide moral content to possession, and his second was to see the introduction of money as an agreement that transformed use rights into property rights. Disentangling the relative importance of labor and consent at this stage is not easy. Locke's purpose was probably not to specify one as preeminent but to establish as firm a foundation for property as possible by having them reinforce each other.

Locke was explicit that the inequality that grew with the application of labor in a money economy was perfectly legitimate. In fact, it seems that the point of chapter 5 was to show that the large and extremely unequal landholdings in Locke's England were consistent with natural law and could be understood to have been derived from God's grant of the earth in a positive community. Only such an argument would have enabled the Whigs "to defend themselves against the accusation of a design to level men's estates, which the Tories repeatedly hurled at them."[15] That the introduction of money was the vehicle that legitimated large and unequal holdings was made clear by Locke the first time he mentioned it: "The tacit agreement of Men to put a value on it, introduced (by Consent) larger Possessions, a Right to them" (2:36). This point was repeated when he reminded his readers that "the exceeding of the bounds of his just Property [is] not lying in the largeness of his Possessions" (2:46). And it was the point with which he ended his discussion of money: "Men have agreed to a disproportionate and unequal Possession of the Earth, they having by a tacit and voluntary consent found out a way how man can fairly possess more land than he himself can use the product of" (2:50). Perhaps it was only in this tradition, which so often imagined contracts, that he could offer the idea that individuals in using money consented to it and to the inequalities that flowed from it. Of course, his assumptions that money "in great part" measured labor and that the labor of employees (or servants) belonged to the employer also helped him link inequalities to natural law (2:28, 50).

Just as the natural law limits were applicable to the stage of use rights but were rarely invoked because it made no sense to violate them, they remained in effect after money was introduced but again were rarely important. This argument is familiar. Gold and silver did not spoil so they could be held and others excluded from them permanently without violating the spoilage restrictions of a use right. And the increased production that came with money assured that larger holdings developed in a process that created more rather than less for everyone, thereby avoiding the leave enough and as good for others limit. Thus temporary rights to use became permanent rights of property not because the restrictions that the earth's resources be used to sustain life were in any way lifted but because the nature of possessions changed in a money economy.

Neither money nor newly cultivated land nor goods produced to be sold to others "did [an] injury, wasted . . . the common stock; [or] destroyed . . . the portion of Goods that belonged to others" (2:46).

Locke's insistence that property should always be understood as a right to use what God gave for the preservation of human life, as well as his emphasis on God and man as workers and makers, brings out the extent to which his theory was meant to urge his readers to overcome their idleness, vanity, contentiousness, and extravagance and to concentrate on using their reason and industry to improve their land (2:34).[16] The moral purposes that property rights had to serve in Locke's theory led him to a defense of commerce and inequality and to an exhortation to all to join in economic activity because of its benefits. This economic theme was secondary to Locke's political purposes in the *Two Treatises*, but in the Scottish Enlightenment, as we shall see, the natural law vocabulary on property, if not exactly Locke's variant, was deployed almost entirely to further an ideology of agricultural improvement.

Like Tyrrell, Locke used the idea of an original community of property and the ability of people to derive property rights from it to guarantee each individual's independence in order to insist that only consent could explain the origin of government. But it was necessary for him to consider three cases in which those with property might be able to exert political control over—deny the natural independence of—those without property. In his consideration of inheritance, conquest, and abject poverty he explicitly adopted practices that would have enabled people to maintain their independence, even in social situations of considerable inequality, because they would have been able to maintain some property.

In the *First Treatise* Locke initially raised the question of inheritance to answer an objection to his assumption of the original community of goods.[17] If such a community existed, the objection went, why did property descend to children instead of reverting to "the common stock of Mankind" at the owner's death (1:88)? Locke's derivation of the right to inherit is interesting because it closely mirrored his derivation of the right to property. He began both arguments by rejecting a consent foundation for right and instead started with an injunction from God in the form of an instinctual endowment—the instinct of self-preservation for property and the instinct for propagating the species for inheritance. From this injunction Locke derived the obligations to preserve oneself and one's children. And from these obligations came the right to property and the right of children to inherit the property of the father. Since the parents had a duty not just to nourish their children but also to extend to them all the conveniences and comforts of life, the children had a right to all of their parents' property and not just to that amount required for their maintenance, as Grotius had argued (1:88). If a man died without children, his property ought to go to his father as a way of repaying him for the care and education he had provided. But if there were no children and no living father, Locke affirmed the origin of property from a common by agreeing that it should revert to the community, which in civil society meant the public magistrate (1:90).

Although children had a right to inherit, this right existed only during their nonage because the duty of the parent upon which the right rested ended with the child's maturity. After the children are "able to shift for themselves" the father can do what he wants with his property, bestowing "with a more sparing or liberal hand" on whomever he wanted (2:72). Locke's position ought not to be overinterpreted. Parents had a duty to care for and educate their children. If parents should die, their property ought to be used to provide for their children, who had a stronger right to it than anyone else. Children also should have a right to inherit, even if they had grown to maturity, if their father had left no will and the laws of the country were silent. Of course, the power of the father was always limited by "the law and custom of each country" (2:72). In all this Locke seems to have thought of himself as simply giving philosophical explanation for what most countries and most people already believed.

Certainly the most important element in Locke's discussion was that *all* the children shared equally in the right to their parents' property (1:93). The political issue at stake was the legal and moral status of primogeniture, which Locke had to show was not commanded by natural law. By stressing the natural right of all the children to inherit, as Grotius and Pufendorf had done, he denied that God had conveyed a superiority to one over the rest. And by insisting that all the children by nature were due a portion of the estate, he guaranteed independence to them all, understanding the possibility of the eldest exercising political power over his propertyless brothers and sisters (1:91). Thus, even if the earth had been given to Adam, at his death all the children would have become property owners and independent of one another. Denying the firstborn a natural superiority in inheriting property was vital to Locke's interpretation of kingly succession. Since he had shown that primogeniture was not part of natural law, it "can . . . have no Right, no pretense to it, any farther than . . . Consent" (1:94). The obvious implication, important in both the Exclusion Crisis and the Glorious Revolution, was that lines of succession could be altered by the legislative power of the community without violating natural law.

Locke also used the rights of the children and wife to the property of the father in his discussion of conquest in the *Second Treatise*. His contribution to the controversy over the meaning of the Norman Conquest for British politics was drastically to limit the rights of even a lawful conqueror. Locke argued that the power of a lawful conqueror could extend only to the lives of those who unjustly opposed him and only to some of their property. The conqueror could not take all of a father's property because of the rights of the wife and children to it (2:182). Thus the sons of conquered soldiers remained free and independent, subject only to a government to which they had consented. From the Norman Conquest, then, it was impossible to buttress absolutist claims based on the argument that the conqueror and his heirs owned all the property of the conquered kingdom.

Locke also recognized as a consequence of the original community the right of necessity. In the *First Treatise* the context for his discussion was primarily political. His argument that political power could not be derived from ownership led him to insist that no one may starve another by withholding food as a means of compelling obedience, "to force him to become his Vassal" (1:42). In fact, the rich man is under a moral obligation to afford relief to the poor out of his "Plenty," and when the rich sin by not giving, the poor have a "Right to the Surplusage of his Goods" (1:42), or as Locke wrote a sentence later, "a Title to so much out of another's Plenty, as will keep him from extreme want" (1:42). It is interesting that the requirement of restitution was not mentioned by Locke, as it was, for example, by Tyrrell. Assuming that this omission was intentional, an assumption by no means certain given how quickly this topic is brought up and left, Locke might have reasoned that in following the will of God to preserve oneself no obligation was incurred to the property holder who should have given but did not.

Locke's argument, then, was that just as individuals had rights to the property they worked for and inherited, they had a right, when no other means of subsistence was available, to take as much, but only so much, from the surplus of the rich as was necessary to keep them from "extreme want" (a concept no doubt analogous to Tyrrell's "ready to perish"). Nothing in Locke's formulation suggested redistribution or constituted an undermining of property rights. Locke ended this discussion with precisely the same point he made with regard to inheritance and conquest—political authority could only be based on consent and could not be derived from wealth or armed force any more than it could follow birth (1:43).

Though the introduction of money extended the period of abundance and thereby legitimated the inequalities in wealth and land that labor created, the period of abundance did not last forever. The event that ended that abundance, especially in land, was the political contract that created nations.[18] The motives for incorporating were various, sometimes described as an extension of the love of society (2:101), or as the need for protection against foreigners (2:107), or because of increased population (2:45), or because of the inconveniences created by men who are "no strict observers of equity and justice" (2:123). But whatever the motives for incorporating, it required setting national boundaries that ended the time during which labor could appropriate without harming anyone. When a nation was founded, its boundaries with other nations and between its own property holders were drawn up in a clear and public way and agreed to by the participants. "The several communities settled the bounds of their distinct territories, and by laws within themselves, regulated the properties of the private men of their society, and so, by compact and agreement, settled the property which labor and industry began" (2:45, 38). Money, then, did not enable Locke to do without an express contract establishing property rights, but it did allow him to postpone the contract until after great inequalities had been legitimated by natural law. As a result, those who were party to the agreement would have strong reasons to make sure large property holdings were protected. Locke, then, like Tyrrell, could rebut the argument that natural law and natural rights constituted an inevitably subversive doctrine.

With the act of incorporation the land that was within the country's boundaries but not owned by any individual underwent a dramatic change in status. It could no longer be appropriated by an individual simply through labor, for given the finite boundaries of any country and the implied scarcity of land, it would not be possible to take and still leave enough and as good for others. Locke noted that "in England, or any other Country, where there is Plenty of People under Government, who have Money and Commerce, no one can enclose or appropriate any part, without the consent of all his Fellow-Commoners. . . . [because] . . . the remainder, after such enclosure, would not be as good to the rest of the commoners as the whole was" (2:35). The property rights of owners, originally based on labor, were also transformed through the creation of a nation. Natural law continued to affirm the need for individual property rights because they were essential to peace and prosperity. But "in government the laws ought to regulate the right of property, and the possession of land is determined by positive constitutions" (2:50). That is, the rights of particular individuals to particular pieces of property could be derived only from municipal law. In entering society, the individual had to resign to the community rights to property or the purpose of the contract, its ability to bring the peace that best protected life, liberty, and estate, would be negated.

> It is fit to consider, that every Man, when he, at first, incorporates himself into any Commonwealth, he, by his uniting himself thereunto, annexed also, and submits to the Community those Possessions, which he has, or shall acquire, that do not already belong to any other Government. For it would be a direct Contradiction, for anyone, to enter into Society with others for the securing and regulating of Property: and yet to suppose this Land, whose property is to be regulated by the Laws of Society, should be exempt from the Jurisdiction of that Government. (2:120; see also 129, 138)

At this point it is clear that Locke's defense of exclusive property rights proceeded through several stages, each one of which brought forth a somewhat different argument. Use rights were founded on labor, property rights to more than any individual could immediately use became legitimate through agreements to use money, and finally in civil society exclusive rights became based on the laws that were enacted by a government people had agreed to join. But this progression did not leave natural law behind. The ultimate justification for property, the only rule that could never change, was that it preserved human life. The specific bases of property rights changed because under new circumstances the preservation of human life required new forms of social organization. Thus, at a certain level of development, government and municipal law were the necessary conditions for peace and economic growth, neither of which could be obtained if people did not "submit to the community" the ability to decide questions of ownership according to the common good. For that reason, natural law validated, perhaps even required, the contracts that established a civil society in which property came to be held by municipal law.

Once in a civil society, then, it was not possible to defend property rights simply by invoking labor. Yet though labor could no longer serve as a particular title, labor still had a role to play in the justification of an overall system of rules. Property rules that discouraged productive labor would not be in the common good. They would be a violation of God's injunction "to increase and multiply." But for labor to contribute to the common good, Locke thought it often needed to be given direction by government regulations, as the following summary of Locke's economic ideas makes clear.

> The state should uphold the value of money, carefully regulate the coinage, never resort to a policy of debasement, allow interest rates to seek their natural level, and keep careful watch over the balance of exports and imports. Through taxation and control of imports productivity might be properly encouraged. A rational colonial policy with regulative acts such as the navigation laws would guarantee sources of raw materials, stimulate home shipping and ancillary industries, and prevent competition with home markets. Finally, a disciplined, industrious, and skilled work force could be developed through an adequate poor law and the provision of institutions for training the unemployed.[19]

The ability of people before government to accumulate property in a way consistent with natural law and the inability of the eldest son, a conqueror, or the rich justly to deny property to others served to underwrite the natural equality in rights established by God. Though some would have legitimately accumulated much more than others in the state of nature, no one could have been starved or bullied into submission. Locke, then, used the original common and the ability of people to derive property from it to argue that individuals who were independent and morally equal would agree to incorporate only under terms established by their consent, rationally given. These terms, at first, were the traditional ones that all decisions had to serve the public rather than private good.

> But though Men when they enter into Society, give up the Equality, Liberty, and Executive Power they had in the State of Nature, into the hands of the Society, to be so far disposed of by the Legislative, as the good of the Society shall require; yet it being only with an intention in every one the better to preserve himself his Liberty and

Property; (For no rational Creature can be supposed to change his condition with an intention to be worse) the power of the Society, or Legislative constituted by them, can never be suppos'd to extend farther than the common good. (2:131)

But not only did natural property rights help guarantee the independence that made consent necessary, they helped give specific content to the common good, the terms under which consent was given. Thus Locke continued by stating that the common good required securing to all people their property (life and liberty as well as estate) through a government of "standing laws . . . known to the people" interpreted by "indifferent and upright judges" (2:131).

To the requirement that government act for the public good through nonarbitrary laws and decisions, Locke added the even stronger condition that because people entered society as property holders their consent must continue to be obtained before the property they held under the law could be regulated or taxed. "Tis true, Governments cannot be supported without great Charge, and 'tis fit every one who enjoys his share of the Protection, should pay out of his Estate his proportion for the maintenance of it. But still it must be with his own Consent, i.e. the Consent of the Majority, giving it either by themselves, or their Representatives chosen by them" (2:140). Here is a notion of consent that seems to require an active and continuous process of agreeing to political decisions that only an elected representative institution could provide. Locke's contribution to property theory not only includes his various technical solutions to questions about appropriation within the state of nature, all of which ended in the expected consensual resignation of rights to the political community, but also his argument that because people were property owners they would have insisted on being part of the political decisions that related to property even after civil society had been established. Thus consent may be the most important shadow that natural rights to property cast over civil society. Locke could not have spoken any clearer than in his statement that "if any one shall claim a Power to lay and levy Taxes on the people, by his own Authority, and without such consent of the people, he thereby invades the *Fundamental Law of Property*, and subverts the end of Government" (2:140).

Prudent people in the state of nature would fear putting the power of making laws in the hands of one person or even a few if they were not elected:

This is not much to be fear'd in Governments where the Legislative consists, wholly or in part, in Assemblies which are variable, whose Members upon the Dissolution of the Assembly, are Subjects under the common Laws of their Country, equally with the rest. But in Governments, where the Legislative is in one lasting Assembly always in being, or in one Man, as in Absolute Monarchies, there is danger still, that they will think themselves to have a distinct interest, from the rest of the Community; and so will be apt to increase their own Riches and Power, by taking, what they think fit, from the People. (2:138)

Locke came even closer to arguing that natural law required the creation of some kind of assembly in his comment that people "could never be safe nor at rest, nor think themselves in Civil Society, till the legislature was placed in collective bodies of Men, call them Senate, Parliament, or what you please" (2:94). On this issue Locke seemed less willing to tolerate constitutional diversity than Tyrrell was. Although Tyrrell thought natural law required understanding government as created by people who would have insisted that its rules promote the public good, he saw England's representative institutions as the result of a unique set of agreements in English history. Locke, however, came very close to arguing that the requirement of natural law that people preserve themselves and others necessitated representative institutions, suggesting that no one should leave the state of nature and join a civil society that was without them. Of course, in either interpretation the king's interventions in parliamentary elections, given in great detail in chapter 19 of the *Second Treatise*, became violations of the original contract and threats against the property of people.

But though the "fundamental law of property" required elected representative institutions, it is still an open question whether Locke thought the franchise had to include all adult males or whether it was possible for the people to be represented by legislators elected by only some of them. Let me just note that Locke had maintained that everyone had property rights in their labor and in the goods necessary for preservation, even if that meant taking from the surplus of the rich. Thus all men, not only the landed, had property rights that might have required representation. As a consequence of these rights, no one could be forced into the dependence that was typically at the heart of seventeenth-century justifications for denying people the vote.[20]

Locke used the natural right to property to recommend to people that they place the legislative power only in the hands of an assembly and that they view taxation without the consent of an assembly as a violation of their rights. For Locke, property led to constitutionalism, not to libertarianism or a radical redistribution. It was an "argument for resistance upon the foundations of the right of the people to have their grievances redressed through their elected representatives."[21] The natural right to property entitled an individual to live under a government that pursued the public good through laws passed by elected representatives; it did not pose any obstacles to or create any presumptions in favor of the regulations or taxation of even an interventionist government. In Locke's work, then, natural property rights cast four shadows over property rights in society. In the first, the laws that regulated property must have been agreed to by representatives; in the second, those laws must be directed to the common good, which included not only the juridical requirements of nonarbitrariness but also the economic requirements of furthering growth; in the third, the law must make certain that no one starve; and in the fourth, a person about to starve because the previous requirement was not fulfilled could take what was needed.

Locke's acknowledgment of the right of necessity in the *First Treatise* was not, as we have seen, unusual. But Locke's concern that God's workmanship not be allowed to perish went deeper. In his early essays on the laws of nature he wrote that among the "outward performances" that the natural law "commanded" were "the outward worship of the Deity, the consolling of a distressed neighbor, the relief of one in trouble, the feeding of the hungry" (*ELN*, pp. 195, 211). These sentiments were expressed in an even stronger and more specific form twenty years later in the opening sentence of the chapter on property in the *Second Treatise*. There his emphasis was on the rights of the poor rather than the obligations of the rich. "Men, being once born, have a right to their preservation, and consequently to Meat and Drink, and other such things, as nature affords for their Subsistence" (2:25). Although it was possible in the natural law tradition to recognize some rights and duties as "imperfect," that is, inappropriate for government regulation, Locke did not put the rights of the poor in this category. Rather, he explicitly enjoined the political community to organize relief. "The first and fundamental natural law, which is to govern the legislative itself, is the protection of the Society, and (as far as will consist with the public good) of every person in it" (2:134).

In 1697 Locke was the author of a proposal to reform the English Poor Law. The Old Poor Law, as it has come to be known, was actually the result of a number of laws enacted between 1597 and 1601, though it was the last of them, the "43rd of Elizabeth," that was taken to be its foundation. This act required each parish to provide for its poor by taxing the landowners within its boundaries. An unpaid overseer was to be appointed in each parish to collect the taxes and to spend them to relieve the aged and infirm poor, to apprentice the children of paupers, and to provide work for the able-bodied poor. In 1662 the Act of Settlement, which enabled the parish overseers, on complaint to justices, to return newcomers back to the parish of their settlement, was added to the laws concerning the poor. This act strengthened even more the local basis of the Poor Law's operation. Preventing vagrancy, relieving distress, and maintaining social stability were the goals of the Old Poor Law, and all can be seen in Locke's plan.

At first glance, Locke's proposals seem extraordinarily harsh. He blamed the poor for their poverty, attributing their situation to a "relaxation of discipline and corruption of manners," "their debauchery" or "idleness."²² To counter their lack of virtue, he recommended a system that used discipline, control, and physical punishment. Paupers would wear badges, children of paupers from the ages of three to fourteen would be put in a "working school" (to be made "sober and industrious"), beggars would be sentenced to "houses of correction," where they would engage in "hard labor," and those found to have violated any of these various rules would be punished by being "soundly whipped," by losing an ear, or by being transported to plantations. It was clearly his belief that if alehouses were closed, vagrancy and begging were punished, and the circumstances of receiving aid were made unpleasant enough, pauperism among those who could work (most of the poor, he thought) would end.

Yet his system did guarantee subsistence and education to the young children of paupers as well as apprenticeships to those children when they reached the age of fourteen. He gave the Poor Law guardians the power to force local artisans and farmers (the wealthiest first) to employ and train these young people. Similarly, if able-bodied adults could not find employment, the guardian was to set a wage below the prevailing rate (after all, Locke said, the unemployed must lack either ability or honesty) and see that they were employed. And if no one volunteered to set such people to work, the guardian could "compel" men of the parish to share in the expenses of providing employment. Locke's insistence that everyone had an obligation to preserve themselves and others was given expression in his Poor Law proposal "that if any person die for want of due relief in any parish in which he ought to be relieved, the said parish be fined according to the circumstances of the fact and the heinousness of the crime."

That allowing people to die was a "crime" also surfaced in a short piece known as the "Venditio" (1695).[23] This essay was a defense of the justice of allowing the market to set prices. "What anyone has he may value at what rate he will and transgress not against justice if he sells it." Locke upheld this doctrine even in the case of selling corn "in a town pressed with famine." That is, it was not wrong to charge a high price to those in desperate need even if the same corn could bring only one quarter as much in a town without famine. Yet again, the injunction to preserve life introduced some limits to economic activity. For if the corn seller refused to sell at all or "extorts so much from their present necessity as not to leave them the means of subsistence afterward he offends against the common rule of charity as a man and if any of them perish by reason of extortion is no doubt guilty of murder." Under these circumstances, the seller is "bound to be at some loss and impart of his own to save an other from perishing." In describing the parish that allowed someone to die as committing a "crime" and the corn seller who let people perish rather than accept a loss as "guilty of murder" Locke was using strong language indeed.

Sidney and Barbeyrac

Algernon Sidney's *Discourses Concerning Government* was written sometime between 1680 and 1682, during the height of Filmer's vogue, but it was not published until 1698. Partly because of Sidney's martyrdom (he was beheaded in 1682 for treason) and partly because of his use of civic humanist themes not found in Locke, his work was probably as well known as Locke's *Two Treatises* to much of the eighteenth century.[24] Sidney, like Tyrrell and Locke, held Grotius in high esteem, naming his *Rights of War and Peace* the most important of all books in political theory, and he too used natural law to criticize Filmer.[25] His main concern was to assert the natural liberty and equality of men to show that all governments had to be understood as originating in the consent of their citizens and could be toppled when a monarch violated the terms under which consent was given. It was popular sovereignty, the unlimited ability of the people to create the kind of government they thought would best guard the public good, that occupied the center of his thought. Thus, implicitly relying on the idea of a negative community, he insisted again and again that "God having given the government of the world to no one man, nor declared how it should be divided, left it to the will of man."[26]

According to Sidney, men were "naturally free" (p. 3) with "an equal liberty of providing for themselves" (p. 59). Moreover, they remained free and equal prior to government because neither birth nor wealth could develop into power. This state continued "till their numbers so increased, that they became troublesome and dangerous to each other; and finding no other remedy to the disorders growing . . . joined many families into one civil body, that they might the better provide for the conveniency, safety, and defense of themselves and their children. This was a collation of every man's private right into a public stock" (pp. 59–60). That property rights were included in this general resignation of rights to the public was clear from his later statement, "My land is not simply my own, but upon condition that I shall not thereby bring damage upon the public, by which I am protected in the peaceable enjoyment and innocent use of what I possess" (p. 482). Of course, people agreed to have their rights "collated" into the public only on the condition that public acts aimed for the public good. But Sidney added, as Locke did, that only those laws agreed to could be said to satisfy the requirement of serving the public good: "He is a free man who lives or best pleases himself, under laws made by his own consent" (p. 386). Sidney's strong sense of what constituted consent can be seen in his specific denial that tacit consent was legitimate, arguing that neither "silent submission" nor "bare suffrance" could signify consent. Only "an explicit act of approbation, when men have ability and courage to resist or deny" (p. 86), could constitute authentic consent. To that end Sidney thought parliaments should be elected annually.

Sidney's sense that a people could consent to set up any government they wanted was mirrored by his sense that they could consent to any law they wanted. Thus he maintained that both the establishment of government and the activity of the legislature were necessarily arbitrary, wholly dependent on the will of men (p. 497). "Societies may regulate themselves as they think fit" (pp. 25, 408). His argument, then, did not require using natural rights to limit what legitimate legislatures could do; rather it was based on allowing a people whose possession of rights made them free and equal to agree through their legislature to virtually any law they wanted. A king who violated their law and their good as they defined it "made his transgressions the legitimate target of the just war of his own people, the only way they had of bringing him to justice."[27] Sidney, like Tyrrell, used an analogy that linked magistrates with servants: "And if I am free in my private capacity to regulate my particular affairs according to my own discretion, and to allot to each servant his proper work, why have not I, with my associates, the freemen of England, the like liberty of directing and limiting the powers of the servants we employ in public affairs" (p. 496).

At the same time that Sidney engaged in a discussion about the natural rights and duties of citizens and magistrates, he also engaged in a historical discussion of English political institutions. This historical argument is beyond the scope of this study, but it is interesting to note the rough parallels that existed in his work between the history of natural man and the history of England. Most important, Sidney interpreted the early history of English landholding as approximating the conditions of an original common. He denied that English kings were ever the owners of all the land or that they allowed others to use land only under the conditions they imposed. From the start the land was open to all. "When the Romans deserted our island, they did not confer the right they had, whether more or less, upon any man, but left the enjoyment of it to the poor remainders of the nation." (p. 436). Later, Saxons settled in England rather than continue their piracy, but the land they were allotted by the Britons was held by them in common, not owned by their king. Though at various times kings may have been given the discretion to distribute land, Sidney insisted it was the people who had given them the right "to dispose of what belongs to the public [for] the common good, and the accomplishment of those ends, for which they were entrusted" (p. 437). Having established the historical reality of an original common, Sidney could understand Magna Carta and the evolution of the English Parliament as part of the process by which a free and independent people consented to their government and its laws.

To Sidney, natural rights to property played a relatively small role. An original community of land and a law of succession that maintained equality by denying that primogeniture had natural law foundations meant that only consent could be a just basis for government. He used the natural law discussion of property to establish legislative superiority and to insist that it was only through elected legislatures that the people could give their consent to laws made for the public good. He displayed little anxiety that legislatures would violate the common good and had little interest in using natural rights to property to limit what legislatures could do.

Sidney's enterprise did not require him to engage in technical arguments over the characteristics of natural property rights. As a result, the prominence he gave to the public and its ability to settle rights in any way consistent with consent was expressed in a very clear fashion. A considerably more technical and somewhat more individualistic interpretation of the natural law tradition can be found in the notes Jean Barbeyrac included with his translations into French of the works of Grotius and Pufendorf. So scholarly and insightful were these notes thought to be that they were added to English translations as if they were as indispensable as the text itself.[28] Barbeyrac thought of himself as a follower of Locke, though he thought highly of Sidney and also recommended him to his readers.

Barbeyrac used his notes on Grotius and Pufendorf to correct them whenever he thought they had not stressed sufficiently that the right to property was the right to exclude others. Not surprisingly, then, Barbeyrac ruled out of consideration a totally public system of ownership. "A universal community of goods, which might have place among men perfectly just and free from all irregular passions, can't but be unjust, chimerical, and full of inconveniences among men so disposed as we are" (*LNN*, p. 368). Barbeyrac's emphasis on the right to exclude can be seen in his criticisms of the rights recognized by Grotius to harmless use, to free passage, to the right to occupy waste land, and to the right to low duties. Barbeyrac denied that anyone should be thought to have these as rights. He argued, instead, that they should be understood as part of the moral obligations of ownership (*RWP*, pp. 152–56). This meant that though a moral person should allow others, for example, to cross his property if it did him no harm, it remained within his right to refuse: "It necessarily follows from the right of property, that the proprietor may refuse another the use of his goods [even though] humanity indeed requires, that he should grant the use to those who stand in need of it, when it can be done without any considerable inconveniency to himself" (*RWP*, p. 152). Barbeyrac also thought that it was wrong for Grotius to say that children had a right to inherit, for this denied owners the right to do whatever they wanted with their property (*RWP*, p. 223). He repeated this point in his notes to Pufendorf, arguing that since it was part of a property right to be able to dispose of goods as owners thought fit, wills derived their force first from natural law and were not the mere creations of civil law (*LNN*, p. 420).

To defend this position Barbeyrac invoked Locke's labor argument, in effect linking the strength of an exclusive property right to its origins in the individual activity of laboring. He particularly used Locke's labor theory to criticize the consent elements in both Pufendorf and Grotius. As Barbeyrac read Locke, individuals first took what they needed from the common in the form of use rights, which excluded others only during the time goods were actually possessed. As population grew and land had to be cultivated, full property rights developed from the labor and industry individuals expended. Consent was unnecessary to the derivation of either use rights by possession or property rights by labor because in both cases people were acting according to God's intention that the earth be used to preserve life. He pointed out that without labor a larger population could not have been preserved and that the only condition under which people would undertake the hardships of labor were if they could be assured of owning what they produced (*LNN*, p. 385). Since neither possessing nor laboring was a seizure, but both were actions in accord with God's intentions, they could establish rights in the absence of tacit consent or an express division. Barbeyrac followed Locke in believing the state of nature was orderly, in part because acquisition in that state was subject to the spoilage and the enough and as good for others limits. What was given by God could not be allowed to perish or become useless. Barbeyrac did not adopt Locke's argument that consenting to money entailed consenting to the inequality that grew with the use of money.

Fulfilling the obligation to God to preserve oneself and others, first through possession and then through labor, seemed to Barbeyrac to be all that was necessary to justify the natural right to property. That this derivation was accomplished through individual acts, without the consent of others, did allow him to see natural rights as somewhat more individualistic than Grotius or Pufendorf did. But however he understood the derivation and nature of rights before the establishment of government, it is clear that he, like Locke, saw the contract that created civil society as requiring individuals to "submit" their property to the community: "After what manner so ever the state is formed, the whole country belongs to all the body; and so it follows, that the laws of union extend so far as to give the people, or them that represent them, right to dispose in divers manners the goods of each particular person, as the public good requires. This is so much the more certain at present, because our kings have for a long time enjoyed this right by the consent of the people" (*LNN*, p. 404).

Barbeyrac was just as explicit as Locke that the natural right to property did not create any difficulties for the public regulation of property. And he accepted that in civil society, regulations may make property "pass from one to another without express consent, nay, sometimes against the will of the ancient proprietor" (*LNN*, p. 442). Barbeyrac's position is perfectly captured in his discussion of wills. Though he began with a more individualistic interpretation, insisting on the right of individuals to leave their property to whomever they wanted in the absence of municipal law, he was just as explicit that in a civil society property was transmitted from one generation to another by positive law. "So that if the civil laws prescribed certain limitations and forms to that power [of making wills], it proceeds from the authority which the sovereign hath to limit the right of property, and to regulate the use that citizens ought to make of their goods" (*LNN*, p. 420).

His intellectual outlook did not include the belief that individual, egoistic actions would spontaneously create public prosperity. His fear that "we must be careful not to extend the rights of property so far as to do a considerable hurt to commerce" attests to his view that prosperity depended on regulations. Thus he seemed to approve of some price controls and laws against idleness (*LNN*, pp. 459–60, 870). And in passages reminiscent of Sidney, motivated in part by the mercantilist fear of imported luxury goods and in part by the fear that an inordinate desire for wealth could lead to dishonesty and weakness, he approved of sumptuary laws (*LNN*, pp. 825, 459).

The dominant value in Barbeyrac and in the tradition he helped pass on to later generations was the preservation of human life. Both property and government derived their legitimacy from their ability to preserve life through the peace and prosperity they brought. As a result, obligations to both ceased when they no longer served their ends. Barbeyrac followed Locke in insisting that people had an obligation to preserve themselves and others and that this obligation justified rebellion or resistance to magistrates (*LNN*, p. 187). And if preservation was threatened by the property rights of others, the right of necessity could be invoked.

Barbeyrac did, however, side with Pufendorf against Grotius in his understanding of this right as using what belonged to others, rather than as having all goods returned to a common status (*LNN*, p. 209).

The natural law discussion of property rights was used by Tyrrell, Locke, and Sidney primarily for political purposes. Their struggle against Charles II (and the intellectual justification of the monarchy provided by Filmer) required that they provide a political theory in which government was created through the consent of people who are by nature free, equal, and independent. Only if people had the right to take what they needed for their preservation from a common would they have been able to require that certain conditions be met before they joined with others and to insist that they retained their right to rebel if those conditions were violated. Because they would have entered society as property holders, they would have insisted that their property could not be taxed and regulated without the consent of representative institutions elected from their community.

To connect the property rules of a developed political society to those that would have been given to man directly by God in the state of nature, this discussion of property rights had to proceed through various stages. As a result, it faced the problem of reconciling the different ways property could be acquired from stage to stage. In the case of Locke, especially, this meant explaining the relationship between the ability of individuals simply to take by their labor what was required for their preservation in the state of nature and their right in civil society to have only what they could acquire under laws passed by a legislature for the public good. The problem posed by the injunction to preserve each and every person under rules that had to guard the public first is nicely illustrated by the parenthetical phrase Locke included in his argument that the purpose of legislatures was "the preservation of the Society, and (as far as will consist with the public good) of every person in it" (2:134). Locke certainly believed that the public good was furthered by publicly funded programs that guaranteed subsistence and work to everyone. To put this point in a more rights-oriented way, Locke believed that the public good required the protection of everyone's property rights, one of which was the right to subsistence, "to Meat and Drink" as Locke put it in the first sentence of his chapter on property. To Locke, then, the welfare of society was bound up with the welfare rights of the poor.

But the relationship between the welfare of society and the welfare rights of the poor, between the overall prosperity that property rights to exclude helped to foster and the preservation of each that property rights to be included guaranteed, could be interpreted in different ways. Natural law, and the relationship it insisted on between property rights and preservation, would continue to play an important role in eighteenth-century Scotland. But under the pressure of trying to modernize a backward economy, many of the social theorists of the Scottish Enlightenment came to think that the welfare of most was not consistent with the welfare rights of everyone.

THREE

Property Rights and Progress

Hutcheson to Smith

The Scottish Enlightenment was dominated by the attempt to understand and promote the progress of society, specifically the economic growth and the cultural changes that had to occur for economic and moral improvement to take place. The founding of the Society of Improvers in the Knowledge of Agriculture in 1720 and the Edinburgh Society for Encouraging Arts, Sciences, Manufactures, and Agriculture in Scotland in 1755 were indicative of this outlook. This interest was prompted in part by the backward state of Scottish economic development and the disastrous famines that occurred between 1695 and 1700 but which were remembered for generations.[1] But also important was the Union with England in 1707, which prompted invidious comparisons between England and Scotland and fostered discussions about how to maintain Scottish cultural and economic independence. Central to the economic program that developed in response to the Union was the need for Scotland to increase its trade and improve its agriculture. But such an improvement seemed impossible unless Scotland moderated its religious passions and rejected the claims of James II and his son, the Pretender. Scotland needed to adopt the moral qualities required by a peaceful, "polite," commercial nation. Thus the philosophers of the Scottish Enlightenment were always concerned about both economic and moral improvement. The difficulty Scotland had in sustaining economic growth in the first part of the century and the periodic outbursts of Jacobite political violence that occurred up to 1745 only made more obvious to many Scottish intellectuals that improvement on both fronts was crucial.[2]

The natural law of Grotius, Pufendorf, and Locke made a particularly strong impression in eighteenth-century Scotland and played an important role in the attempts to improve it. In part, this occurred through the influence of Gershom Carmichael, who introduced his 1718 edition of Pufendorf's *Duties of Men and Citizens* into the center of the Scottish university curriculum.[3] Carmichael was a strong supporter of the Whig cause in 1688–89 and later of the House of Hanover in 1714. His interest in using Pufendorf to teach "those duties of men and citizens which are demanded in the individual circumstances of human life" reflected the instability of Scottish society.[4] He shared with those who would follow him in Scottish universities the hope that a knowledge of natural rights and duties would inure Scottish society to the appeal of the Jacobites.

> But the need for a thorough grounding and training in moral science should be sufficiently evident when one considers the innumerable delusions which tend to creep into questions of this kind and divide men every day into parties not without great disturbance of public peace. Nay, one may affirm that that perverse and malignant spirit which inspires evil citizens among us to unsettle the public happiness . . . and agitates the same individuals to initiate endless rebellions in favour of the papal pretender to the throne has no other source (so far as this source can be imputed to opinions more than to evil passions) than ignorance of the true principles of natural law. (P. 5)

Carmichael helped transmit to eighteenth-century Scotland the Whig interpretation of natural law, including its understanding of property. He criticized Filmer's contention that God gave the earth to Adam alone and instead asserted that it was given to all mankind. He used a negative community to express the nature of God's grant and under the influence of Locke found in labor the origin for some of the rights of individuals to what they appropriated (pp. 38–43). Thus Carmichael rejected Pufendorf's use of contract and consent to derive property rights, maintaining that Pufendorf was inconsistent to argue for both a negative community and the need for a contract. The consent of others would be required only, Carmichael held, if they were co-owners, as in a positive community. "Pufendorf was not consistent with himself," Carmichael wrote, "when he denied that the original community of things was positive and insisted at the same time that one could acquire a right of ownership only with the aid of agreements" (p. 40). But though he adopted Locke's position that labor established property rights independently of consent, he ignored the mixing argument and emphasized the link between labor, property rights, and "the safety and utility" of the human race.

The work of Gershom Carmichael is an especially clear indication that Locke's labor theory was not read by his near contemporaries as an ideological justification for unlimited accumulation. Carmichael insisted that people needed only a finite amount of goods and that to strive for more was contrary to human nature. "Things once obtained should be considered as bulwerks against necessity and as material for doing good for others, not as things to be piled up endlessly and merely to titillate the imagination" (p. 43). Carmichael also upheld the right of necessity, and he explicitly preferred the stronger formulation of Grotius to that of Pufendorf, arguing that the right of necessity inhered even in those who were poor because of their own fault. The legacy of the natural law of Pufendorf and Locke, at least according to Carmichael, was an affirmation of the need to preserve human life, the continuation of an ethic in which property rights and morality were intertwined, and, most important, given the threat of Jacobite rebellion, the moral requirement of citizens' devotion to the public.

Carmichael was not alone among Scottish natural law philosophers in thinking that the natural law understanding of property carried with it moral and legal restraints. The same understanding can be found in the two great attempts at a rational compendium of Scottish law written during this period, the first by Lord Stair (James Dalrymple) in 1681 and the second by John Erskine published in 1773.[5] In summarizing the thought of Stair and Erskine as having "followed the natural law line," Peter Stein has written that they "considered the holder of property to be subject to such restrictions imposed by nature in the public interest that he was theoretically almost a trustee of his property on behalf of the community."[6] The theorists this chapter will consider—Francis Hutcheson, David Hume, Thomas Reid, Lord Kames (Henry Home), Adam Smith—more often wrote against legal restrictions on property than for them. But that was not because they thought that property rights were no longer tied to the public interest and the preservation of human life. Rather, they had come to believe that certain restrictions and regulations, such as those of the Poor Law, were incompatible with the moral, political, and economic development that was needed for private and public life to flourish.

Hutcheson

Gershom Carmichael's successor in the chair of moral philosophy at the University of Glasgow was Francis Hutcheson. Hutcheson, a Presbyterian minister, brought the oratorical skills of the pulpit to his classroom and as a result became one of the most famous teachers of his time. Moreover, his *Short Introduction to Moral Philosophy* (1747) was the most popular textbook in moral philosophy in Scotland and America in the eighteenth century. Hutcheson's moral philosophy, like Carmichael's, was meant, at least in part, as an attack on the Jacobites and a defense of the Glorious Revolution. In fact, Hutcheson's defense of rebellion was so widely used in the American colonies later in the century that it is often taken as his most influential teaching.[7]

But his outlook is most appropriately described as that of an economic and moral improver. His property theory was both an explicit defense of inequality and an effort to educate those in "polite" society to the moral, political, and economic virtues that would justify their eminence. He attacked the wasteful ostentation of the wealthy, favored putting them in jail if they fueled their conspicuous consumption by bad debts, and railed against their gaming and idleness.[8] He hoped that "the mechanick trades should be held in high reputation, so that people of better fortunes and families may not deem it below them to be concerned in them" (*SI*, p. 323). And he urged his readers to undertake "cleaning forests, draining marshes, maintaining foreign commerce, making harbors, fortifying cities, cultivating manufactures and ingenious arts, and encouraging the artisans" (*System*, 2:250).

In the controversy over who should choose ministers to lead local churches, known as the patronage dispute, Hutcheson's political and social position is clearly indicated. In 1712 the British Parliament, with its three Scottish representatives dissenting, restored the power of patrons (the few largest, usually absentee, landowners in the parish) to pick ministers and reignited a conflict that had occurred periodically since the Reformation. Although the disagreement traditionally pitted the gentry and elders of the church ("moderates" in this period) against the patron, in the early eighteenth century a new element was added with the emergence of an evangelical "popular" party that maintained that the right to elect ministers inhered in the whole congregation, propertied and propertyless alike. Hutcheson considered the plan to allow all the adult males in the congregation to vote on the choice of a minister in his pamphlet *Considerations on Patronages. Addressed to the Gentlemen of England.* He strongly rejected that plan, arguing that

> the populace are by no means the fittest and best judges of ministerial qualification. Preaching, for instance, is one main thing to be noticed in a right choice. Now what kind of preachers are they

whom the vulgar chiefly admire . . . if the choice of ministers were chiefly in the vulgar, I would be much afraid this would be one bad effect among others, that it would be too violent a temptation to preachers in order to gain the applause of the electors, to suit themselves to their mean and depraved taste.[9]

Hutcheson preferred the "moderate" method of selection, which he described as limiting electors to "the principal men of interest in each parish" and the church elders. Hutcheson opposed the "popular" method because it did not give sufficient weight to the local landed interest and argued against the patronage system for the same reason. According to his calculations, the vast majority of the patrons would not be residents of the parish in which they would exercise their right. By identifying these absentee patrons with the "court" interest, Hutcheson raised the specter of patrons basing their decisions on political rather than religious grounds and the possibility of their being bribed through the offer of places and pensions. Not only did the patronage system suggest the corrupting influence of the "court" and the violation of the gentry's ancient rights, it also threatened the local system of social control. He understood that picking a minister was an important way to form the "temper and minds" of "tenants." His fear was that ministers chosen by absentee patrons would not have the respect of the gentry and would lose influence with the populace. The result would be a people without virtue, by which he seems to mean without deference, soon to fall to the mischiefs of the "populars."

The social perspective that Hutcheson adopted in this pamphlet—the desire "to enlarge the power of the body of the landed gentleman"— informed all of his work on property. He defended the gentry against both the few in the high aristocracy, behind whom he saw the corrupt methods of the court, and the many who owned no land. Like most of the professors of the Scottish Enlightenment, Hutcheson saw the gentry as the group most likely to be improved and most able to improve their society. His description of public life as an arena in which "men of finer genius and capacity exert their abilities and improve them by exercise in the service of mankind" was certainly meant to make it as alluring as possible (*System*, 2:250).

The language of natural law was not the only one available for political discussion, or, in fact, the only one Hutcheson used. But it did address a number of issues important to Hutcheson's enterprise of consolidating the Whig establishment and improving Scottish society. Only the language of natural law could combat Hobbesian views of natural man and the state of nature and demonstrate against Hobbes and Bernard de Mandeville that morality and society were not the result of convention or artifice but were part of an order established by God. Natural law vindicated God's providence and the Scottish social order. It established moral duties appropriate to each social position. It helped to justify the revolution of 1688. But most important to a discussion of property, it established the duties of those who owned property and explained why others were propertyless. Because the "lower orders are always imitating the manners of their superiors" (*SI*, p. 322), it seemed especially important to Hutcheson that those with property fulfill their economic, political, and moral duties.

Hutcheson did not simply accept the natural law bequeathed to him. Under the influence of the Third Earl of Shaftesbury, he thought the natural law theories of Pufendorf and Locke were excessively rationalist and selfish. Hutcheson denied that people did what was right because they were aware of the advantages that would accompany acts in conformity with God's law.[10] Instead, he defended the reality of social affections which moved people to act in virtuous ways prior to and independent of any selfish or legal considerations. As a result, he thought of natural rights as based on the requirements of a human constitution that was most fully developed when it served others as well as the self. The importance of the sociable passions is immediately evident in his discussion of the origin of property rights. He began with the "desire of self preservation" and added "tender affections [to] those we love" as motives for "occupying or acquiring things necessary" (*SI*, p. 150; *System*, 1:310). Hutcheson hoped to find in these passions an empirical foundation for natural law, which could be based on "observations and conclusions discoverable from the constitution of nature" (*System*, 1:1). The social passions also provided Hutcheson with reason to think people could act on the principles of the public good. "Our natural taste is so formed," he wrote, "that we immediately approve and esteem all such affections or powers, the more in proportion as they are of greater importance to the general good" (*SI*, p. 62).

Hutcheson did not understand property rights to be natural rights. He used the distinction, as had Pufendorf, between natural and adventitious rights. The former "nature itself has given to each one" whereas the latter "depends upon human deed or institution." Among natural rights were a right to life, to an unblemished character, to liberty, to the sacrifice of one's self for the public, to private judgment, and to the same access as others to acquire adventitious rights (*System*, 1:293; *SI*, pp. 141–42). Though these were perfect rights and therefore had to be secured through the force of the state, Hutcheson's constant reminder that they applied only if the public good did not require otherwise (*System*, 1:320) shows how far natural rights were in Hutcheson from expressing a strongly individualistic point of view. Since property depended upon the activity of occupying or laboring, it was an adventitious right. Hutcheson was clear that adventitious rights had their foundation in the nature of man; they simply needed human acts or "deeds" to take form. That marriage as well as property holding was for him an adventitious state should convey the solid foundations of adventitious rights and obligations.

Since God created people with senses and desires that "naturally lead to the use of external things," His intentions conferred on them a right to subordinate plants and animals to their purposes. Hutcheson explained the origin of individual property rights in two ways. First, just as the physical senses and appetites in the constitution of people impelled them to use the products of nature, another part of their constitution—their moral sense—reacted with disapprobation if what they had acquired from nature was taken by someone else. "Our sense of right and wrong also shows, that it must be inhuman and ill natured, for one who can otherways subsist by his own nature, to take by violence from another what he has acquired or improved by his innocent labours" (*SI*, p. 150). Although the moral sense reacted immediately and was not the result of a chain of calculations, it was implanted by a benevolent God to direct people to act in ways consistent with the public's happiness and their own.

Hutcheson's second explanation for the legitimacy of property rights was based on demonstrating more directly the relationship between property rights and the public good. His argument with regard to property was simply that to preserve themselves and others, especially under the circumstances created by population growth, people had to be industrious. Since "no man would employ his labours unless he were assured of having the fruits of them at his disposal: otherwise all the more active and diligent would be a perpetual prey, and a set of slaves, to the slothful and worthless," all persons must have rights to what they had acquired through their labor (*SI*, p. 150). In the absence of a property right, neither self-love nor the love of others would result in industry.

The passions implanted in human nature prompted people to use the products of the earth for themselves and their families and to believe they had rights to what they were using against the encroachments of others. The legitimacy of these feelings was reinforced by reason when they thought about the benefits of property rights to the public good. In this way the mutual recognition of property rights developed peacefully from a negative community through individual acts of occupation, possession, and labor. Hutcheson's general point was that the rights approved by the moral sense and the public good were consistent with one another, but he did recognize the possibility of conflict. When that occurred, the public good seemed to take priority over the initial promptings of the passions and senses. Hutcheson wrote that though the "several rights of mankind are therefore first made known, by the natural feelings of the heart, and their natural desires . . . all such inclinations or desires are to be regulated by right reason, with a view to the general good of all" (*SI*, p. 119).

Private property rights were necessary to engage the passions that were part of the human constitution created by God. Although this argument was much concerned with motivating people to labor, its relationship to Locke's labor theory is problematic and depends primarily on how one interprets Locke. Even in Hutcheson's early *Inquiry* (1725) in which he appears to have relied specifically on Locke (and repeated, for example, the point that nine-tenths of what is useful to people resulted from industry), he focused on the benefit of industry and the approval of the moral sense.[11] In neither the *Inquiry*, the *Short Introduction*, nor the *System* did Hutcheson's theory rely on the mixing argument. In fact, Hutcheson's argument that "tis trifling to imagine that property is any physical quality or bond between a man and certain goods" was not only a rejection of older disputes about which actions conferred property rights—seeing, touching, enclosing, discovering, throwing a spear into—but also a rejection of Locke's mixing argument (*SI*, pp. 132–33). No physical activity by itself could create the moral quality that constituted a property right. Hutcheson concluded that "a certain person should be allowed the full use and disposal of certain goods; and all others excluded from it" only when the individual had acquired those goods under rules required by "the maintenance of amicable society" (*SI*, p. 153). But though Hutcheson explicitly criticized the technical role that labor played in Locke's theory, he was at one with Locke in wanting to emphasize that property ownership brought with it the moral obligation to work diligently and to use property efficiently. His emphasis on labor and improvement as well as his justification of inequality were summarized in his statement, "If great occupation and much labor employed, intitles the vigorous and active to great possessions; the weak and indolent have an equally sacred right to the small possessions they occupy and improve" (*System*, 1:299–300).

Hutcheson's criticisms of Grotius and Pufendorf also were based on the overriding moral status of the public good. He took them to have argued that property rights began in contracts. But Hutcheson followed Carmichael in believing that contracts were unnecessary if the original grant from God was in the form of a negative community. Under those circumstances the good of mankind was reason enough to justify both the original taking from the common and the injunction against taking what another had acquired. The common good or the requirements of continued industriousness also demanded that the first rights to be derived from the original community should be full property rights, not use rights (*System*, 1:328).

The arguments that enabled Hutcheson to justify property rights because of their contribution to the public good also allowed him to limit property rights. Since property was needed to engage the passions to labor, it could not be invoked with regard to goods upon which labor need not or could not be expended (*SI*, p. 158). The open sea fell into this category. It also would be illegitimate to claim more land than a family and its servants could cultivate in a reasonable length of time (*SI*, p. 156). Since property in land was justified because it increased production, land could not be claimed as private and taken out of the common to lie unused when doing so would keep others from cultivating it. Hutcheson was here explaining why neither individuals nor states could claim as their own continents or islands they had discovered. But it is hard to imagine that he was not also expressing disapproval of those who did not cultivate or cultivate efficiently the land they owned in Scotland.

Hutcheson imagined political society arising from the state of nature through a series of contracts. The first contract united disparate individuals into a civil society, the second created a government, and the third bound the rulers to administer for the good of society and the people to obey (*SI*, p. 286). Since the purposes of the agreement to create a civil society could not be achieved if the land owned by individuals remained outside the new government's jurisdiction, "tis justly presumed that when any body of men possessing such a district of land constitute a civil power, each one thus subjects his lands to it" (*SI*, p. 287). But since the public good in civil society still required peace and industriousness, he insisted that laws encourage labor by protecting the right to exclude others from what one had produced. Hutcheson argued that individual property rights would always provide better motivation than magistrates could, for magistrates would be more likely to distribute goods produced in common to their friends and favorites than to the diligent. Hutcheson defended Aristotle against Plato and More in his argument that education rather than communism was the proper remedy for the problems of private property (*SI*, p. 151; *System*, 1:323).

But just as the good of mankind required limits on appropriations in the state of nature, the public good required limits to private property in political society. Hutcheson's defense of an agrarian law was a strong expression of the need for such limits. His concern was not only with the rich owning land they did not or could not cultivate, it was also with the rich owning so much land that their economic power threatened the nation's liberty. The idea that very large landholdings could threaten liberty Hutcheson took from Harrington's political science. "'Tis vain," Hutcheson wrote, "to talk of invading the liberty of the rich, or the injury of stopping their progress in just acquisitions. No public interest hinders their acquiring as much as is requisite for any innocent enjoyment and pleasures of life. And yet if it did, the liberty and safety of thousands or millions is never to be put in the balance with even the innocent pleasures of a few families" (*System*, 2:248; *SI*, pp. 295–96).

Though Hutcheson mentioned the legitimacy of an agrarian law more than once, his approval was always hypothetical or theoretical rather than programmatic. He seems to have thought that changing the laws of primogeniture and entail would accomplish the same result. "Without any such [agrarian] laws some mixed states are safe, provided the lords can sell their estates, and trade and manufactures flourish among the plebians, and they have access to the places of greatest profit and power. By these means, without any law, wealth may be sufficiently diffused" (*System*, 2:259). Hutcheson carried into Scotland the natural law argument that primogeniture and entail were purely human contrivances, not found in natural law (*SI*, p. 168).

Hutcheson's interest in the agrarian law was not based on the injustice of many being propertyless. He invoked the principle of limiting the political and economic power of the very wealthy few primarily to guard the political power of the gentry and the Protestant establishment. But he fully accepted the propertyless situation of many and used the public good to justify increasing society's control over them. He argued that with population increase "all lands of easy culture must soon have been occupied, so that there would remain none in common; and that many would have no other fund than their own bodily strength or ingenuity" (*SI*, pp. 163–64). Hutcheson seemed to maintain that the employment contracts that must arise between the propertyless and the propertied should conform to standards of fairness that stood above or at least outside the market. For example, the wages of an employee hired for a long period should not be decreased because of the employee's illness, and, more generally, all contracts should be for more than mere subsistence (*System*, 2:200; *SI*, pp. 272–78). His concern for the treatment of the propertyless reached its limits when he considered those who were unemployed. In this case, the public good justified forcing the unemployed to work. His statement that "slothful wretches are to be compelled to labour" nicely captures his attitude. And in another place he suggested (certainly under the influence of Andrew Fletcher's reaction to the famines of the 1690s) placing vagrants into servitude (*SI*, p. 247; *System*, 2:202).[12]

In discussing limits on appropriation in the state of nature, limits on the amount of land a colony could claim, and limits that justified an agrarian law, Hutcheson invoked the common rights of mankind: "Mankind must not for ages be excluded from the earth God intended they should enjoy, to gratify the vain ambition of a few who would retain what they cannot use, while others are in inconvenient straights" (*System*, 1:328; *SI*, pp. 241–47). The existence of common rights meant that political communities could override private rights if they were protecting illegitimate uses of property. For example, the community could force an inventor to part with his invention or a doctor with a new cure for diseases (*SI*, p. 235) so long as compensation was paid. It could also keep individuals from destroying their own goods out of "caprice or ill nature" on the grounds that goods should be used and not allowed to perish (*SI*, pp. 246–47). But Hutcheson never considered the case of whether a poor person without food could take from the rich, an extraordinary omission considering its standard place in discussions of the right of necessity. Instead, immediately after listing charity as an imperfect right, he cautioned against exercising it too much (*SI*, p. 136), and he stressed repeatedly that sloth and vice could render the poor unfit to receive private charity (*System*, 1:305, 321). If we compare Hutcheson's theory to that of his predecessor at Glasgow, Carmichael, it is striking how much harsher Hutcheson's attitudes toward the poor were. Hutcheson's emphasis on the public good meant that he could formulate reasons for a community to suspend private property rights if it were required for the survival of many. But he found it impossible to justify an individual breaking rules to feed only himself. "One may use or destroy the goods of another without his consent," he wrote, "when tis necessary for the preservation of multitudes" (*SI*, p. 244). Thus Hutcheson did not recognize, as Locke did, an individual, inclusive property right to subsistence. Individuals shared in inclusive common rights with others, which meant that a government created to protect rights had to protect common rights as well as individual rights and see to it that the land was used for the benefit of the community. But this formulation of inclusive rights did not guarantee preservation to every individual in the community.

Justifying property rights because of their contribution to peace and prosperity was a strong element in the writings of all the seventeenth-century natural law theorists. And this led them to see that governments could adjust property rights to bring peace and prosperity to the specific conditions they encountered. Of course, this utilitarian element existed in a complicated relationship to the language of natural rights. In Hutcheson, however, this relationship was much clearer, for he defined both the laws of nature and the particular rights they conferred in a more utilitarian way. Thus he wrote that "the laws of nature are inferences we make, by reflecting upon our inward constitution, and by reasoning upon human affairs, concerning that conduct which our hearts naturally must approve, as tending either to the general good, or to that of individuals consistently with the general good" (*System*, 1:284, 253; *SI*, pp. 109–11, 118). As a result, his constant reminders that general rules "may justly be altered and limited under civil polity, as the good of the state requires," are not as jarring as such statements were in the seventeenth-century theorists (*System*, 1:329, 339; also 2:327).

But it would be wrong to think that Hutcheson's more straightforward acceptance of the public good jeopardized property rights. By linking the obligations and rights of natural law to the psychological constitution of people and seeing behind that constitution an unchanging God, Hutcheson's combination of moral sense and public good provided an extremely stable foundation for property rights. And to make it even stronger, Hutcheson invented a new category of rights, which he called external rights, to add to the usual distinction between perfect and imperfect rights. The problem he faced was that both the moral sense and the public good immediately considered could not be trusted to uphold rules allowing, for instance, a wealthy miser to recall the loan of an industrious tradesman. But though neither God nor man would approve of the lender ruining the tradesman, his right (an external right) must be upheld because even greater problems would be created if the state had the power to void such contracts (*System*, 2:259).[13]

According to Hutcheson, both the wealth and the poverty that accompanied the operation of property rights were affirmed by the moral sense. "Wealth and power," he wrote, "are the great engines of virtue" (*SI*, pp. 53–54). He thought people respected wealth because they associated it with "a mixture of moral ideas, of benevolence, of abilities kindly employed" and were embarrassed by poverty because it suggested "avarice, meanness of spirit, want of capacity, or conduct in life, of industry, or moral abilities" (*Inquiry*, pp. 137–39; *SI*, p. 54; *System*, 1:104). He accepted the social hierarchy of his world and wrote only to urge those with wealth and power to involve themselves in public rather than private pursuits, to contrive "wise forms of polity," and to encourage "the more ingenious and useful arts" (*System*, 2:113). So strongly did he feel about the legitimacy of the social hierarchy that he counseled individuals to moderate their ambition and accept a station lower than their abilities might merit rather "than to be set in a station too high" (*System*, 2:114). Consistent with these attitudes were his frequent Stoic admonitions to keep the passion for money calm and moderate and to guard against avarice (*System*, 1:163–64). Hutcheson emphasized the relationship between property rules and the public good to provide a stable foundation for the traditional precepts of natural jurisprudence and Christian virtue, not to undermine them through a calculus based on economic efficiency. He was not aware that the economic development he desired would require more than the commitment of the gentry to the civic task of economic and moral improvement.

Hutcheson's social thought also denied to property one of the most important roles it played in Locke's thought. Since individuals acquired property independently of others, according to Locke, any common activity requiring the use of economic resources had to be based on their consent. As a result, Locke could use his discussion of property to insist that natural law required representative institutions and to defend rebellion against a monarch who tried to subvert those institutions or tax property without obtaining the consent of the representatives. In Hutcheson, however, the common good led directly to both the creation and the regulation of property and did not necessarily have to proceed through the consent of owners or their representatives. Thus Hutcheson wrote that when an individual left the state of nature and consented to join or to create a civil society, he did so "not only for himself but for his posterity: and in this, tho uncommissioned, did them a most important service. They are bound therefore, whether they consent or not, to perform to the body of the state, as far as their power does, all that which could reasonably be demanded from persons adult for such important benefits received" (*SI*, p. 287).

Hutcheson certainly thought there were good reasons for a society in which land was widely held to have representative institutions, but at no time did he suggest that property rights brought with them the requirement of consent or representation. Owners with or without representation were bound to pay their taxes "provided they are no more than what are requisite for the prudent administration of public affairs; as this public expense is made for the behoof of all" (*SI*, p. 330). Not surprisingly, then, Hutcheson's defense of rebellion turned primarily on utilitarian concerns rather than simply on rights violations. It was to "safety," "security," and "felicity" that Hutcheson appealed when he suggested that colonies could rebel against their mother country (*SI*, pp. 316–17).

The Hutchesonian project for moral and economic improvement infused the work of David Fordyce, professor of philosophy at Marischal College in Aberdeen. Fordyce's *Dialogues Concerning Education* (1745–48) and "The Elements of Moral Philosophy" (which appeared in Robert Dodsley's *Preceptor*) were widely read both in Scotland and in America.[14] So closely related was the work of Fordyce and Hutcheson that Benjamin Franklin mistakenly attributed Fordyce's *Dialogues* to Hutcheson when he first read them.[15]

Fordyce's educational ideas have been described as above all "gentlemanly."[16] Any number of quotations from his work confirm this view, but none more clearly than his opinion that it is better to learn how "to use a fortune right, than how to acquire it" (*Dialogues*, 2:338). Though his primary concern was with the sons of the landed gentry, he was willing to consider the education of "a merchant of the first class, who enters upon business with a handsome capital, and has leisure and genius to think of such subjects: for it is chimerical to think an ordinary trader should find time for such improvements" (*Dialogues*, 2:318). It must be remembered that though Hutcheson and Fordyce gave the moral sense to all, they still insisted that wisdom (especially that needed to govern) was found only in the few (*System*, 1:243). Fordyce adopted Hutcheson's view that in the course of economic development and in a way consistent with natural law some will end in "opulence" while others will be landless. Between these groups will grow a system of employment contracts, which if they are vague or general must be interpreted as providing the employee with a wage consistent with justice ("Elements," p. 315).

The goal of the education Fordyce envisioned for the sons of gentry and wealthy merchants, who were "above a servile dependence," was primarily good citizenship and devotion to the public good. First, it required an allegiance to and participation in the Whig establishment and a repudiation of all Jacobite loyalties. These were the sentiments behind his desire "to raise a veneration for order, government, and law . . . and the subordination to the community" (*Dialogues*, 1:296). Of course, this political project was saturated with the literature and philosophy of classical civilization. Not far below this attempt to improve the culture of the Scottish gentry was the concern with Scottish backwardness and the desire to educate a class of economic improvers. Fordyce suggested a course of study that included mechanics, chemistry, fortification, architecture, navigation, surveying, designing, manufactures, agriculture, and gardening. He also recommended that in his students' grand tour of the Continent they inspect the manufactures, workhouses, arsenals, and markets of the countries they visited (*Dialogues*, 2:303, 308). But Fordyce, like Hutcheson, insisted that his notion of utility was not measured by preference. His point was to show that virtue was useful, not to argue that what was useful was virtuous. It was the skeptic Hobbes, he said, who "measures virtue by mere utility" ("Elements," p. 265).

Hutchesonian social theory was heavily influenced by economic and political considerations, but in both cases the consequences were toward strengthening obligations to the public. To understand the relationship between human passions, private property, and the public good as Hutcheson and Fordyce did was most of all to have an increased appreciation of the priority of the public good. Thus Hutcheson's project for the economic improvement of Scotland did not involve using the natural law discussion of property rights to free people from social responsibilities, to limit government to protecting private rights, to limit morality to respecting privacy, or to allow a free rein to acquisitive desires. Even when he adopted the harsh attitudes of Fletcher toward the poor it was not from an individualism that eliminated social duties, including those to the poor, but rather from a sense that their idleness was a barrier to social improvement. He approved individual labor and economic development precisely because of their contribution to the prosperity of society and the virtue of the individual. Moreover, he thought they would be undertaken with the greatest effort and concentration when the motivation for them was a deep commitment to the public good. Just as Carmichael before him saw the importance of natural law for political stability, Hutcheson thought a greater awareness of the moral duties of ownership, made clear by an understanding of why natural law approved of property, would play an integral role in a program of economic and moral reform.

Hume

It was once an intellectual commonplace that Hume's skepticism and utilitarianism required understanding his thought as outside the tradition of natural jurisprudence. But this view of Hume's place in intellectual history has been challenged. Duncan Forbes, for example, has bridged the chasm thought to divide Hume from natural law by pointing to the utilitarian elements in the work of Grotius, Cumberland, Pufendorf, and Hutcheson, while at the same time emphasizing in Hume's work the origin of moral rules in the unchanging characteristics of the human mind—the principles of association.[17] It is important to this interpretation that Hume never identified artificial (or man-made) rules with rules that were unnatural, that he saw his work as protecting rather than shaking social foundations, and that he linked his work not just to Hutcheson but also to Grotius and Pufendorf. Thus in a letter to Hutcheson he emphasized that "I have never called justice unnatural, but only artificial."[18] His careful distinction between unnatural and artificial is also found in *A Treatise of Human Nature* (1740) in which he wrote, "Though the rules of justice be artificial, they are not arbitrary. Nor is the expression improper to call them Laws of Nature."[19] In *An Inquiry Concerning the Principles of Morals* (1751), he wrote that his theory "is in the main the same with that hinted at and adopted by Grotius."[20] And in *A Letter from a Gentleman to His Friend in Edinburgh* (1745), he explained that it was legitimate to call justice natural and added that the laws of justice were "universal and perfectly inflexible."[21] Thus Forbes has argued that Hume's concern was with what "lies behind legal fiction and conventional usage, and in trying to show how the rules of justice and property are grounded on universal principles of human nature, and whatever the differences between Hume and the natural lawyers may be, they are not adequately summarized in a nature versus convention dichotomy."[22]

Hume's project was to uncover the general characteristics of human nature and social circumstance that explained the existence of the major institutions of his society, including private property. His immodest comment in the *Treatise* that his "considerable achievement has little or no influence on politics" (*Treatise*, p. 469) was consistent with the famous distinction he made in a letter to Hutcheson between his own role as an anatomist and Hutcheson's as a painter, a distinction that nicely separated Hutcheson's style of exhortation from Hume's more "rational, critical, and detached" stance.[23] But Hume may have underestimated the consequences of his novel explanations. By providing a thoroughly naturalist account of the origin of property rules he removed property from the rich (if ambiguous) moral context that had surrounded it. His naturalism seems to have had a particularly strong impact on his understanding of inclusive rights. Hume's work contained neither an individual right to subsistence as Locke's had nor a common right that the earth be used to sustain life as Hutcheson's had.

We can begin to understand the ways in which Hume's naturalistic assumptions required changes in the traditional categories used to understand the origin of property by considering the consequences of not discussing primitive common ownership. Hume's refusal to involve God in his account of how moral rules evolved meant that he did not begin with the nature of God's grant of the earth to mankind and whether such a grant was in the form of a negative or positive community. Such a question was clearly outside the areas Hume thought worthwhile to ponder. In the *Treatise* he called the state of nature "a mere philosophical fiction," "an idle fiction" (*Treatise*, p. 493–94). But this refusal did more than enable Hume to avoid some unanswerable questions. The absence of an original common was important both to Hume's reduction of justice to the rules of property and to his definition of a property right as only the right to exclude. Without acknowledging an original grant of the earth from God, Hume omitted one way natural law had accounted for a right of necessity and a right to common property. Similarly absent from his work was the idea of a right to self-preservation based on the obligation to God to preserve oneself. This omission also meant that a traditional path to an inclusive right was unavailable.

Whereas the classic texts in seventeenth-century natural law discussed the circumstances that led from common to private property rights through hypothetical histories (often following a roughly biblical outline), Hume dealt more abstractly with these circumstances. His work does not mention a movement from friendship and simplicity to discord and desire or anything about increasing population putting pressure on increasingly scarce land. Hume attempted to avoid these contestable and perhaps unnecessary discussions by simply specifying the fewest possible conditions that explained the need for property rules. In the *Treatise* his argument was that the experience people had in their families taught them they had to live with others in order to satisfy their "wants and necessities." But they also learned from the experience of living with others that the society they needed to form was constantly threatened by the instability that came from avaricious individuals stealing the scarce goods others had acquired through "industry and good fortune." The resultant instability inhibited the improvement of goods. Thus in the *Treatise* property rules were "intended as a remedy to some inconveniences, which proceed from the concurrence of certain qualities of the human mind with the situation of external objects. The qualities of the mind are selfishness and limited generosity. And the situation of external objects is their easy change, joined to their scarcity in comparison to the wants and desires of men" (*Treatise*, p. 494).

The specific and perhaps peculiar psychology behind this argument has often been noted.[24] So impressed was Hume in the *Treatise* with avarice, calling it "insatiable, perpetual, universal," that it seems to have eclipsed all other emotions and left Hume with an extraordinarily narrow view of the range of human passions (*Treatise*, p. 492). His argument that there were no "advantages" to injuring another person's body, as opposed to stealing that person's goods, seems based on a commercial view of advantage and to have ignored all the ways the desire for honor and reputation, for example, can lead to conflict.

When Hume considered the same question in the *Inquiry Concerning the Principles of Morals* the emphasis both on avarice and the transferability of goods was gone. Here we find the more famous of Hume's discussions of the origin of property, a discussion so parsimonious that it avoided virtually any psychological assumptions. Hume argued in this work that limited benevolence and limited resources gave rise to property and justice. These conditions defined the situation of moderate competition that could have peace brought to it by rules. Situations without competition, those of plenty and benevolence, did not need rules, but situations of life-and-death competition, complete egoism, and extreme scarcity could not generate motives to follow rules (*PW*, 4:179–82).

Outside the situation of moderate competition and the rules of justice that protected property rights and produced order was the rightless world of necessity and commonality. Hume did not deny that in necessity people would take what they could. But this situation existed for him outside the realm of property and justice and of rights and obligations:

> Suppose a society to fall into such want of all common necessaries that the utmost frugality and industry cannot preserve the greater number from perishing and the whole from extreme misery: it will readily, I believe, be admitted that the strict laws of justice are suspended in such a pressing emergency and give place to stronger motives of necessity and self-preservation. Is it any crime, after a shipwreck, to seize whatever means or instrument of safety one can lay hold of, without regard to former limitations of property? Or if a city besieged were perishing with hunger; can we imagine, that men will see any means of preservation before them, and lose their lives, from a scrupulous regard to what, in other situations would be the rules of equity and justice? . . . Every man may now provide for himself by all the means, which prudence can dictate, or humanity permit. The public, even in less urgent necessities, opens granaries, without the consent of proprietors. . . . Would an equal partition of bread in a famine, though effected by power and even violence, be regarded as criminal or injurious? (*PW*, 4:182)

The situations described here by Hume were ones of social breakdown and give no indication that a starving individual in an otherwise orderly world could invoke necessity. Even more important, it is indicative of Hume's outlook that situations others would have located within a system of justice (the opening of granaries or the distribution of food to the famine-stricken) were for Hume beyond justice—no different than when the drowning grab planks in the sea. Preservation, prudence, and violence filled the moral vacuum left by the absence of individual or common rights to life.

Earlier natural law theorists usually saw a contract standing between an original common and property that was private. Not surprisingly, because the common had disappeared from Hume's thought, so had the idea of a contract that would divide it. Like Hutcheson, Hume rejected the contract theory of property used by Grotius and Pufendorf. Hume thought of property developing from the slow recognition that it was to everyone's benefit to leave what others possessed alone so that they in turn would be left alone. But in this understanding there was no room to explore the stipulations that reasonable people might have insisted upon before they allowed their rights to the common to be given up. Since there were no promises, there was no investigation of what terms people would or would not have promised to obey. The contract origin of property was another often used path to the right of necessity. It did not depend on theological assumptions but only on the plausible belief that reasonable people would not agree to a division that might require their own starvation. A contract could establish that the obligation to obey rules of property ceased when the minimal benefit of the property system—subsistence—ceased. But without a common to which all had access, without an obligation to preserve what God had created, and without a contract with terms that could be interpreted, Hume had no way to express the idea of an inclusive right.

For people to enjoy the benefits of organized social life, possessions must be stable. Hume's identification of the rules of property that accomplished this with all of justice was a variant of the natural law attempt to specify the minimum conditions necessary for social order. These conditions were usually subsumed under the idea of perfect rights and duties, the observance of which was the virtue of justice. In contrast to justice was charity, a virtue that required fulfilling imperfect rights and duties. Though it was Hume's identification of justice with the rules of property that usually created controversy, it was at least as important that his discussion did not include the idea of imperfect rights and duties. To describe a virtue as an imperfect duty was necessarily to recommend and urge its fulfillment. But it was precisely the recommendation or "preaching" of virtues that was ruled out of Hume's project by his naturalist methodology. "It is not my present business to recommend generosity and benevolence, or to paint in their true colors all the genuine charms of the social virtues" (PW, 4:175). Again, at one level, Hume's acknowledgment of social virtues but his refusal to describe them as imperfect duties was simply a technical issue. But on another level,

Hume's method resulted in a discussion of property without the moral resonance found in previous discussions. Some confirmation of this is provided by his view of giving voluntary aid to the poor. The situation typically described in the natural law tradition as involving the imperfect right of the poor and the imperfect duty of the rich was transformed by Hume into a situation without any rights or duties. And in the absence of even imperfect moral duties economic logic could dominate. Thus he wrote, "Giving alms to common beggars is naturally praised, because it seems to carry relief to the distressed and indigent. But when we observe the encouragement thence arising to idleness and debauchery, we regard that species of charity rather as a weakness than a virtue" (PW, 4:178). What had been ambiguity in Hutcheson—a moral recommendation to be charitable with a caution not to be too charitable—in Hume became a revaluation of charity from a completely economic viewpoint.

Hume saw in a way that others did not that the public need for property rules did not account for the motives that would lead individuals to adopt and obey them. He found only difficulties behind traditional explanations of rationality, promises, self-interest, benevolence, and the public good. It is not surprising that readers accustomed to a more straightforward route to justice became lost trying to follow the convoluted path that led in Hume's works from the mind, the passions, and social circumstance to justice. Furthermore, it is unlikely that those who concluded that no such path existed, that Hume could not ground justice securely, were comforted when Hume in the *Inquiry* perversely denied that chastity and fidelity were based on either self-interest or benevolence. In all of these cases Hume's general point was the same. The advantages of the rules upholding justice, chastity, and fidelity were "general and distant" (PW, 4:197) and therefore sometimes contrary to the individual's immediate self-interest and benevolence. Benevolence, for example, might lead virgins to acquiesce in the pleas of their suitors or the kindhearted to oppose repayment of debts from the unfortunate poor to the miserly rich. Similarly, self-interest could lead the "sensible knave" to desire only that everyone else observe rules so that he could violate them.

Since the immediate promptings of nature could not account for the motives that engaged people to obey rules, justice to Hume was an artificial rather than a natural virtue. Hume was not the first to deny that the rights and obligations of ownership arose directly from nature. Both Pufendorf and Hutcheson had argued that property belonged to a class of adventitious rights that had to be created by the actions and institutions of people. Perhaps it was Hume's early desire to shock that accounts for his use of artificial instead of adventitious. But it was not simply Hume's argument that people created rights that involved him in controversy. As important was his refusal to state (as Hutcheson did) that God created people and did so in a way that inevitably led them to create rights.

According to Hume, property rights existed because of their usefulness, their contribution to the absolute necessity "that possession must be stable" (*Treatise*, p. 502). Though Hume occasionally remarked on the role of sagacity and reflection in understanding this usefulness, his general theory was that a system of property rules grew slowly, like speech, without design or intention. To buttress this point he used a quotation from Grotius (though one from Pufendorf may have been more appropriate) that property was not created "through a single act of the mind" (*PW*, 4:275). It was precisely because the system of rules did not reflect any individual's design or any society's choice that it often ran afoul of people's sense of interest or benevolence. Inevitably, Hume argued, "particular hardships" would result. "But however single acts of justice may be contrary, either to public or private interest, tis certain, that the whole plan or scheme is highly conducive, or indeed absolutely requisite, both to the support of society, and the well-being of every individual" (*Treatise*, p. 497). But placing justice outside of the design or choice of individuals in a society had an important consequence: it meant that justice was left with the sole task of protecting the status quo in property holdings.[25]

For a system of rules to bring stability to possessions, it must assign particular goods to particular individuals. In the *Treatise* Hume's discussion of the specific rules that governed ownership centered on the traditional principles of Roman law—possession, occupation, prescription, accession, and succession. Hume proceeded in a way typical of Scottish philosophy in the eighteenth century; that is, he linked property rules both to their usefulness and to a faculty of the human constitution that operated more immediately than rational considerations of public benefit. To Hutcheson this other faculty was the moral sense; to Hume it was the principles of association that "are principally fixed by the imagination." The interesting and innovative aspect of Hume's argument in the *Treatise*, then, was his attempt to derive Roman law principles from the operations of the imagination. For example, his explanation for the most basic rule, "that everyone continue to enjoy what he is present master of" (*Treatise*, p. 503), moved from custom to cause and effect to the principle of association he called constant conjunction. But since this rule, which legitimated present possession, was appropriate only at the start of society, when there could not have been a previous owner, it had to be modified. Hume also interpreted the initial modification, first possession, to be a "species of cause and effect; possession being the power of a person to use, move, alter, or destroy the thing possessed" (*Treatise*, p. 506). If first possession was unclear because of the shrouds of history, long possession or prescription became the rule.

Hume used "the natural propensity [of the mind] to join relations, especially resembling ones," to discuss the particularly important principle of accession (*Treatise*, pp. 509–11). The natural tendency of the imagination to join smaller to greater objects with which they were connected explained the traditional natural law argument that nations can own bays and firths. Though Hume noted that the right of inheritance (the right of children to inherit if a parent died intestate) was usually based on the "presumed consent of the parents" and on the interest of the public in promoting industry and frugality, he suggested the further influence of the association of ideas: "These goods must become the property of some body: but of whom is the question. Here tis evident the person's children naturally present themselves to the mind" (*Treatise*, pp. 512–13).

Throughout this discussion in the *Treatise* it is clear that Hume's concerns had little to do with property and a great deal to do with vindicating his epistemology. Property was an opportunity for him to demonstrate the power of the principles of association and their ability to explain why the categories of Roman law were so widely used. Yet a theory that explained the origin of property rules in an imagination that could not help but link people to their present or long-held possessions could not do more than uphold a current distribution. Hume's well-known emphasis on the power of habit reinforces Knud Haakonssen's conclusion that in the Humean system "the possessions which justice is introduced to protect cannot be required to be redistributed in any way."[26]

The most obvious rule not used by Hume was that of labor. In the *Treatise* Hume understood Locke as having used the mixing argument to explain why occupation had moral force. Hume's first response was to reinterpret labor to explain its relationship to the principles of association. He argued that labor did not involve mixing so much as altering or having an effect, a change that allowed him to emphasize the mind's natural propensity to join things related by cause and effect.[27] He also provided an alternative to Locke's tenuous extension of labor to the activity of a servant or an animal. Acquiring property this way, Hume averred, was better understood through the idea of accession and the association of ideas upon which it was based (*Treatise*, pp. 505–06). In general, Hume argued against Locke, as Hutcheson did, that property was a moral relationship rather than a physical one and that only utility (the public good) could create a moral justification for a system of property rules. Locke was no doubt included in his comment that "the writers on the law of nature" ultimately rested their systems on "the convenience and necessities of mankind," whether they admitted it or not (*PW*, 4:189, 277; *Treatise*, p. 527). If we can contrast Hutcheson's and Hume's criticisms of Locke's labor theory with Carmichael's acceptance of it, a general pattern emerges. When the labor theory was seen as distinctive because of its mixing argument, it was rejected, and it was endorsed when it was tied to the public benefit or the utility of industry.

In the *Inquiry Concerning the Principles of Morals* Hume used the categories of Roman law and the principles of association much less. Instead, he emphasized the more direct link that must exist between particular rules and their utility, a relationship he had only mentioned in the *Treatise*. Hume rejected both distribution according to moral merit and equality because of their pernicious consequences. The first would create severe disagreement and ultimately a civil war; the second, by depriving different degrees of industry and care of different rewards, would result in tyranny and poverty (*PW*, 4:187–89). Hume's calculations of utility to arrive at these conclusions were quite specific and included a recognition of marginal utility, incentives, and disincentives. In the *Treatise* he seemed to think that to be useful property rules could not be consciously chosen for their usefulness, yet in the *Inquiry* he seemed much more willing to have a people "establish" or "search for the rules which are, on the whole, most useful and beneficial" and to have "different utilities proposed by the legislature" (*PW*, 4:189). He asserted that only "vulgar sense and slight experience" were required to make such laws. Presumably, then, most people could understand that individuals would work harder if they were able to enjoy the fruits of their labor, that people would be industrious and save in their later years if they knew their savings would descend to their children, and that fulfilling contracts "promotes the general interest of mankind" (*PW*, 4:189).

Hume was much more explicit about the need for government actively to adjust property rights in the *Inquiry Concerning the Principles of Morals* than he had been in the *Treatise*. It is likely that the calculation of utility and the greater role for government were linked in Hume's mind, the first providing the rationale for the second. Hume's reading of Montesquieu may have been important to his new awareness that the general principles of property had to be made consistent with the peculiar characteristics of each country. Montesquieu was referred to as "a late author of genius" at precisely that place in the *Inquiry* where Hume wrote that "we may observe that all questions of property are subordinate to the authority of civil law, which extend, restrain, modify, and alter the rules of natural justice, according to the particular convenience of each community" (*PW*, 4:190). Hume's *Inquiry* ended, then, with a greater sense of utilities actually being calculated than can be found in any of those in the natural law tradition who preceded him. Yet Hume's general points, that the rules of nature had to be modified by legislatures or princes to be useful to particular countries and that the civil government was the ultimate definer of property rights, were natural law commonplaces.

Just as Hume's methodological innovations in the *Treatise* had consequences for the substance of property rights, so did his increased sense of utilitarian calculation in the *Inquiry*. But though his demonstration in the *Treatise* of the link between the principles of the mind and the rules of property seemed to limit justice to a very conservative defense of the status quo, his emphasis on utilitarian calculation in the *Inquiry*, especially insofar as it could take into account marginal utility, added a potentially powerful redistributive principle into discussions of property:

> It must, indeed, be confessed that nature is so liberal to mankind that, were all her presents equally divided among the species and improved by art and industry, every individual would enjoy all the necessaries and even most of the comforts of life. . . . It must also be confessed that wherever we depart from this equality we rob the poor of more satisfaction than we add to the rich, and that the slight gratification of a frivolous vanity in one individual frequently costs more than bread to many families, and even provinces. (*PW*, 4:188)

Yet Hume went on to point out that any attempt to realize equality would be impracticable and pernicious. And at the end of the *Inquiry* he insisted that once a distribution was settled the pain all present owners would feel if the property of even a few was taken created a barrier to any redistribution. "By the laws of society, this coat, this horse is mine and ought to remain perpetually in my possession; I reckon on the secure enjoyment of it; by depriving me of it, you disappoint my expectations and doubly displease me and every bystander" (PW, 4:278). In his essay "Of Commerce" (1752) Hume again acknowledged the relationship between equality and happiness but used it only to praise England and to oppose higher taxes (PW, 3:296–97). Only Cumberland, the most utilitarian of the seventeenth-century natural law philosophers, rivaled Hume in equating virtually any current distribution with public happiness.

Hume's greater reliance on utility in the *Inquiry Concerning the Principles of Morals* did not satisfy his critics, who were worried about the foundation of property in the "frivolous" imagination, as he provocatively described it in the *Treatise*. Nor were they satisfied when Hume played down his distinctiveness by interpreting the natural law tradition as fundamentally utilitarian. His protest in the *Inquiry* that the grounding of property in the general interests of society did not diminish "anything from the most sacred attention to property" (PW, 4:194) would remain ineffective as long as he refused to see behind the imaginative or passionate constitution of people the work of a benevolent and unchanging God.

One of the first criticisms of Hume's work to appear was James Balfour's *A Delineation of the Nature and Obligation of Morality* (1753). Balfour concentrated on the *Inquiry* and as a result read Hume as a utilitarian, who found the "sole origin of justice" in "public utility."[28] Against Hume's position, Balfour, who was professor of moral philosophy at Edinburgh University, asserted that justice was an original principle of human nature, implanted by God to regulate all human actions, not just those that arose from limited benevolence and limited resources. He denied that justice was confined to upholding property and contracts and that property was based solely on its beneficial consequences. "It is not true," he wrote, "that the product of a man's art or industry ought to be secured to him, for no other reason, but to give encouragement to such useful habits and accomplishments, for the good of society . . . for such encouragement previously supposes an affection for property to be natural to man, without which, he must be entirely indifferent about the security of it" (pp. 86–87). Balfour saw that Hume's derivation of property rights from the contingent circumstances of limited benevolence and limited abundance meant first that in other circumstances there would be no rights or duties and second that when rights did develop from the circumstances that made them necessary it occurred without divine assistance. In both cases the implication was that social life could proceed without religious sanction. Balfour's defense of a natural right to property was, then, a reaffirmation of God's providence and the constant need for religion to buttress justice. Since the purposes of God could not include starvation, Balfour's defense of a natural right to property ended with his recognition of an imperfect duty on the part of the wealthy to give charity to the poor. And if the poor were not helped, they could claim a right of necessity. "Everyone is bound to supply the wants of the poor, according to his abilities: This obligation is, however, imperfect so long as the poor can make a hard shrift to provide themselves; but in case they cannot, the obligation becomes perfect; and if not complied with a poor man may take what belongs to another, in order to preserve his life, without being unjust" (p. 57).

Perhaps the most thorough attack on Hume's philosophy in eighteenth-century England was by Thomas Reid, a professor first at Aberdeen and then at Glasgow University. His criticisms of Hume's property theory are particularly interesting because he self-consciously adopted a perspective he took to represent the teachings of the natural law tradition. According to Reid, this tradition was a "modern invention" based on "the genius of the immortal Hugo Grotius."[29] Systems of morals, he wrote, taught men their duties, but natural jurisprudence focused on the rights people had. Reid, however, began with the difference between systems of duty and systems of right only so that he could explain how a system of rights properly conceived could perform the same function as a system of duties. But if modern natural law was to teach moral duty, Reid saw that it had to recognize the existence of imperfect rights and duties. For though "a system of the perfect rights of men, or the rights of strict justice, would be a lame substitute for a system of human duty, yet, when we add to it the imperfect and the external rights, it comprehends the whole duty we owe to our fellow man" (p. 644).

Reid's target here was Hume's decision to limit justice to the rights of property and to limit property rights to perfect rights. Not only did Reid affirm the existence of imperfect rights and duties, but he argued that a legislature may rightfully change imperfect rights to perfect ones. "In all civilized nations," Reid wrote, "laws are intended to encourage the duties of humanity" (p. 645). According to Reid, the natural law tradition saw property as only one of the natural rights—others being the right to self-preservation, to liberty, to reputation, and to the fidelity of contracts. All of these rights, he argued against both Hume and Hutcheson, existed prior to and, therefore, limited considerations of utility (p. 638).

Reid began his derivation of property by assuming that "the earth [was] given to men in common for the purposes of life, by the bounty of Heaven" (p. 657). Reid described the act of first taking variously as occupying, improving, or laboring. Both the right to life and the right to liberty justified these acts of individual appropriation. The right to life, he argued, implied a right to the means necessary for life, and the right to liberty enabled individuals to engage in the innocent labor of their choice and to acquire a right to the fruits of that labor. Since "God has made man a sagacious and provident animal," property included whatever sustained life and could be stored up for future sustenance (p. 658). To take what another had innocently acquired was an injury, even in the absence of civil law. Thus, though property was required for useful activity and was fully understood only in society, Reid denied that its justification came from its usefulness or that it made any sense to think of it as artificial. "Property must exist wherever men exist," Reid concluded (p. 658). Although both Balfour and Reid reasserted natural property rights against Hume, neither fell back on Locke's mixing labor argument or used the idea that rights were the result of reason perceiving the link between property and the public good. Both worked in the intellectual space cleared by Hutcheson in which rights were traced directly to a moral capacity that was part of the human constitution created by God.

Reid maintained that property was held on the condition that no one was "deprived of the necessary means to life" (p. 659). The right to subsistence, he wrote, was superior to the right to the "riches" anyone had accumulated and stored. "Justice . . . as well as charity requires that the necessities of those who, by the Providence of God, are disabled from supplying themselves, should be supplied from what might otherwise be stored for future wants" (p. 659). This led him to insist (specifically against Hume) that in an emergency the equal partition of goods was a requirement and not a suspension of justice (pp. 659–60). It also led him to affirm the right of necessity: "The man who breaks my fences, or treads down my corn, when he cannot otherwise preserve himself from destruction, who has no injurious intention, and is willing to indemnify me for the hurt which necessity and not ill will, led him to do, is not injurious, nor is an object of resentment" (p. 655).

Reid had no trouble explaining why individuals with property rights were subject to the civil laws that might regulate property. To enter civil society, Reid averred, it was necessary to agree to subject individual property to civil authority (p. 659). Reid's analogy of the state to a family that must care for its children and sick, his belief that imperfect duties may be made perfect ones, that states must be able to regulate the property of its citizens, and that justice is served by assisting the needy who have a right to life together constituted the Scottish Enlightenment's strongest reassertion of inclusive rights against Hume.[30]

Kames

In his first important work, *Essays on the Principles of Morality and Natural Religion* (1751), Henry Home, Lord Kames, interpreted Hume as Balfour and Reid had. All held Hume to say that property would not exist in a state of nature, that it came to exist only through individuals consulting their interest in public tranquillity, and that the only foundation for property in civil society was municipal law.[31] Against this theory, Kames, like the others, attempted to find a basis for property rights that was ultimately independent of self-interest or public law.

More than any of the Scottish writers we have considered so far, Kames explicitly tied his theory of property to his interest in the economic improvement of Scotland. The need to improve Scottish agriculture, to facilitate commerce, and to abolish those aspects of the legal system that impeded growth were the goals of his theory. Nor were his interests only theoretical. Crop selection, weed elimination, mulching, plow shape, forestry, drainage, and manure were just a few of the more practical areas he studied in the attempt to make Scottish farming more scientific. Kames was famous for actually working in the field at a time when many landlords were absentee. His commitment to modernizing Scotland is also evident in his participation on the Board of Trustees for the Encouragement of Fisheries, Arts, and Manufacture in Scotland and the Board of Commissioners for the Annexed Estates.[32]

Kames's interest in economic improvement also reflected deeply held moral beliefs. His attitude toward ownership, with its characteristically Scottish mixture of moral obligation and economic utility, is captured in a letter he wrote in 1767:

Upon succeeding to a pretty opulent fortune well stocked with people, some sentiments began to display themselves which had formerly lain in obscurity. I clearly discovered the true meaning of the term proprietor or landholder, not a man to whose arbitrary will so much good land, so many fine trees, and such a number of people are subjected, but a man to whose management these particulars are entrusted by Providence, and who is bound to answer for that trust. It is his duty especially to study the good of his people and to do all in his power to make them industrious, and consequently virtuous, and consequently happy.[33]

Kames's desire for improvement led him to attack the institutions he thought promoted idleness—primogeniture, entail, and the Poor Law. But the development Kames sought so hard to foster was primarily agricultural and rural, not commercial and urban. Especially in Kames's later work, he seemed more and more troubled by the moral consequences of urban individualism. "What judgement then are we to form of the opulent cities London and Paris," he asked, "where pleasure is the ruling passion, and where riches are coveted as instruments of sensuality? What is to be expected but a pestiferous corruption of manners? Selfishness, engrossing the whole soul, eradicates patriotism, and leaves not a cranny for social virtue!"[34]

When Kames began his discussion of property in the *Essays* by writing, "Man is by nature fitted for labor, and his enjoyment lies in action" (*Essays*, p. 104), one cannot help but think that he was exhorting as much as describing. He saw evidence of divine providence in the fact that this inward disposition to gain pleasure from active improvement was perfectly appropriate to an external world that yielded its wealth only to labor and industry. But though labor could bring satisfaction, it was first undertaken simply to feed, clothe, and shelter people and their families. Property, which Kames called that "peculiar connection" that exists between "a man and the fruits of his industry" (*Essays*, p. 105), was based at first on preservation. But in a way that was characteristic of the Scottish Enlightenment Kames did not rely on the ability of people to use abstract or "cool reason" to apprehend the link between property and preservation (*Essays*, p. 118). Instead, he thought that people made this connection more immediately and with less reflection through their passions and dispositions. A "sense of property" (sometimes called the "hoarding principle") was proposed by Kames and thought to operate in such a way as to lead people naturally to consider goods they acquired through their industry as their own. So deeply did he want to embed this principle in nature that he suggested that humans shared it with other animals, including beavers, bees, sheep, monkey, cattle, and roosters. To these emotions he added the most powerful of all—the moral sense. If what people had acquired because of their disposition to work and hoard was taken from them, they immediately experienced "the feeling of wrong and injustice." Because he thought people could not fail to have these feelings, "property is established by the constitution of . . . nature" (*Essays*, p. 108). This argument enabled Kames to conclude against Hume that property existed prior to society and to any agreements individuals may have entered into to preserve society. So strong was this "peculiar connection" that people conceived their goods "just as much as we conceive our hands, our feet, and our other members to be our own" (*Essays*, p. 108). In this early work his eagerness to prove that private property was natural led him to deny that common rights to property ever existed. "There never has been, among any people or tribe, such a thing as the possession of goods in common" (*Essays*, p. 107). The emotional ties that individuals must come to feel toward that part of nature under their control seems to have made a common inconceivable to Kames.

Though Kames accepted Hume's limitation of justice to the rules upholding property and contracts (*Essays*, pp. 103, 129) and criticized Hutcheson for not appreciating the special status of justice, he tried to distance himself from what he saw as Hume's insecure grounding of property rules in conventions based on utility. The particularly strong assertions of the natural right to property Hume provoked from Balfour, Reid, and Kames were rooted in the need to affirm the importance of God's providence and to buttress the social edifice. But in defending the natural right to property by linking it to a right of self-preservation, it was hard to avoid also recognizing property in its inclusive form. Thus even Kames, whose antipathy to common property knew no bounds, affirmed in this early work that a person had a right "to seize upon food whenever he can find it, to keep himself from dying of hunger" (*Essays*, p. 124). He also insisted that everyone was "strictly bound" (*Essays*, p. 129) to relieve those in distress through private charity.

But it is hard to avoid the conclusion that Kames's affirmation of the right of necessity was completely formal, forced on him by the logic of his argument and accepted as merely a standard part of the natural law vocabulary. That it appeared at all attests to its almost unavoidable status in an argument that takes self-preservation seriously. Only Reid among the Scottish critics of Hume seems to have thought of inclusive rights as requiring action on the part of the propertied and perhaps even government programs.

Kames believed that the property sense and the moral sense were firmer foundations for property, and more deeply rooted in human nature, than utilitarian calculations. But in using the idea of senses intrinsic to human nature, Kames had to deal with the problems presented by the historical diversity of property rules. His attempt to show that property had changed dramatically in its forms while still remaining consistent with the unchanging plans of providence spoke to a problem confronted by all modern natural law theorists as they tried to explain how property could move from use rights to a common through full property rights in the state of nature to the rights conferred by civil law. At the very start of the modern natural law tradition Filmer had used historical change to discredit the laws of nature explicated by Grotius. But though the confrontation between natural law and history predated Scottish natural jurisprudence, it was examined in this period, especially by Kames and Smith, with more detail and interest than ever before. Kames argued that though the specific content of the laws of nature changed, they were not less natural because they always represented the requirements of the social life for which man was intended by God. Since the circumstances under which people lived together changed, "The law of nature, which is the law of our nature, cannot be stationary. It must vary with the nature of man, and consequently refine gradually as human nature refines" (*Essays*, p. 147).

The theme of a gradual refinement in the moral sense was central to Kames's argument in the *Principles of Equity* (1760). Perhaps because he was a judge and in that capacity had to balance incommensurable values in particular cases, he seemed more aware than his contemporaries that justice as the protection of private rights could conflict with utility, or, to put it another way, that the moral sense, which reacted with disapprobation when something was taken from someone who rightfully owned it, could conflict with the rational calculation of the public good that might require such a taking. He used the classic example of a recently developed "manufacturing village" which might need so much of the water in a river that there would no longer be enough to power mills owned by individuals downstream. In this case and in others Kames thought it was proper to use the general principle that "property, which is a private right, must yield to what is essential for the good of the nation."[35] But at the same time that social and economic development created conflicts between private rights and the public good, Kames thought that economic improvement also was responsible for a refinement in human sentiments which enabled moral duties and the public good to play a more important role in individual action and public law. The increased awareness of the public good that came with refinement also made it appropriate, Kames thought, for some imperfect rights and duties to become legally enforceable. Kames, then, shared with Hutcheson the idea that though property rights were originally derived from the immediate reaction of an emotion or a sense, they came to be based increasingly on a broader consideration of the public good.

Kames's optimistic appraisal of historical development ran throughout his *Historical Law Tracts* (1758) in which his purpose was to use a theory of property based on historical stages to evaluate contemporary property rights. The theme he pursued was that of a progressively stronger emotional attachment of people to their property. Though all people had a "remarkable propensity for appropriation"[36] in the earliest stage of society, when economic activity was limited to hunting and fishing, this propensity would have been confined almost entirely to animals captured. Nothing would have led people to extend property beyond the goods that were physically possessed for immediate use. In the second stage, shepherding, the difficulty and length of time involved in rearing sheep and looking after the flock enabled a "very strong affection for property" to grow (*HLT*, p. 93). Because a shepherd was not always in close physical proximity to all of his flock, property came to be less dependent on actual possession. The growth of a government able to administer justice in this stage brought greater stability to property relations, which in turn fostered even more intense attachments to property. The transition from use rights to modern property rights was completed in the third stage, agriculture. With the inclusion of land in the moral and legal relationships of property, the sense of ownership reached its full development. Kames's extraordinary feeling for land and farming is captured well in the following quotation: "A man who has bestowed labor in preparing a field for the plough, and who has improved this field by artful culture, forms in his mind a very intimate connection with it. He contracts, by degrees, a singular affection for a spot, which, in a manner, is the workmanship of his own hands. He chooses to live there, and there to deposit his bones. It is an object which fills his mind, and is never out of thought at home or abroad" (*HLT*, p. 95).

Because Kames associated moral and economic improvement with individuals coming to have these sentiments about their property, he always expressed antipathy to the idea of common property. What Kames saw in common property was common poverty, an absence of culture and refinement, and therefore an inability to act for the common good. Only with private property was there economic development, moral improvement, and the ability to take the good of others into account. Since people were intended for these achievements, and common property impeded their development, it was "unnatural." The association of private property with selfishness and common property with sharing was not part of Kames's understanding at this time in his career.

In the *Historical Law Tracts*, an essay entitled "Considerations upon the State of Scotland with Respect to Entails" (1759), and *Sketches of the History of Man* (1774), Kames deployed his historical analysis against entails, the practice of settling the succession of landed estates so that the possessors could neither sell nor bequeath them according to their pleasure. He argued that though entail may have been appropriate to feudalism, a period he never tired of painting as being as bloody as possible, it was inconsistent with the economic and moral possibilities of modern society. Improved manners, political liberty, and economic development all seemed to be at stake in this discussion. Thus the legal institution of entail stood directly in the path of the project of the Scottish Enlightenment and was criticized by virtually all of the philosophers we associate with this period.

Only ambition, avarice, and arrogance, Kames thought, moved landowners to try to maintain control over their estates after their death (*HLT*, p. 120). Entails were born in the ambition of one generation, and they created and recreated it in generations that followed. As more land became entailed, it fell into the hands of fewer people. These few would grow in arrogance while slavishness would grow in the vast majority, now dependent on the few. Neither the idle rich nor the poverty-stricken many were fertile ground for the growth of the arts and sciences. And because entailed land could not be used to secure loans, entails made it increasingly difficult for landowners to raise the capital needed for agricultural improvement. Kames repeated again and again the charge that great wealth among the few and poverty among the many, the inevitable outcome of entails, would destroy the spirit of industry, liberty, and independence.

Entails were also inconsistent with the logical requirements of a property right as it had developed in the modern world. Kames argued that the right to alienate was inherent in a full right to property and that neither will nor agreement could set it aside. The right to alienate had to reside with the person who exercised all other aspects of the property right (*HLT*, p. 120). Since the development of a full property right that included the right to alienate was consistent with natural law and served the purposes of natural law in modern society, Kames could argue that the Scottish legislature in legalizing entails in 1685 was ruinously tampering with the law of nature.

Kames developed his ideas about property, at least in part, to attack the inequality protected by entails and to approve the redistribution of land to smaller farmers that he thought a more open market in land would engender. That Kames's vision of social life was firmly tied to rural values can be seen in his belief that "every prosperous trader will desert a country where he can find no land to purchase; for to raise a family by acquiring an estate in land, is the ultimate aim of every merchant, and of every man who accumulates money" (*Sketches*, 4:445–46). The benefits of a "small landholder," a "gentleman of moderate fortune," and "middle-sized proprietors" extended to politics, economics, and manners. In politics people of this rank had the "true spirit of liberty," in contrast to the despotic spirit of the very rich and the slavish spirit of the poor (*Sketches*, 4:447–48). Using Harringtonian political science, Kames argued that nothing was more likely to subvert liberty than the accumulation of property in the hands of the few. The rich and the poor hampered economic development for both groups tended to idleness. Only the industrious and frugal middle-sized proprietor was interested in economic and moral improvement. Moreover, the middle rank was necessary "to complete the social connection," to tie together all the gradations in the social hierarchy so that both duty and benevolence were possible.[37]

In Kames's *Sketches* he joined to his attack on entails, the institution that allowed the rich to be idle, a complementary attack on the institution that he thought had the same effect on the poor, the Poor Law.[38] Since men were made to labor, he argued, the law of nature could not include rules that promoted idleness. "When a lawgiver ventures to tamper with the laws of nature, he hazards much mischief . . . we have a pregnant instance . . . in many absurd regulations for the poor . . . the law authorizing entails is another instance of the same kind" (*Sketches*, 4:438). By removing the only incentive the laboring poor understood, fear of want, the Poor Law subverted industry. Taxing the industrious to support the profligate added another disincentive to labor. His recommendation that begging be prohibited, even if it might cause the loss of "a few lives by neglect or oversight" (*Sketches*, 3:103), shows that he no longer took seriously the right of necessity he had at least formally affirmed in the *Essays*. Workhouses, charity schools, and foundling hospitals should also be abolished. Other inefficiencies occurred because much of the money raised was lost to embezzlement, wages were pushed artificially high, and barriers to the mobility of labor were created. But just as important, the Poor Law subverted the morality of the poor by keeping them from learning the virtues of industry and destroyed the morality of the rich by providing them with excuses not to engage in benevolence and charity. Though Kames did not think the Poor Law could be abolished all at once, and believed that the sick and aged should be supported in public hospitals, it is clear that in the long run he favored a system of care for the poor based almost entirely on private charity. "Leave nature to her own operations," he implored his readers. "By what unhappy prejudice have people been led to think that the author of our nature, so beneficent to his favorite man in every other respect, has abandoned the indigent to famine and death" (*Sketches*, 3:93). Kames was certain that pity and charity would guarantee the deserving poor appropriate support.

Kames's attack on Poor Law administrators because they lacked the proper "birth," his argument that the Poor Law raised wages over "customary" levels, and his support for a hospital for servants who served in the same household for over twenty years make clear that his social world was still precapitalist. His criticism of the Poor Law, then, was not the result of his individualism or of a natural rights philosophy freed from the obligations of natural law. Instead, like Hutcheson, his hatred of the idleness of both the rich and the poor stemmed from his deep sense of the obligation the people of Scotland should have to the development of their society. Since Scotland's welfare, both moral and economic, was inconsistent with the legally granted welfare rights of the Poor Law, such rights could not be required by natural law.

The *Sketches* also defended the British Parliament in its dispute with the American colonies and criticized Locke's argument that the natural right to property brought with it the right to consent to taxation through elected representatives. He referred to Locke's doctrine as "a very crazy foundation" for public finance and "totally subversive of government"

(*Sketches*, 2:357). Kames recommended the more utilitarian principle that people who benefited should pay the cost of the government that protected them. The colonists received protection from the British and so were obligated to pay taxes, with or without their consent. Kames also focused on the weaknesses of Locke's idea of consent, pointing out that most people subject to taxes in England could not be said to have actually consented to them. Kames used the good of society not only to justify taxes but to explain the principles that should govern their collection. "Because so many vices that poison a nation, arise from inequality of fortune; I propose it as a . . . rule to remedy that inequality as much as possible, by relieving the poor [of taxes] and burdening the rich" (*Sketches*, 3:384).

Throughout the history provided in the *Sketches* Kames was concerned with the interaction between idleness and industry, terms that had deep moral as well as economic meaning for him. In the history of property rights found in the *Sketches*, this interaction occurred through the repeated substitution of private rights for various common rights. Thus keeping herds in common encouraged the "idle and indolent" to consume what they did not help to produce and for this reason was replaced by every family rearing its own animals. The increased productivity that resulted led to a greater population, which caused conflicts over scarce pasture. The solution to feeding more people was the introduction of farming. Again, land was at first held in common, sown in common, the product stored in common, and distributed according to need. Because a system of common agriculture did not adequately motivate people, it gave way to a permanent division of land in which the produce belonged to the owner. With the perfection of government and the protection to property it afforded, the attachment between the owner and his land grew ever stronger (*Sketches*, 1:93–94). But this history of a progressively stronger emotional tie between an owner and his land could be told from another perspective. Since the land was located in a particular country and protected by a particular government, this was also a history of increasing patriotism as the owner's love for his country grew from the particular and concrete love he had for his land.

Patriotism for Kames encompassed all of those values—benevolence, courage, and heroism—that countered selfishness. Thus he argued that by the growth of "a regular government, by husbandry, by commerce, and by a common interest" patriotism increased (*Sketches*, 2:313). Presumably government made property secure, farming and commerce complemented each other as commerce provided markets that allowed agriculture to flourish, and with an awareness of the close tie between these two activities there developed a sense of common interest, the willingness to help others and defend the nation. In England, patriotism broke forth at the end of Elizabeth's reign, "when manufacture and commerce began to flourish" (Sketches, 2:317). People were put to work and learned the values associated with work, a middle strata free from poverty and sensuality was created, and affection for property and the government that protected it grew. Under these circumstances people's natural benevolence was able to assert itself. Throughout this analysis ran the belief that love of country and love of others occurred only when individuals were secure and independent, values Kames associated with the growth in private rights to property.

But as society successfully achieved prosperity and peace, it also made room for the vices of luxury and hoarding. The following quotation captures the tone and nature of Kames's argument:

> Luxury, a never-failing concomitant of wealth, is a slow poison, that debilitates men, and renders them incapable of any great effort: courage, magnanimity, heroism, come to be ranked among the miracles that are supposed never to have existed but in fable; and the fashionable properties of sensuality, avarice, cunning, and dissimulation, engross the mind. In a word, man by constant prosperity and peace degenerates into a mean, impotent, and selfish animal. Figure a man wallowing in riches and immersed in sensual pleasure, but dreading the infection of a plague raging at his gate; or figure him in continual dread of an enemy, watching every opportunity to burn and destroy. This man represents a commercial state, that has long enjoy'd peace without disturbance. (Sketches, 2:296)

Kames's denigration of an urban, luxurious, and commercial society started with his overriding hatred of idleness, a hatred that reached its zenith in his remark that one of the benefits of war was that it rid a country of idlers (Sketches, 2:305). With luxury came extreme inequality, a wealthy few who did not work, and an unemployed many who could not find work. But even worse, Kames found in idlers in particular and commercial society in general a selfishness that severely limited the ability of citizens to engage in benevolent and patriotic actions.

Natural law's emphasis on the secure enjoyment of full property rights might be thought to preclude an understanding of the common good and individual sacrifice. But this was certainly not the case with Kames. It was because of the strong link that existed between property, industry, and progress that Kames (like Hutcheson) was so hard on the idleness of the rich and the poor. Security, industry, benevolence, patriotism, and refinement were the values Kames thought were embedded in the ownership of landed property, not economic or moral individualism.

Smith

That Adam Smith would share with the rest of the Scottish Enlightenment a deep interest in the relationship between moral improvement and economic improvement is not surprising. He was taught by Hutcheson, Kames served as his patron, and Hume was one of his closest friends. The specific targets of Smith's improving spirit were the regulations that dampened and misdirected economic activity in the rural and commercial economy. Smith used the tradition of property theory inherited from Grotius to attack property restrictions on the grounds that they were inconsistent with the principles of natural law that should govern ownership. Smith was eager to end these restrictions so that Britain would reap the political and moral benefits resulting from an increase in the number of independent farmers and mechanics. His goal for the rural economy, "the multiplication of small proprietors" because "of all improvers [they were] the most industrious, the most intelligent, and the most successful," was shared with Kames.[39] Smith's reference to the "affection which property, naturally inspires" to explain the success of "small proprietors" was similarly Kamesian. But Smith extended this logic to "independent workmen" because they were more hardworking than "even a journeyman who works by the piece" or "servants who are paid by the month or by the year" and less likely to have their morals "ruin[ed]" (*WN*, I:101).

To make certain that his students understood the moral context of his economic analysis, Smith opened his first lecture on "police" (or public policy) by setting out the relationship between moral and economic improvement.

Nothing tends so much to corrupt and enervate and debase the mind as dependency, and nothing gives such noble and generous notions of probity as freedom and independency. Commerce is one great preventive of this custom. The manufactures give the poorer sort better wages than any master can afford; besides, it give[s] the rich an opportunity of spending their fortunes with fewer servants, which they never fail of embracing. Hence it is that the common people of England who are altogether free and independent are the honestest of their rank any where to be met with. The gentry and nobility of France are no doubt as good a set of men as those of England or other countries, but the commonality as being more subjected are much less honest and fair in their dealings. The gentry of Scotland are no worse than those of England, but the common people being considerably more oppressed have much less of probity, liberality, [and] amiable qualities in their tempers than those of England.[40]

His comparison of the level of economic development and honesty in England and Scotland must have been an embarrassment to his Scottish students. Similar arguments existed in his well-known history of the transition from a feudal to a commercial society in the third book of *Wealth of Nations* and in his comments on the honesty of the "middling" classes in *Theory of Moral Sentiments*. His hope was that a market economy with fewer barriers to agricultural and commercial activity would provide such powerful incentives "to truck, barter, and exchange" that everyone would be transformed through work.

Smith had little directly to say about property rights in *The Theory of Moral Sentiments* (1759), but in his short discussion of justice and beneficence he provided an introduction to the issue. He argued that individuals had rights "antecedent to the institution of civil government,"[41] that these rights were based on the moral equality of individuals, and that the resentment that individuals felt when their rights were violated led them justly to defend themselves and punish the wrongdoer. He listed rights in the following order of importance as requiring punishment if they were violated: "life and person . . . property and possessions . . . personal rights" (*TMS*, p. 163). Smith argued that maintaining these rights was justice and that Hume (a "great and original genius") was correct to point to the difference in the obligation to justice and to beneficence. For though beneficence was necessary for a society to flourish and be happy, justice "is the main pillar that upholds the entire edifice" (*TMS*, p. 167). Thus a man who shut "his breast against compassion, and refuses to relieve the misery of his fellow creatures, when he can with ease," deserved blame (*TMS*, p. 158). But since such a man chose only not to do good, he could not be coerced, as could the person who caused an injury by violating the rules of justice. The usefulness of justice was not, however, the motive individuals had in following its rules. Smith's theory of natural resentment and the impartial spectator here joined Hutcheson's and Kames's use of a moral sense and Hume's principles of association as a way of linking justice to dispositions more immediately and intensely felt than the public good.

Smith's distinction between justice and virtue in the *Theory of Moral Sentiments* was not meant to belittle virtue. Instead, he emphasized the extent to which a worthwhile life depended on "love . . . gratitude . . . friendship . . . and esteem" (*TMS*, p. 166). Under some circumstances, Smith even thought it would be permissible for the law to "command mutual good offices," that is, the performance of imperfect duties.[42] In keeping with the general tenor of the Scottish Enlightenment, Smith suggested that these virtues were most accessible to people of the middling ranks (*TMS*, p. 128). Indeed, he dealt harshly with those in the "superior stations of life," describing them as "ignorant and presumptuous" and the objects they surrounded themselves with as "frivolous" (*TMS*, p. 129). He never tired of reminding his readers that it was wrong to confuse virtue and wealth. And he thought that if the rich fell into poverty it was because of their own "considerable misconduct" (*TMS*, p. 243). Although Smith added to his warning that wealth not be confused with virtue, the parallel caution against confusing poverty with vice, it is nonetheless surprising how little there is the in *Theory of Moral Sentiments* about the poor. Smith noted that beggars were despised (*TMS*, p. 242) and that the poor were most often simply ignored. As if to prove this last point, in Smith's system of ethics, spelled out at great length in the *Theory of Moral Sentiments*, neither compassion nor charity for the poor seemed to occupy any place at all.

In his lectures on jurisprudence (one from 1762–63 and one from 1763–64) he discussed in much more detail the relationship between justice, property rights, and natural law. In both lectures he divided the rules of jurisprudence into four categories—justice, police, revenue, and arms. Under justice were those rules that kept the members of a society "from encroaching on one another's property" (*LJ*, p. 5), property here used in the wide sense of all the rights people possessed. In 1763–64 he rephrased this definition to "the end of justice is to secure from injury" (*LJ*, p. 399). Since a man may be injured in his "body, reputation, or estate" (*LJ*, p. 8, 399), justice required the protection of property rights. Like Hume and Kames, Smith saw justice as concerned with the protection of perfect rights. To talk of imperfect rights was not "proper," Smith argued, but "metaphorical" (*LJ*, p. 9).

In both lectures rights to person and reputation were described as natural. Injuries to the person included not only physical harm but also restraints placed on individual liberty. Smith's listing of the "right to free commerce" or the "right of trafficking with those who are willing to deal with him" (*LJ*, p. 8) under the rights to liberty is reminiscent of Grotius's attack on the monopolies in colonial trade the Portuguese had claimed. Between 1762–63 and 1763–64 Smith moved the right to one's estate from a natural right to an adventitious right. As with Hutcheson, it would be wrong to think this distinction had ideological overtones because natural law required the protection of one as much as the other. To call a right adventitious was just to point out it could exist only through human action in a social setting. Smith seemed to have a stronger sense by 1763–64 that "there is no such state" as "the state of nature" (*LJ*, p. 398) and that therefore the tie between property and government was virtually impossible to disentangle. His own description of this change did not suggest that a great deal should be read into it:

> Acquired rights such as property require more explanation. Property and civil government very much depend on one another. The preservation of property and the inequality of possession first formed it, and the state of property must always vary with the form of government. The civilians begin with considering government and then treat of property and other rights. Others who have written on this subject begin with the latter and then consider family and civil government. There are several advantages peculiar to each of these methods, tho' that of the civil law seems upon the whole preferable. (*LJ*, p. 401)

Yet insofar as the idea of an adventitious right rests on mutual recognition and government action, it more accurately reflected the explanations he gave, for example, for rights to land and last testaments. That property rights were adventitious also makes sense of the fact that when Smith, especially in *Wealth of Nations*, invoked a natural right against a current practice, he used the right to liberty and not to property.

Smith's discussion of the creation of property rights was based on the way the five categories of property in Roman law—occupation (or possession), accession, prescription, succession, and exchange—changed through the four stages of economic and political development. His emphasis was on the progressively weaker tie between possession and property and on the way an active government had to create new property rules and abolish old ones to foster economic growth and moral improvement.[43]

Smith began his discussion of property in the 1762–63 lecture with a paradox. Why should something that would benefit another more belong to me simply because I possess it (*LJ*, p. 13)? Smith eschewed both a labor mixing argument and a straightforwardly utilitarian argument. Instead, he deployed the apparatus developed in the *Theory of Moral Sentiments* to show that property was based on the concurrence of the impartial spectator with the reasonable expectations of individuals that they should be able to use and defend from others what their "time and pains" had enabled them to possess (*LJ*, pp. 17–18). No doubt Smith, like so many others, thought the labor argument failed because it merely described a physical act and the utilitarian argument could not resolve (and in fact created) the paradox with which he began.

Hunters worked with the expectation they could use the prey they captured for food. Insofar as there were property rights in such a society, they would be entirely confined to clothes, the game hunters caught, and the weapons they used. Since game would have been plentiful in this early stage and, when caught, clearly possessed, theft would occur infrequently and inflict little hardship. In such a society there would be little reason for government to develop as an agency to protect against injury.

The relationship between property and possession changed with the advent of herding. Among shepherds expectations would grow that they would own all of their herd even when they were separated from and could not be said physically to possess all or a part of it. So long as sheep had a distinguishing mark, Smith thought they would be considered to be privately owned. With property no longer limited by what an individual actually possessed, inequality would grow to the point that some owned all the animals in an area and others owned none. Under these circumstances, violence would characterize relations between the rich and the poor and would provide reason for government to be created. Smith wrote in 1762–63 that "the appropriation of herds and flocks, which introduced an inequality of fortune, was that which first gave rise to regular government. Till there be property there can be no government, the very end of which is to secure wealth, and to defend the rich from the poor" (*LJ*, p. 404). In this lecture he credited Rousseau with helping him to see the relationship between property and government. Not surprisingly, then, he described property as "the grand fund of all dispute" (*LJ*, pp. 203, 313).

In the shepherding stage a new understanding was also given to the huts in which shepherds lived. A hunter would have a right to a cave only when he dwelt in it, but the huts made by shepherds, like the sheep they herded, would come to be theirs with or without their occupation. The considerable change this represented could not be accounted for by the individual labor involved in building. At first, an unoccupied hut like an unoccupied cave would have been used by anyone in need. Only "the *common consent* of the several members of [the] tribe or society," Smith insisted, conferred a property right in huts (*LJ*, p. 21).

In the third stage of society, when agriculture was introduced, property was slowly extended to include land. Since an agricultural society emerged from a society of shepherds, it began with the tribe owning the land, cultivating it in common, and distributing the produce according to individual status and family size. With "fixt habitations" and the growth of cities, this situation would change because people would cultivate the land closest to them. Finally, individuals would receive rights to land through the express agreement of the people or their leaders (*LJ*, pp. 20–22, 460). Smith cited Homer, Aristotle, and Tacitus as providing historical evidence for an express agreement. But it is clear that the model he used in moving from use rights to full property rights by an express agreement was Grotian, which is not surprising from someone who praised Grotius as the best natural law theorist (*LJ*, p. 397).

Smith discussed the division of commonly held land into individual plots without any evidence of the animus that Kames had toward common property. Although the course of economic progress meant the narrowing of what was common, Smith did not deny that common property was natural. Rather, he affirmed the continued existence of common property in air and running water and called "tyrannical" the efforts of "feudal lords" to make wild (and common) animals private (*LJ*, pp. 22–23).

There was no need for Smith to consider possession in commercial society, for after the first three stages ownership had been separated both theoretically and practically from possession. He did discuss briefly the way prescription and accession developed through these stages, primarily to emphasize how small a role utility played in the definition of either one. Changes in succession, however, were more important.

In the stage of hunters no property would pass from the dead to the living. The few personal effects people may have accumulated would be buried with their bodies. Shepherds, however, did accumulate property, and thus they posed for the first time the question of how it should be divided at the death of the father, the head of the family. Smith made two points here that were important. The first was that succession occurred according to rules that existed independently of the will of the owner (*LJ*, pp. 38, 465). He explicitly argued that succession by a testament was a relatively recent invention that carried no particularly strong moral presumption in its favor. His second point concerned the content of the rule which he described as "the natural law of succession" (*LJ*, p. 361). According to this rule, a shepherd's property would be divided equally among the wife and children, both male and female. As Smith said (again reminiscent of Grotius and Locke), "All the members of the family come in for an equal share in it on his death, as they all contributed their assistance to the support of it" (*LJ*, p. 39). Though the logic of identifying as a natural law the method of succession appropriate to the shepherding stage is unclear, its rhetorical value is obvious: it gave Smith a perspective from which to criticize primogeniture.

Primogeniture was first understood by Smith to be a reasonable response to the chaotic conditions in feudalism, which were caused by the lack of a government able to protect the security of individuals. What peace did exist was primarily owing to the power exercised by the owners of very large landholdings who were able to use their wealth to create private armies. If property were divided at the death of such a lord and then again at the death of his sons, holdings would soon be too small to maintain the private armies required for security. But if property had to be kept intact from generation to generation, the question arose as to how to pick the individual in the next generation who would inherit. Succession to the eldest son was adopted as a rule, according to Smith, simply because it was least capable of being misunderstood and of causing conflict.

As was true for Kames, the four-stage theory was an excellent apparatus for discrediting practices by demonstrating that they were outmoded. Smith's argument was that primogeniture grew under feudalism because it provided security, but it was obsolete in commercial society because the state guaranteed protection to the person and property of every Englishman (*WN*, 1:383). Since primogeniture was no longer necessary for the secure enjoyment of rights, there was no reason to maintain it rather than equal division, the natural law of succession. Moreover, primogeniture was a hindrance to the second object of law, the production of inexpensive commodities (*LJ*, p. 398). Primogeniture maintained property in the hands of people who had little incentive or inclination to improve it and kept property from those "small proprietors" who would. Smith concluded that primogeniture was "contrary to reason, to justice, to nature" (*LJ*, p. 49).

Though succession by the laws of nature was originally used by the community to pass property from the dead to the living, in the course of moral development succession by last testament took precedence. Smith explained the late introduction of wills by linking them to the growth of piety to the deceased, "a pitch of humanity, a refinement on it, which we are not to expect from a people who have not made considerable advances in civilized manners" (*LJ*, pp. 64, 467). In England, Smith wrote, testaments came to play an important role only during the reign of Henry VIII.

Tracing wills to piety gave Smith his first argument against the practice that controlled land into perpetuity—entails. Just as piety was felt most strongly immediately after death and then lost its power, so should a testament of the deceased honored out of piety lose its power over time. It was absurd, said Smith, that a will should govern property long after the person who made it had been forgotten. Entails also impeded agricultural improvement in the same way that primogeniture did by keeping land from going to smaller proprietors who would cultivate it efficiently (*WN*, 1:385–88). Smith's desire to elevate tenants to independent owners is evident in this discussion. But behind his attitude toward both primogeniture and entails was the most basic assumption of the tradition we have been considering, that is, that God gave the earth to *all* people for their sustenance. Rights to private property justly grew only because they, better than common rights, allowed the efficient production of food and other commodities. Entails and primogeniture were condemned because they allowed a few to monopolize land to the detriment of others. In his lectures and in *Wealth of Nations* Smith invoked the principle that "the earth and the fullness of it belongs to every generation" (*LJ*, p. 486, *WN*, 1:384).

Smith's approach to property rights, considering whether they served the values of security, preservation, and prosperity, is also evident in the enterprise for which he is most famous, the attack on government regulation of business activity. He noted that many of the "exclusive privileges" that limited free trade once performed valuable functions and in some areas (e.g., patents and copyrights) were still worthwhile (*LJ*, pp. 86, 472). Civil law, then, was correct to create them in "the first stages of society," should continue to guard some, but should abolish others because they no longer fulfilled a function sanctioned by natural law. Insofar as these regulations, especially those that created monopolies, tended to raise prices and lower quality, they violated the injunction of natural jurisprudence that law should promote the cheapness of provisions. Like Kames, he had a special interest in rural economic development and was especially critical of restrictions that impoverished the countryside to the benefit of cities.[44]

In *Wealth of Nations* Smith considered both the regulation of apprentices and the regulations of the Poor Law. To evaluate both sets of rules he adopted the point of view of the laborer and asked whether the limits placed on labor could be justified. His objection to the English Poor Law was not that taxes paid by the propertied to support the poor violated the property rights of the propertied. In fact, he never objected to the provisions of 43rd Eliz. under which the poor were given aid. His focus was entirely on the laws of settlement that had been added later. He argued that in inhibiting mobility and distorting the wage structure these laws violated the rights of the poor. "To remove a man who has committed no misdemeanor from the parish where he chooses to reside, is an evident violation of natural liberty and justice." As a result of this law, "There is scarce a poor man in England of forty years of age . . . who has not in some part of his life felt himself most cruelly oppressed by this ill-contrived law of settlements" (*WN*, 1:157, 470). Smith made a similar argument against laws that regulated wages and set bread prices. He noted that "masters" had more political power than laborers and for that reason wage regulations often treated workmen unfairly. He also suggested that though regulating the price of bread might once have made sense, competition would now do a better job of limiting the profits of merchants (*WN*, 1:158).

Throughout Smith's discussion of "police" in the *Lectures* and in *Wealth of Nations*, there was a concerted effort to link the accomplishments of a less regulated market to the realization of the moral values that others invoked to regulate economic activity or limit property rights. For example, Smith echoed Hutcheson's belief that the goals of an agrarian law could be achieved by opening land to the market through the abolition of primogeniture and entail. He also suggested that taxes on luxury goods could serve the same purpose as sumptuary laws (*LJ*, p.

823). This effort was repeated in his consideration of famine and the rights of necessity. Smith recognized neither the individual right of necessity nor the common rights of the community to take from those with more than enough to feed others during a famine. Like Hume, he noted without judgment that people suffering famine "will break open granaries" (LJ, p. 197). Smith's contribution to the discussion of famine and natural rights was to try to demonstrate how the laws that created public granaries or regulated the sale of corn were causes of famine (WN, 1:526). He argued for a free grain trade on the grounds that it "is not only the best palliative of the inconveniences of a dearth; but the best preventative of that calamity" (WN, 1:532).[45] To add weight to his economic arguments for a free market in grain, he invoked the natural law vocabulary, in effect turning the "right to free commerce" against inclusive rights. The laws that hindered the trade of the corn merchant "were evident violations of natural liberty, and therefore unjust" (WN, 1:530). Here as elsewhere in Wealth of Nations Smith relied on the natural right to liberty rather than property rights to limit government activity.

Since tax policy could be as important as government regulation in hindering or facilitating market activity and moral improvement, Smith discussed taxes in considerable detail. Just as he had rejected Locke's mixing argument, he (like Hutcheson, Hume, and Kames) also refused to use Locke's argument that property rights entailed the right to be represented in deliberations about taxation. Neither the obligation to law in general nor the obligation to pay taxes in particular was based on consent, according to Smith (LJ, p. 323). He noted that people were not aware of having consented to obey or to be taxed. An accurate account of why people *did* obey must be more sociologically acute than a consent theory. It would have to take into account the role of authority, deference, and utility. At the same time, an account of why people *should* obey required an investigation of the laws of nature, which could not be established or set aside by consent. "There are some things," Smith said, "which it is unlawful for the sovereign to attempt and entitle the subjects to make resistance" (LJ, p. 320). One act that justified rebellion was "a very exorbitant tax." The reason, however, had nothing to do with the presence or absence of consent. Rather, such a tax would be a "gross violation of power" because it was antithetical to the purpose of government, which was the defense of property. Dugald Stewart was not unfair to the thrust of Smith's argument when he used Smith to insist that "the happiness of mankind depends not on the share which the people possess, directly or indirectly, in the enactment of laws, but on the equity and expediency of the laws that are enacted."[46]

Natural law constraints applied to the impact taxes had on different parts of society as well as to the overall level of taxation. The first maxim Smith gave to judge alternative tax policies was that "the subjects of every state ought to contribute towards the support of the government, as nearly as possible, in proportion to their respective abilities; that is, in proportion to the revenue which they respectively enjoy under the protection of the state. . . . In the observation or neglect of this maxim consists what is called the equality or inequality of taxation" (*WN*, 2:825). Smith returned to this theme of equity every time he discussed taxes. In general, his sense of fairness and proportion required that taxes fall on the wealthy rather than on the poor and on luxuries rather than on necessities (*WN*, 2:842; *LJ*, p. 821).

At the start of his lectures on jurisprudence Smith listed "the four great objects of law." The first was justice, to secure people from injury; the second was police, to provide for the "cheapness of commodities" or "the opulence of the state"; the third concerned revenue or taxation; and the fourth was protection from foreign invasion or attack (*LJ*, p. 398). In effect, these objects were the natural law goals of security, prosperity, and peace, all of which required a government funded by taxes. The possibility that this account of jurisprudence may have contained contradictory elements, that protecting property, for example, might be at odds with the economic, public health, educational, or taxing policies necessary for opulence seems not to have occurred to Smith. In part this was because he believed that reduced government regulation, justice, and economic growth were fundamentally consistent with one another. Connecting these three principles was independence. People who were independent because their rights were protected had incentives to improve their economic situation and in so doing learned the virtues associated with a market economy.[47]

The Scottish Enlightenment used the natural law discussion of property rights to exhort owners to improve their land and to criticize legal barriers to economic development. This much was shared with John Locke's theory of property. But in other ways the Scottish philosophers' understanding of what natural law required with regard to property rights was quite un-Lockean. In general, their perspective was consistently more public and less individualist than Locke's. They all objected to his derivation of property rights from individuals mixing their labor with nature. Except for Reid, they were antagonistic to the idea that the poor had individual inclusive property rights that required public assistance or legitimated the exercise of the right of necessity. A commitment to the public welfare seemed to them to be inconsistent with individuals having welfare rights. Kames and Smith, especially, made arguments against the English Poor Law that became influential. In their view, there was work for all to do and in its doing all would be improved. Common property inhibited growth, poor laws were inefficient and unjust, rights of necessity were dangerous excuses for idlers, and charity could not be forced. Moreover, they rejected the idea that natural property rights required individual consent through representative institutions. Yet if the program of Hutcheson, Kames, and Smith accomplished the goals they set for it, larger estates would be broken up, more people would become owners, and economic efficiency would guarantee that more food would be available to all. Though they did not defend individual inclusive property rights, they continued to work from the central assumption of the natural law tradition that the earth was given for the preservation of human life and that all systems of property rights were to be judged by their ability to meet this standard.

FOUR

Paternalism and the Poor Law

Paley and Others

The Scottish interpretation of the natural rights and duties of property, with its general antagonism to common and inclusive rights, was not the only interpretation of Grotius, Pufendorf, and Locke that came to have political importance. This tradition of analysis also passed through a group of eighteenth-century English writers who took a paternalistic attitude toward ownership. Their interest in conserving the institutions of their society by linking those institutions to the laws of nature included a philosophical defense of the Elizabethan or Old Poor Law through the use of the idea that the poor had a right to welfare. It is especially important that in the work of two of these writers—Richard Woodward and William Paley—a welfare right was explicitly presented as a claim on the wealth of the nation and not just a liberty to take what was necessary. That such conservative writers should transmit ideas that would be put to radical use in the late eighteenth century and beyond is a paradox well known to intellectual history. And in a more straightforward way their work provides the background to the Tory paternalism of the early nineteenth century.[1]

Rutherforth and Blackstone

In 1754–56 Thomas Rutherforth, Regius Professor of Divinity at Cambridge University, published a series of his lectures under the title *Institutes of Natural Law; being the substance of a course of lectures on Grotius' De Jure Belli ac Pacis*. Though it is difficult to assess the impact of these lectures, if any, they must have impressed some readers, for a second American edition was published in Baltimore as late as 1832. Considering Rutherforth briefly will provide some insights into how Grotius and Locke were read in eighteenth-century England as well as a more general sense of how property rights were understood.

The center of Rutherforth's discussion was the meaning of the original grant of the earth to mankind and the implications of that grant for the development of private property. For reasons that are impossible to know, Rutherforth did not invoke Pufendorf's distinction between a positive and negative community. But only the idea of an original positive community makes sense of his discussion, which is not surprising because he worked within a Grotian framework. He argued that "all things belonged originally to all mankind" and that individuals in the state of nature had "a common right in a joint stock."[2] According to Rutherforth, everyone shared a right to the common and they could take what was necessary to subsist. In doing so they were simply taking that which they partly owned. But because they were only part owners, they could not take more than they could use. To do so would be to injure others by depriving them of what they had a right to. Rutherforth argued that the exercise of a primitive use right in a situation of common ownership did not require waiting for the approval of others and that only the idea of common ownership explained why those private rights were limited to use.

Rutherforth interpreted Grotius as maintaining that the only way use rights to the common could be transformed into property rights was through consent, either express or tacit. The reasons Rutherforth thought people would give their consent are familiar—to settle disputes and to provide a motive for increasing productivity. These same reasons justified any inequalities in property that later developed. Like Grotius, he saw express consent as given through a contract and tacit consent as given through the mutual recognition of one another's occupancy: "What a man seizes upon, with a design to make it his own, or to appropriate it to himself, will become fairly his own, or will be made his property; when the rest of mankind, as far as they have an opportunity of observing him, understand what his design is, and show by their behavior, in not molesting him, that they agree to let his design take effect" (p. 25). Rutherforth saw Locke's labor and mixing arguments as intellectual competitors to Grotius's theory because they did not require consent for property to develop.

For labor to establish a property right to what had been held in a positive community, which was the way Rutherforth understood Locke's argument, it must have been able to "overrule or set aside the right of others." But to set "aside the right of an individual, without his consent, is an injury to him; so setting aside the common claim of mankind, without their consent, is an injury to them" (pp. 26–27). Just as it would not be permissible to claim that laboring on someone else's property transferred its title to the laborer, so it could not be claimed that laboring on what was owned by all could make it the property of the laborer. And if it were possible for labor to make private what belonged to all, Rutherforth thought Locke would not have been able to defend the spoilage and as much and as good for others limits he put on acquisition (pp. 27–28). In effect, Rutherforth argued that if labor could create private property rights, others must not have had rights to the common, but if others did not have rights to the common, there was no reason for there to be limits on how much could be taken. Conversely, if there were limits, others must have had rights, and if others had rights, consent must be obtained before what belonged to all could belong to anyone. That Locke's use of labor to derive rights from a positive community occurred in a situation of abundance must have seemed irrelevant to Rutherforth.

Behind these theoretical disagreements with Locke was another issue. Rutherforth detected in the labor argument a danger to landlords. Thus he was at pains to deny Locke's contention that labor was responsible for virtually the entire value of goods. First, he pointed out that laborers worked with materials supplied by the landlord. "If neither the timber of his plough, nor the horses that draw it, nor the meat which they eat, nor the manure which he lays upon his land, nor the grain with which he sows it, are his own, what will you rate his labor at" (p. 30)? But his anxiety at the possible consequences of the labor argument also led him to consider the example of a tenant who "plows and sows the land" using his own material as well as his own labor to raise wheat. He denied that even under these conditions labor conferred rights. "But no one will be led to conclude from hence, that because . . . ninety-nine parts in a hundred are owing to the labour of the occupier, the property, which he has in his own labor, will swallow up the property which the landlord has in the soil; and that the land, because he has cultivated it, will for the future become his own" (p. 31). As we shall see, Rutherforth was right to see these radical possibilities within the Lockean theory.

Though Rutherforth thought the original positive community cast some shadows over property after it had been made private, and precluded oceans from ever becoming private, he made certain that exclusive rights were not jeopardized (p. 38). For example, though wild animals continued common, to make sure this did not open possibilities for the poor to hunt and fish in ways that might disturb the wealthy, Rutherforth quickly added that one could not trespass on land that was owned to get to these animals (pp. 39–40). Rights of harmless use similarly continued, but Rutherforth insisted that it was up to the proprietor to decide if a use was harmless (p. 43).

Grounding property in consent avoided the problem of finding ways to "domesticate" a theory that emphasized labor, especially in a period still dominated by absentee landlord-tenant relationships. But consent also had problems, and these centered on whether people would have consented to a distribution in which they or their children could find themselves left out altogether. Since Rutherforth thought that people would have "agreed to the introduction of property for the convenience of all, and not for the destruction of any," and were, in any case, barred from alienating the right to "the necessary means of [their] own preservation," he upheld the existence of a right of necessity. "When a man must have starved otherwise, it is naturally no theft if he takes victuals which is not his own" (p. 41). Rutherforth attached to this right the usual conditions that a starving person must ask individuals and then the magistrate for assistance and could exercise the right of necessity only if help was not forthcoming. He also must make restitution. But here, again, Rutherforth found a way to make certain that the right of necessity did not become dangerous. By interpreting the English Poor Law as guaranteeing that magistrates would aid the poor, he could conclude that in England it was illegitimate ever to invoke this right. "Indeed in our own country, where the civil laws have provided for the poor, there can be no necessity which the civil law will allow to be sufficient ground for taking" (pp. 42–43). Although Rutherforth's discussion of property ended in a defense of the English status quo, he saw that the property theory he inherited from Grotius and Locke presented opportunities for criticism that those less enamored with the current arrangement of holdings could exploit. His criticism of Locke's labor theory and his interpretations of the Poor Law so as to make illegitimate the invocation of the right of necessity were his attempts to control the way natural property rights were understood.

William Blackstone's *Commentaries on the Laws of England* (1764) is primarily known for its attempt to bring some order to English common law, but it included a brief general discussion of the law of nature as well as a natural law justification of property rights. Blackstone was explicit about the audience for whom he wrote. In his introduction to Volume 1 he addressed himself to "gentleman of independent estates and fortunes [who are] the most useful as well as considerable body of men in the nation."[3] The Scottish philosophers of the eighteenth century addressed a similar audience in the hope that their public spirit could be awakened and the economic reform of society undertaken. No such sentiments moved Blackstone. Instead, he desired to educate English gentlemen in the intricacies of property law so they would be able to "check and guard" their property from their "inferior agents," who might cheat them. His more conservative aims are revealed in the roles that he thought well-educated gentlemen could play on juries, as justices of the peace, and as members of Parliament. As jurors they should reverse the trend of judges who were enhancing judicial power. As justices of the peace they needed to maintain "good order in [their] neighborhood; by punishing the dissolute and idle; by protecting the peaceable and industrious." And as members of Parliament they must be "guardians of the English constitution," a job that required them "to watch, to check, and to avert every dangerous innovation" (1:7–9). Both Rutherforth and Blackstone used the natural law discussion of property to buttress English institutions by grounding them in the laws of nature.

Blackstone opened his derivation of private property from the principles of natural law with a paragraph so extraordinary it deserves to be quoted in full:

There is nothing which so generally strikes the imagination, and engages the affections of mankind, as the right of property; or that sole and despotic dominion which one man claims and exercises over the external things of the world, in total exclusion of the right of any other individual in the universe. And yet there are very few, that will give themselves the trouble to consider the original and foundation of this right. Pleased as we are with the possession, we seem afraid to look back to the means by which it was acquired, as if fearful of some defect in our title; or at best we rest satisfied with the decision of the laws in our favor, without examining the reason or authority upon which those laws have been built. We think it enough that our title is derived by the grant of the former proprietor, by descent from our ancestors, or by the last will and testament of the dying owner; not caring to reflect that (accurately and strictly speaking) there is no foundation in nature or in natural law, why a set of words upon parchment should convey the dominion of land;

why the son should have a right to exclude his fellow creatures from a determinate spot of ground, because his father had done so before him; or why the occupier of a particular field or of a jewel, when lying on his death-bed and no longer able to maintain possession, should be entitled to tell the rest of the world which of them should enjoy it after him. These enquiries, it must be owned, would be useless and even troublesome in common life. It is well if the mass of mankind will obey the laws when made, without scrutinizing too nicely into the reasons of making them. But, when law is to be considered not only as a matter of practice, but also as a rational science, it cannot be improper or useless to examine more deeply the rudiments and grounds of these positive constitutions of society. (2:2)

In the first sentence of this paragraph Blackstone gave expression to as thoroughly private a definition of property as it ever received. Only Kames seems to have had as much reverence for private rights in land as Blackstone. But just as interesting is the sense of fear expressed that an inquiry into natural law might call into question current property rights, the reason he thought such inquiries would be "troublesome in common life" and ought not to be undertaken by "the mass of mankind." Ownership based on inheritance, the title most of his readers would be relying on, was mentioned as a potential problem because it could not be traced directly to the commands of natural law. Of course, Blackstone did not think that natural law properly understood was subversive of current property rights, and it was to demonstrate this that he engaged in the natural law discussion.

As we have seen, Locke's mixing argument had been rejected by virtually everyone in the eighteenth century who had considered it. It is, therefore, noteworthy that after providing a very brief and conventional account of God's original grant of the earth (negative or positive community left unspecified) and the way use rights became property rights because of population growth and conflict, Blackstone described the process by which movables became subject to exclusive rights: "Few of them could be fit for use, till improved and meliorated by the bodily labor of the occupant; which bodily labor, bestowed upon any subject which before lay in common to all men, is universally allowed to give the fairest and most reasonable title to an exclusive property therein" (2:5). Whether he thought labor conferred rights because of its usefulness or whether he accepted the mixing argument is hard to know. But given the widespread rejection of Locke's labor argument by previous philosophers, Blackstone's approving use of labor in a book that became so authoritative must have been one of the most important ways in which Locke's labor theory was transmitted to the late eighteenth century, especially in America.

Blackstone was somewhat more cautious in his discussion of property rights in land. He noted that Grotius and Pufendorf used consent to explain why occupancy created rights, whereas Barbeyrac and Locke saw occupation itself as sufficient to create a just title to land. Blackstone, no doubt hoping to create a consensus, suggested that this disagreement was "too nice and scholastic" and that the important point was the shared understanding that occupancy, for whatever reason, was an appropriate foundation for property rights in land (2:8–9). But though occupancy began the process of establishing full property rights in land, this process came to an end only through the laws of society. "Necessity begat property," he wrote, "and, in order to insure that property, recourse was had to civil society" (2:8). Or, as he summarized in another place, "the permanent right of property . . . was no natural, but merely a civil right" (2:11). In this last quotation Blackstone was explaining that the right to dispose of land in a will was a creation of civil law and therefore a fit subject for regulation. His emphasis on the civil law foundations of property was consistent with his recognition that natural rights were given up when people joined society (1:52, 121), with his celebrated description of Parliament's power as "absolute and without control" (1:157), and with his defense of a sovereign power that must be a "supreme, irresistible, absolute, uncontrolled authority" (1:49). Unfortunately for clarity's sake, Blackstone also described property as a "despotic dominion" or an "absolute" right (1:134) and argued that absolute rights could not be abridged by human law (1:54).

Theoretically, it was possible for him to reconcile the power he gave to Parliament to promote the "general advantage of the public" (1:121) with the "absolute" right to property he seemed to give to individuals by the argument that "the public good is in nothing more essentially than in the protection of every individual's property rights" (1:135). But given all the restrictions on property Blackstone actually approved, he must be credited with handing down to the generations that read him the confusion of believing that property rights were "a despotic dominion" and at the same time subject to the "long and voluminous" regulations of a sovereign Parliament. In only two cases did Blackstone seem to believe that government regulation was explicitly limited by individual property rights. A government could not justly tax without the consent of Parliament, nor could it confiscate property, even for a public purpose, without paying compensation (1:134–35).

Blackstone did not follow Locke, however, in finding a right of necessity implicit in a property right. He disagreed with "Grotius, and Pufendorf, together with many other of the foreign jurists . . . and some even of our own lawyers" by calling the right of necessity "unwarranted" because it would put property "under a strange insecurity." His general point, that property was necessarily private and exclusive, is neatly captured in the final sentence of the section devoted to the discussion of natural law when he comments that "the legislation of England has universally promoted the grand ends of civil society, the peace and security of individuals, by steadily pursuing that wise and orderly maxim, of assigning to every thing capable of ownership a legal and determinate owner" (2:15).

Blackstone's recommendation that all things be made private was completely consistent with the abolition of common fields and common rights to pasture, wood, and turf that was brought about by parliamentary enclosures, the use of which accelerated dramatically in this period. In the twenty years before 1760 Parliament adopted 151 enclosure acts, and in the twenty years after 1760 this number rose to 776.[4] Though the commissioners appointed to oversee the enclosure could recognize the customary rights of the poor who used the common, "in by far the greatest majority of the cases, they chose to disregard these rights and to make no provision whatsoever for the dispossessed."[5] If we can hear in Blackstone the echo of landowners praising enclosures for the gains in agricultural efficiency and profits that they brought, we will hear in paternalists like Paley and then radicals like Thomas Spence echoes of protest from the small landowners, cottagers, and squatters who suffered when commons and common rights were abolished.

But though Blackstone denied the existence of the right of necessity, he did not completely jettison the idea of a welfare right. Instead, he discussed it as part of the right to personal security guaranteed by English law, a right that included the right to life, limbs, and reputation. Not only should civil laws guard life and limb insofar as that was consistent with "the general advantage of the public" but they should furnish people "with everything necessary for their support" (1:127). English law gave this support through the Poor Law, "for there is no man so indigent or wretched, but he may demand a supply sufficient for all the necessities of life, from the more opulent part of the community, by means of several statutes enacted for the relief of the poor." The Poor Law was also "dictated by the principles of society," a reference probably to the idea that obedience to the law could not be expected from people who were starving (1:127). Like Rutherforth, Blackstone pointed out that the existence of the English Poor Law meant that dire necessity that might justify "thieving" could not occur in England (4:32). It is difficult to know how to read these short comments, whether Blackstone was recommending the Poor Law as good policy or as required by natural justice. His comments took up only a paragraph or two, which must tell something of their importance to him. P. S. Atiyah has captured the cynical element in the paternalism of Rutherforth and Blackstone in his comment that "the Poor Laws were perceived as part of the price paid by the landowners for the acquiescence of the mass of the people in the eighteenth-century system of government."[6]

Woodward and Paley

In the work of Richard Woodward and William Paley, both Anglican clergymen, we find a less cynical paternalism, a greater concern for the well-being (as opposed to the passivity) of the poor, and an explicit defense of the Poor Law on the grounds that it was required by justice. Woodward moved to Dublin in the early 1760s and soon became concerned with the conditions of the Irish poor. He was one of the founders of the House of Industry in Dublin and the author of two essays that advocated the establishment of a poor law in Ireland and defended its continued existence in England. He saw Kames as the most important critic of the English Poor Law and against him tried to show that the poor had a right to aid and that aiding them was in the best interest of a country. Thus, though Woodward was adamant that the poor should be deferential, he insisted that they had a claim-right to the goods necessary for their subsistence.

Woodward was explicit that the duty the rich had to the poor could not be fulfilled through private charity alone. Instead, he described this duty as similar to the payment of a debt and as required by "strict justice."[7] The implication was that just as the legislature was bound by justice to pass laws that guaranteed people paid their business debts to one another, it had a duty to require that the rich paid their debt to the poor.

Though Woodward's argument was not as clear as it might be, its main outlines are straightforward. It was useful, he thought, to think of society as having originated in a contract. In a precontractual period people should be thought of as having had a right to gather their subsistence from property owned in common. To reduce conflict, people would have agreed to private shares and a government to protect them. But no one could be thought to have entered civil society to be in a worse position. It was consistent with natural law that land became privately owned and some became landless only under the assumption that the landless were able to earn a subsistence from their labor. But individuals who were both landless and unemployed continued to have an obligation to the laws of civil society only if that society guaranteed their subsistence through a system of taxation and aid. Individuals could not have agreed to enter a society in which obedience to the laws against stealing required their own starvation. In a statement that was often cited later in debates over the Poor Law, Woodward asked rhetorically whether the rich

> are or are not, bound in justice to provide for him [a poor person] a competent maintenance? If not, by what right did they take upon them to enact certain laws (for the rich compose the legislative body in every civilized country), which compelled that man to become a member of their society; which precluded him from any share in the land where he was born, any use of its spontaneous fruits, or any dominion over the beasts of the field, on pain of imprisonment, or death? How can they justify their exclusive property, in the common heritage of mankind, unless they consent in return to provide for the subsistence of the poor, who were excluded from those common rights by the laws of the rich, to which they were never parties? (Pp. 32–33)

As Blackstone's recommendation that all things be made private reflected approval of the policy of parliamentary enclosure that was occurring in this period, Woodward's argument that "those excluded from . . . common rights" should be maintained by government aid reflected an awareness of the social costs of that policy. Woodward's argument, then, was that the rich owed a debt to the landless poor as compensation for the common rights that all men had but which had been taken from the poor.

Woodward's sense that landlords lived off wealth created by the laboring poor and his recognition that the poor were unrepresented in Parliament never added up to a radical critique. Lest his strictures be interpreted wrongly, he more than once insisted upon "the reasonableness of [the poor's] subordination in society, and their obligations to obedience." He also stressed that his analysis applied to "those persons only who, though willing to work, cannot subsist by labor" and not to "idle vagrants" (p. 9). Moreover, the aid given to the eligible should be the lowest rate earned by those working. He thought that aid was best given in a house of industry because it improved the morals of the poor, which indicates the primarily paternalist nature of this argument.[8]

Two good examples of the way Blackstone and Woodward were used can be seen in Thomas Ruggles's *History of the Poor* (1793) and J. G. Sherer's *Remarks upon the Present State of the Poor* (1796). Both works championed the rights of the poor within a paternalistic context. Sherer insisted that the relief that was owed to the sick, old, and disabled had its foundations in justice, not charity. He argued that these rights "are not mere legal claims, dependent only on the varying laws of custom, and capable of being cancelled or annulled at pleasure, but rational, permanent, indefeasible rights, founded on the very principles that support society, and independent of any change of time or manner."[9] In support of this position, he cited Blackstone's comment that the Poor Law was "dictated by the principles of society" (p. 30). His attitude toward the able-bodied poor was more ambivalent. Insofar as they were lazy he argued that they had no rights at all, yet he criticized landlords who undertook enclosures and suggested instead that they build cottages and rent land in half-acre allotments to the unemployed. Whether the able-bodied who were willing to work but were unemployed had rights was left unclear. That Sherer's defense of the poor's rights remained paternalistic is clear from his insistence that "it is the duty of the poor, to behave to their superiors with reverence, to serve them with fidelity, and to obey them with cheerfulness" (p. 10).

Ruggles's work was one of the most well-known examinations of the Poor Law in the 1790s. So respected was he that William Pitt consulted him before submitting his ultimately unsuccessful Poor Law Reform Act to Parliament in 1797. Though the basis for welfare rights varied throughout Ruggles's long and rambling work, its status as a claim-right never did. In his opening essay, "To the public," he stated immediately that the rights of the poor had the same status as "security or political liberty or private property."[10] Ruggles drew on both Woodward and Blackstone to defend this position. From Woodward he took a contract argument, maintaining that there was "a tacit contract between men, when societies, states, and kingdoms, are in their infancy; that to him whose only patrimony is his strength, and ability to labor, that patrimony should be equal to his comfortable existence in society" (1:24). And he argued that if the laborer could not find work, the social contract granted the laborer a right to relief. His debt to Blackstone is apparent later in his work where he linked welfare rights to protection from personal injury, exactly the argument given by Blackstone (2:60–61).

By far the best example of the way the natural law discussion of property was used to defend the right of the poor to aid within a paternalistic social view is to be found in the work of William Paley. Paley lectured on moral philosophy at Cambridge University from 1768 to 1776. He wrote *The Principles of Moral and Political Philosophy* (1785) in the hope that it would be more interesting to students than the textbooks they were using, and he succeeded completely. In America it was "the most popular text on moral philosophy from the 1790s to the Civil War."[11] In England it was the "classical manual of morals at Cambridge University" and, more generally, "the acknowledged representative of the utilitarian philosophy" for half a century.[12] In 1814 Paley's text went into its twenty-eighth edition in England; in America at least ten editions had been printed by 1821. New editions came out throughout this period, one appearing in London as late as 1859, in Boston in 1846, in Hartford in 1850, and in New York in 1849 and 1867.

Paley was drawn to Dissenters and opposition politicians. He opposed the slave trade and compensation to slave traders, he tried to organize the wealthy to limit their consumption of food during the 1799 scarcity, and he abolished the tithes and extended the leases of his tenants at Bishopwearmouth. But he burned a copy of Paine's *Rights of Man* when he found a member of his family reading it, defended rotten boroughs, and consistently disappointed those who wanted him to become more involved in politics. His most famous biographer has concluded, "His principles have been thought to lead to more extensive conclusions than he himself was willing to pursue."[13]

Though Paley's text was well-known for its utilitarian foundations, his utilitarianism was always theological. Thus the major premise of Paley's thought was that a benevolent God had constructed the world in such a way that the individual's eternal happiness (the motive for acting morally) was consistent with the greatest happiness of the greatest number (the criterion of moral rules).[14] Paley's argument that happiness consisted in the pursuit of salvation, benevolence, prudence, and health is a clear indication that his utilitarianism differed from Bentham's. And lest Paley's epigram, "What is expedient is right," should be interpreted as in any way critical of existing institutions, he was at pains to emphasize that he meant "expedient upon the whole, at the long run, in all its effects collateral and remote, as well as in those which are immediate and direct."[15] Paley believed that this notion of expedience could not be captured by a felicific calculus but, instead, required following rules and respecting the rights they conferred. "The moral government of the world," Paley asserted, "must proceed by general rules" (1:77). Because Paley considered habits deeply inculcated rules, he maintained that virtue consisted in forming the right habits. Paley's attempt to build a rule utilitarian theory was not lost on his contemporaries, who used against him the arguments that have now become the standard criticisms of all rule utilitarian theories.[16]

Paley used two examples to illustrate the importance of following rules in moral life—telling the truth and being charitable. He introduced the question of charity by asking his readers to consider the situation in which a beggar, appearing to be in extreme distress, asked for aid:

> If we come to argue the matter, whether the distress be real, whether it be not brought upon himself, whether it be of public advantage to admit such applications, whether it be not to encourage idleness and vagrancy, whether it may not invite impostors to our doors, whether the money can be well spared, or might not be better applied; when these considerations are put together, it may appear very doubtful, whether we ought or ought not to give anything. But when we reflect, that the misery before our eyes excites our pity whether we will or not; that it is of the utmost consequence to us to cultivate this tenderness of mind; that it is a quality, cherished by indulgence, and soon stifled by opposition: when this, I say, is considered a wise man will do that for his own sake, which he would have hesitated to do for the petitioner's; he will give way to his compassion, rather than offer violence to a habit of so much general use. (1:75)

Charity was a theme Paley returned to again and again in his sermons, but his sense of social hierarchy, his definition of charity as "promoting the happiness of our inferiors" (1:237), makes clear that his appeal was thoroughly paternalistic.

The sympathy Paley expressed for the poor throughout this text was in contrast to his more critical attitude toward the wealthy. The best example of this attitude opened his discussion of charity and served as a general justification of it. "It is a mistake to suppose, that the rich man maintains his servants, tradesmen, tenants, and laborers: the truth is, they maintain him. . . . All that he does is to distribute what others produce; which is the least part of the business" (1:240). Paley suggested to his wealthy readers a wide variety of charitable acts. Doctors, lawyers, and ministers ought to give their services freely to the poor. Annuities should be bestowed on families in distress, public charities supported, beggars given aid, fuel and food given to the poor during temporary scarcity, wages augmented if the market price for labor dropped too low, and cottages built by the proprietors of large estates (1:249). These were some of the ways of exercising compassion, a feeling implanted in human nature by God because He wanted the distress of the poor remedied.

The passages from Paley considered so far were from a section of his treatise devoted to the imperfect duties owed to others. Although Paley was clear that imperfect duties were as important to moral behavior as perfect ones, it is nonetheless true that they need not result in rights enforced by the government. But Paley, like Woodward, argued that private charity was not enough.

The poor have a claim founded in the law of nature, which may be thus explained. All things were originally common. No one being able to produce a charter from heaven, had any better title to a particular possession than his next neighbor. There were reasons for mankind's agreeing upon a separation of this common fund; and God for these reasons is presumed to have ratified it. But this separation was made and consented to, upon the expectation and condition, that every one should have left a sufficiency for his subsistence, or the means of procuring it; and as no fixed laws for the regulation of property can be so contrived, as to provide for the relief of every case and distress which may arise, these cases and distresses, when their right and share in the common stock were given up or taken from them, were supposed to be left to the voluntary bounty of those who might be acquainted with the exigencies of their situation, and in the way of affording assistance. And, therefore, when the partition of property is rigidly maintained against the claims of indigence and distress, it is maintained in opposition to the intention of those who made it, and to *his*, who is the Supreme Proprietor of every thing, and who has filled the world with plenteousness, for the sustentation and comfort of all whom he sends into it. (1:252–53)

The structural similarity of this argument to Woodward's is obvious. Both upheld the justice of private property by suggesting that there were good reasons people living in common would have agreed to it. But they also insisted that part of the agreement to allow the common to be divided would have had to be the general recognition that if people's economic situation became desperate they would have a valid claim on the community for the resources necessary for life. That Paley's purpose in this passage was to defend private charity as a necessary complement to, rather than a substitute for, the Poor Law was clear from his advice to magistrates that "the care of the poor ought to be the principal object of all laws; for this plain reason, that the rich are able to take care of themselves" (1:247). His response to those who justified their lack of charity by using the excuse that they paid the poor rates is also consistent with this interpretation. These individuals, Paley said, "might just as well allege that they pay their debts" (1:264).

But justifications for government aid to the poor, particularly for the claim that the poor had a right to such aid, inevitably were met by counterclaims on behalf of the right to property. Paley used the natural law discussion to construct a property theory that escaped this charge and to assert that government aid to the poor was not just acceptable but required. Paley's argument was that though a particular individual's right to landed property was based only on positive law, the poor's right to subsistence was based on natural law or the invariably useful rules established by God to preserve all of people.

The section on property opened with an extraordinary analogy, one probably designed simply to interest the student in a formal philosophical problem. But the irony was so heavy and the description so vivid that Paley was read as giving away some strongly held sentiments.

If you should see a flock of pigeons in a field of corn: and if . . . you should see ninety-nine of them gathering all they got into a heap; reserving nothing for themselves, but the chaff and the refuse: keeping this heap for one, and that the weakest, perhaps worst pigeon of the flock; . . . and, if a pigeon more hardy or hungry than the rest, touched a grain of the hoard, all the rest instantly flying upon it, and tearing it to pieces: if you should see this, you would see nothing more than what is everyday practiced and established among men. (1:111–12)

Thus did the Reverend William Paley get the nickname Pigeon Paley. And in case the reader did not get his message, Paley continued: "Among men you see ninety and nine, toiling and scraping together a heap of superfluities for one; (and this one, too, often times the feeblest and worst of the whole set, a child, a woman, a madman, or a fool) getting nothing for themselves . . . looking quietly on, while they see the fruits of all their labor spent or spoiled; and if one of the number take or touch a particle of the hoard, the others joining against him, and hanging him for the theft" (1:112). Considering the description of the one for whom all the others worked, it is not surprising that rumors blamed this passage for the king's supposed refusal to appoint Paley as bishop of Gloucester in the 1790s.

The radical conclusions that might be drawn from this description were not drawn by Paley. Private property was, he wrote, "paradoxical and unnatural," but it provided so many advantages to society—increasing production and decreasing conflict—that it was absolutely necessary (1:113–16). Yet he found flaws in those arguments that justified the natural rights to property that might carry strong presumptions against their regulation by government. His strategy was to show that natural rights arguments could not justify the extensive property rights in land that actually existed (and should exist) and that the utilitarian arguments that did justify very large landholdings could not be invoked against the rights of the poor to government aid.

The central problem in the natural law discussion of property rights was to understand how an individual could come to have an exclusive property right in land that was once held in common. Paley began by dismissing the argument that property rights were the result of tacit consent allowing those who occupied land to have a property right in that land. He distrusted the notion of tacit consent and argued that consent could never be taken from silence (1:123). The implication seems to be that the poor could not be thought of as agreeing to a distribution of property rights that would leave them without property or the right to aid.

Paley was more sympathetic to the position that since God provided the earth for every person's use, he gave all a right to take what they needed without having to ask others. But this right extended only to the amount of property necessary for a "comfortable provision"; it could not justify property rights to large landholdings. The situation was analogous to that of a banquet given for the freeholders of a district. No one had to ask permission to sit down and eat; the food and drink were provided for that purpose. But though the freeholder would have, in effect, a natural right to satisfy his appetite at the banquet without asking others, he could not "fill his pockets or his wallet, or carry away with him a quantity of provision to be hoarded up, or wasted, or given to his dogs, or stewed down into sauces, or converted into articles of superfluous luxury; especially if, by so doing, he pinched the guests at the lower end of the table" (1:124).

"Mr. Locke's solution" to the problem, basing the natural right to property on labor, also had some merit, according to Paley. But this argument justified property only "where the value of the labor bears a considerable proportion to the value of the thing; or where the thing derives its chief use and value from labor" (1:121–22). Labor might confer rights to fish caught, utensils fashioned, and land cleared, plowed, sowed, and harvested, but it could not, Paley argued, provide a foundation for the extensive property rights in land that appropriately characterized eighteenth-century England.

Paley concluded that there was no natural right to property in land. Instead, he argued that "the real foundation of our right is the law of the land" (1:124). Individuals had adventitious rights to land and to the produce of the land, created and regulated by positive law. Although Paley was clear that some form of private property was required by God's will because He gave the earth to people for their subsistence and comfort, both of which were best accomplished through a system of private property, the particular forms of property rights that existed in particular societies were wholly dependent upon the utilitarian considerations appropriate to each society. One consequence of this view was that Paley believed that the right to dispose of landed property in a will was given only by municipal law (1:226). There may be good utilitarian reasons for such laws to respect the wishes of a testator, but in some cases utility may require violating those wishes. The extent to which Paley saw economic activity generally as subject to the laws of the state, rather than limited by natural rights to property, can also be seen in his treatment of regulating interest, exporting corn, encouraging families, and balancing the advantages and disadvantages of luxury goods (2:366–67, 407). Limiting natural rights "to the produce of a personal property," those objects that were the direct result of labor (e.g., tools, weapons, the "hut that he builds," the "flocks and herds which he breeds and rears" [1:276]) had the consequence of drastically limiting when natural rights could be invoked against government action.

Proprietors of land could not claim that their rights to property had been violated when the state that created those rights regulated or taxed the land or the income derived from it, but those with little or no land could invoke their natural rights if the laws that created property did not direct it to the uses intended by God. Adventitious rights must be consistent with the will of God, which was expressed in the natural right of each to life and in the general right of all that "the productions of the earth should be applied to the sustentation of human life" (1:103). In the sense that all share in this general right equally, Paley derived from it a presumption in favor of common property and equality, presumptions that could only be overridden when it could be shown that private property and inequality increased prosperity. Although Paley thought that the property and inequality that existed in his society fulfilled these requirements, he maintained that "any great inequality unconnected with this origin . . . ought to be corrected" (1:116).

Paley's insistence that landed property was subject to the general rights shared by everyone can be seen in his statement that "all waste and misapplication of these productions [of the earth], is contrary to the divine intention and will; and therefore wrong, for the same reason that any other crime is so" (1:103). Some examples of "crimes" that he listed were converting manors into forests for hunting, "letting large tracts lie barren, because the owner cannot cultivate them, nor will part with them to those who can" (1:104), and destroying food to keep the price up. Paley's antagonism to the laws that restricted the right of the poor to hunt probably also stemmed from this position, as did his opposition to the enclosure of farmland and to absentee owners (2:168, 373, 415). Paley considered absentee ownership as so detrimental to economic production that his most general prescription for the laws that created property rights was "to secure this right to the occupier of the ground, that is, to constitute such a system of tenure, that the full and entire advantage of every improvement go to the benefit of the improver; that every man work for himself, and not for another; and that no one share in the profit who does not assist in the production" (2:373–74). Paley also affirmed the right of necessity (1:109). He understood the situation of dire emergency as one in which the immediate, particular advantage derived from violating private property rights—maintaining life—exceeded the general advantage of respecting those rights.

Government regulation of property to aid the poor was sometimes thought to violate property rights. Paley's response was to argue that because government created property, it could regulate it. It could also be argued that government regulation of property violated the natural right to liberty. But as Paley pointed out, "to do what we will, is natural liberty: to do what we will, consistently with the interest of the community to which we belong, is civil liberty" (2:167). And though he was sympathetic to the idea that "restraint itself is an evil," he turned this maxim into an argument for the poor and excluded by using it to criticize laws that "lay unnecessary restrictions on the poor" and denied tolerance to Catholics and Dissenters (2:168).

Blackstone's comment that "charity is . . . interwoven in our very constitution" (4:32) expressed the way the Poor Law had come to be accepted as part of English political life and helps explain the continued existence of a conservative, paternalistic defense of government aid to the poor. Paternalist theorists may have wanted only, as Sherer wrote, "to plead the cause of the needy and afflicted, and to excite the benevolent exertions of the rich and prosperous" (p. 7). But in pleading the cause of the poor, they were led to assert an individual natural right to be included in the wealth of the nation. Moreover, this right required more than the recognition of the right of necessity. It required a government-funded relief program to guarantee that no one would fall into the circumstances that could justify their taking from others. John Locke may have held a position similar to this, but its development in Paley and Woodward had little to do with his ideas. Woodward's argument relied on the un-Lockean idea that property came from a contract, whereas Paley's was built on an explicit rejection of the idea he associated with Locke that labor could create property rights. Whether the paragraph in Blackstone that linked welfare to the right to life was derived from Locke is hard to know. But it remains important that by the end of the eighteenth century the institution of the Poor Law, regardless of its origins in social control, had come to be understood through the perspective of natural law and as fulfilling a natural right.

FIVE

Property Rights, Utility, and Political Economy

Bentham to Longfield

S uggestions for reforming the Poor Law had been made throughout the eighteenth century. But because of the economic problems of the 1790s and the threat some thought the ideas of the French Revolution posed to property, pamphlets written during that decade proposing changes in poor relief inundated the reading public.[1] The Speenhamland system of 1795 in which local government revenues were used to supplement wages, Samuel Whitbread's attempt to enact minimum wage legislation in 1795 and 1800, and Pitt's Bill for the Relief of the Poor, which was debated in Parliament in 1796, all added to the controversy. The economic problems that England experienced after the end of the Napoleonic War in 1815 and the agricultural distress that occurred around 1830, the first dramatized by the appearance of the Luddites and the second by the exploits of Captain Swing, kept the condition of the poor at the center of public attention. A sense of the problems England faced can be gathered from the Poor Law expenditures, which were under £700,000 in 1750 and had climbed to £18 million in 1818.[2] Poor relief was not the only difficulty England faced in the early nineteenth century, but it remained central to political argument up until at least 1834, when the Poor Law that had existed more or less intact since Elizabeth was reformed by men deeply influenced by utilitarianism and the emerging discipline of political economy.

Throughout this period arguments raged not only over the details and policies of poor relief but also over whether the poor had a right to relief. This chapter will first set out the utilitarian and political economy attack on natural rights, especially those to welfare. Those who thought that high levels of aid or any aid at all was to the detriment of the poor and their community had to confront the idea that aid was a right and deny it in terms equally theoretical. This usually meant arguing that a property right could only be a right to exclude others. The idea of an inclusive property right derived from natural law was held by these theorists to be incoherent, inefficient, and anarchical. By far the most astute, forceful, and important of these critics was Jeremy Bentham. His attacks on natural property rights, developed against the American revolutionaries and later used against the French, had an enormous impact on the way political representation and aid to the poor were understood.

Although utilitarianism, political economy, and evangelical religion initially combined to oppose all aid to the poor, by the 1820s a reevaluation had occurred which resulted in justifications for some, though often minimal, state-funded provision of such aid. By the early 1830s the case for aid had become so compelling that a group of political economists returned to the language of natural law to describe the Poor Law as fulfilling the rights of the poor. This chapter and the one that follows, should make clear that natural property rights were understood in this period to require redistribution or welfare, that the attack on government provision for the poor was developed from a utilitarian perspective, and that even those utilitarian arguments for the elimination of aid to the poor soon gave way to a utilitarian defense of welfare rights.

Bentham

The relationship between social utility and individual rights in the modern natural law tradition had always been extremely complicated. After all, the long-term usefulness of private property—its ability to bring peace and prosperity—explained why property rights were required by natural law. Either God was presumed to have approved them or men simply using their reason were understood to have consented to them for these reasons. Our modern attempt to distinguish sharply between rights-based theories and utilitarian theories hardly existed before Bentham and probably owes its existence to Bentham's treatment of natural law as the competitor to utilitarianism. To Bentham the language of natural law and natural rights was not just ambiguous, it was incoherent. And as a result of this incoherence it was anarchical and subversive of all social order. Bentham, it should be remembered, was a staunch Tory through the 1790s—a critic of John Wilkes, the American Revolution, and the French Revolution.

Though Bentham was an admirer of Joseph Priestley's *Essay on the*

First Principles of Government (1768), that book illustrates some of the confusions to which Bentham thought the use of rights and utility were liable. Priestley's purpose in this essay was to defend religious toleration and the ability of parents to educate their children without interference from the government. To accomplish this, he began with a state of nature in which people were endowed with natural liberty. Because of "inconveniences," they resigned part of their natural liberty to a political community. Bentham's praise for this essay came from its argument that the only legitimate standard the community could use in its political decisions was "the good and happiness of the members."[3] Priestley went so far as to say that "virtue and right conduct consist in those affections and actions which terminate in the public good; justice and veracity, for instance, having nothing intrinsically excellent in them, separate from their relation to the happiness of mankind" (p. 19). He maintained that the magistrate could do anything that served the good of the society (p. 172), he denied that any individual could have a legitimate claim against the public good (p. 59), and he gave a straightforward utilitarian argument for property: "Nothing is properly a man's own, but what general rules, which have for their object the good of the whole give to him" (p. 41).

Having established the primacy of the public good, however, Priestley continued to invoke not just natural rights but inalienable natural rights as if they rather than the public good limited government activity. Especially regarding the liberties he was most eager to defend, he chose to speak of natural rights and to suggest that they had a status independent of and superior to the public good: "If there be any natural rights which ought not to be sacrificed to the ends of civil society, and no politicians or moralists deny but that there are some (the obligations of religion, for instance, being certainly of a superior nature) it is even more natural to look for these rights among those which respect a man's children" (p. 85).

Priestley was a utilitarian thinker who could not resist using natural rights when he wanted to express the importance of a liberty in the strongest way possible. Richard Price, on the other hand, was a rights theorist, at times explicitly antiutilitarian, who could not avoid the complications of invoking the public good. It is instructive to look at Price's work for another reason. At least in Bentham's eyes, it not only demonstrated the incoherence of rights theory but also its inevitably subversive nature. Price was one of the most important defenders of the American

Revolution in England and for that reason became the object of Bentham's criticism.

Richard Price's major work in moral theory was *A Review of the Principal Questions in Morals* (1757). Against ethical theories based on a moral sense, the will of God, individual advantage, or public happiness, Price argued that "the power within us that perceives the distinctions of right and wrong ... is ... the understanding."[4] The mere perception of truth, he maintained, is both a spring and a guide to action. Like Hume, Price narrowed the virtue of justice to that "which regards property and commerce" (p. 263), though unlike Hume, he saw the requirements of reason granting property rights to individuals prior to any considerations of the public good. "The origin of the idea of property," Price wrote, "is the same with that of right and wrong in general. It denotes such a relation of a particular object to a particular person, as infers or implies, that it is fit he should have the disposal of it rather than others, and wrong to deprive him of it. This is what everyone means by calling a thing his right, or saying that it is his own" (pp. 263–64).

Among the fit relations that established property rights were first possession, the fruits of labor, donations, and succession. To take from someone whose possession was based on one of these foundations was immediately understood to be wrong. Thus the injunction against theft was not based on any consideration of its consequences (p. 265). As in contemporary criticisms of utilitarianism, Price pointed out that without a theory of rights it was at least theoretically possible to imagine an acceptable utilitarian policy that would reduce a small number of people to misery in order to confer benefits on a large number. Price's moral theory ended in an extremely strong defense of private property rights:

> The limbs, the faculties, and lives of persons are theirs, or to be reckoned amongst their properties, in much the same sense and upon the same grounds with their external goods and acquisitions. ... Were nothing meant, when we speak of the rights of beings, but that it is for the general utility, that they should have the exclusive enjoyment of such and such things; then, where this is not concerned a man has no more right to his liberty or his life, than to objects the most foreign to him; and having no property, can be no object of injurious or unjust treatment. (P. 266)

In addition to the obvious difficulties involved with the meaning of "fit relations" and how the understanding motivates people to action,

Price's work was further complicated by his use of the public good. Having constructed his own theory in large part around a critique of utility, he nevertheless could write, "What will be most beneficial, or productive of the greatest public good, I acknowledge to be the most general and leading consideration in all our enquiries concerning right ... it may set aside every obligation which would otherwise arise from the common rules of justice" (p. 256).

Reconciling the public good with private rights seemed to Price especially difficult on the question of conflicting claims about property rights. Yet he was unable to provide any method by which hard cases could be decided. In the end, the public good was important but not all-important; the principles of right and wrong were self-evident but so difficult to apply that "we should frequently be in the dark" (p. 282).

To the confusions over rights and utility found in Price and Priestley we can add one more as proper background to Bentham. I refer to the famous passages in Blackstone in which the right to property was described as a "sole and despotic dominion" while at the same time Parliament's sovereign power was understood as "so transcendent and absolute, that it cannot be confined, either for causes or persons, within any bounds." Bentham may not be the clearest writer, and in his desire to create a new science of morals he could multiply new words and categories in a way very difficult to follow. But he saw clearly the confusions in the way Priestley, Price, and Blackstone used rights and utility, natural law and municipal law, and he understood the political danger of that confusion.

Bentham encountered the subversive nature of natural rights (and especially the natural right to property) in the claims of the American colonists in the 1760s and 1770s and, specifically, in the many pamphlets Price wrote to defend them. Price relied on Locke's linking of property to representation to argue that the only government consistent with the natural and inalienable rights of men was one in which people directed their own actions through freely chosen representatives. In a just government "all taxes are free—gifts for public services—all laws are particular provisions or regulations established by common consent for giving protection and safety."[5] Since the colonists were not represented in Parliament in a way consistent with his requirements for legitimate representation, Price agreed with them that the Stamp Act was "a direct attack on their property" (p. 62). To the charge Price knew would be made, that England itself did not satisfy his rules for representation, he responded by saying to the English, "You are only enslaved partially— were they to submit, they would be enslaved totally" (p. 100).

In 1775 and 1776 Bentham collaborated (though without acknowledgment) with John Lind, a longtime friend and newly hired pamphleteer for Lord North, to defend British policy.[6] In their first work, *An Englishman's Answer to the Declaration of the American Congress* (1775), their target was the doctrine that Americans possessed the right to be taxed only with their consent. Bentham and Lind, however, described the property rights of Englishmen as follows: "The proprietors of the soil of Great Britain, are, indeed, lords of their own property, subject only to the regulations of the legislature; but the legislature has power to dispose of any part or all of it, without the consent of the owner; and this power they do exercise, when they judge it necessary for the public good."[7]

They pointed out that without the ability to regulate property in the absence of (or against) the owner's consent, government could not undertake economic improvements or collect taxes necessary for the armed forces that protected both colonists and Englishmen. Not twenty-nine out of thirty Englishmen could be said to give their consent to the laws they must live by. To be taxed *without* representation and consent was, in fact, at the heart of the British constitution. Government could not act to protect or regulate property if real consent were required of all those affected. The last paragraph of this essay perfectly captured Bentham's view: "The main end of government in every society, is to produce security to its members: For without security no man can be happy in the enjoyment of anything which he possesseth" (p. 26). Throughout his career, Bentham believed that the doctrine of a natural right to property was the enemy of secure possession, not its guarantor.

In their next collaborative work, *Remarks on the Principal Acts of the 13th Parliament of Great Britain* (1775), Lind and Bentham continued to criticize the idea (which they attributed to Locke and Blackstone) that property could not be taxed without consent. They denied that taxes were a gift from the governed to their magistrates and instead boldly asserted that property was a gift from the magistrates to the governed. The House of Commons was "invested with the whole property of the kingdom, in trust that they shall apportion and distribute to the supreme executive magistrate, that which is necessary to the support of his department of the government; and that they shall cooperate in securing to each man his share of the remaining parcel; which share alone is his property." When individuals paid taxes, they were not giving what was theirs to someone else. Since their property was only the amount the legislature said it was, they had no prior claim to that portion of the common stock the legislature had reserved for itself. "Taxes then cannot in a proper sense, be called a gift, much less a free gift. For in the strict and proper sense nothing is given, if by given is meant ceding that which is our own, that which we have a right to withhold."[8] Lind and Bentham knew that this theory of property would seem to many to deny the essence of English liberty. But they insisted that it was not the origin of rights that set nations apart but the way rights were apportioned by sovereign powers and whether a particular apportionment helped people to prosper or become poor.

Bentham and Lind took Price on directly in 1776 with their *Three Letters to Dr. Price*, a critique of his *Observations on the Nature of Civil Liberty*. Natural right, they maintained, required a natural law, and natural law required a lawgiver. "But where is this Law of Nature to be found? Who has produced it." When Lind and Bentham pointed out that natural rights and natural laws were fundamentally theological, requiring a God who willed law, they did not do so with the intent of saving it. "When men talk of a law of nature, they mean only certain imaginary regulations," Bentham and Lind concluded. Rights, they argued, must have their origin in municipal law. And for rights to land and goods, this meant that before law "a man may have the use and enjoyment of them, but he cannot have the right to them; that is, he may have possession, but he cannot have property."[9] Bentham, then, answered two important questions in property theory in the negative. Individuals could not have rights to property independent of the municipal laws under which they lived, and, as a result, the ownership of property did not confer a right to be represented in the making of that law.

Knowing that Bentham was engaged in an offensive against the claims of the American colonists in 1775 and 1776 helps to provide the appropriate context for understanding his *Fragment on Government* (1776). Though his concern in this pamphlet with Blackstone and the law far transcended the particular controversy over America, the publication in 1776 of a book that discussed just those Lockean aspects of Blackstone germane to questions of sovereignty and obedience was obviously meant to educate Americans and their British supporters to the incoherence of the natural law vocabulary. That he understood the political edge of the *Fragment* to be directed against the colonists is clear from the many references to the *Fragment* that were made in *Three Letters to Dr. Price*, the pamphlet he and Lind wrote against Price's defense of the colonists.

In the *Fragment* Bentham acknowledged his debt to Hume, writing in a footnote that it was in reading Book III of the *Treatise of Human Nature* that Bentham felt "as if scales had fallen from my eyes."[10] The theory of obligation in the *Fragment* was virtually indistinguishable in its broad outlines from Hume's. They both took as their target the idea of an original contract and the use of consent to explain political obligation. Bentham labeled these fictions. As might be expected, he pointed out that there was no record of such a contract. Just as predictable, but still worthy of note because of the verve with which it was expressed, was Bentham's comment on consent. Here he scored a direct hit on the idea of consent found in Locke. "As to 'submitting my will' to the wills of the people who made the law you are speaking of,—what I know is, that I never intended any such thing: I abominate them, I tell you, and all they ever did, and have always *said* so: and as to my 'consent,' so far have I been from giving it to their law, that from the first to the last, I have protested against it, with all my might" (1:285). Neither promises nor contracts were needed to explain obligation or rebellion. The happiness of the people should be the object of sovereign power and the standard the people should use to decide whether to obey. Disobedience was justified when "the probable mischiefs of resistance appear less than the probable mischiefs of submission" (1:287). No doubt Bentham hoped the American colonists would apply this standard to their situation, rather than the hopelessly unrealistic natural law standards they were using.

The great benefit of the utilitarian standard, Bentham thought, was that it referred parties in a dispute to matters of fact. "The footing on which this principle rests every dispute, is that of matter of fact; that is, future fact—the probability of certain future contingencies" (1:291). Arguments over facts—forgetting for a moment the problems presented by the notion of future facts—were more likely to be settled than arguments over natural law and natural right or fictitious contracts and promises. Claims based on natural rights were "but so many ways of intimating that a man is firmly persuaded of the truth of this or that moral proposition, though he either thinks he need not, or finds he can't tell why" (1:269). Controversies between people who cannot or will not provide reasons can only take the following form: "I say, the legislature cannot do this—I say, that it can. I say, that to do this, exceeds the bounds of authority—I say, it does not" (1:291). When the argument was between an individual and a government, the inability of the natural law vocabulary to provide a standard for finding a solution meant that "the natural tendency of such a doctrine is to impel a man, by the force of conscience, to rise up in arms against any law whatever he happens not to like" (1:287). Thus he thought the doctrine of a natural right to property was one of the reasons the American colonials were in rebellion.

Bentham's most famous attack on natural rights was presented in *Anarchical Fallacies*, three essays written about the events in France during the 1790s. Bentham and Edmund Burke are not often linked in political philosophy, but their criticisms of the use of natural rights to justify the French Revolution were similar. They both suggested that the abstractness of rights made them inappropriate for discussing the particular problems politics presented. They denied that it made sense to assume either natural equality or a state of nature. They associated the use of rights with a lack of intellectual modesty or, as Bentham said, with "power turned blind . . . self conceit and tyranny exalted into insanity." And they thought that a people who believed in natural rights would be ungovernable. Bentham called natural rights a "terrorist language" and said its use was a "moral crime" (2:501, 524).

In 1791 the French National Assembly promulgated the Declaration of Rights, which included a provision affirming a natural right to property and insisting on consent before taxation. As in his attack on the colonists, Bentham thought the idea of a natural right to property was incompatible with the taxation and regulation of property that were required in any organized society. But against the Declaration of Rights he argued that a natural property right was incompatible with the very existence of private property. To give all men equal rights and to give them all a right to property was to suggest, Bentham argued, that all should have an equal amount of property. "If I have a right to be on a par with everybody else in every respect, it follows, that should any man take upon him to raise his house higher than mine . . . I have a right to pull it down about his ears, and to knock him down if he attempts to hinder me" (2:518, 523). Even if it were explicitly stipulated that the equal right to property did not require equal property, danger could not be avoided. Thus in the last of the *Anarchical Fallacies* essays he replied to the assertion of Sieyès, "Every citizen who is unable to provide for his own wants, has a right to the assistance of his fellow-citizens." But this, Bentham insisted, would "overturn every idea of property" (2:537) and give "the indigent class the most false and dangerous ideas" (2:534). According to Bentham, then, the natural right to property as either exclusive or inclusive was incompatible with men actually enjoying the fruits of their labor. Both interpretations were destructive of the peace and prosperity that only a government able to define, regulate, and enforce property rights could bring. It is no wonder that Bentham could write, "The repose of Grotius and Pufendorf and Barbeyrac and Burlemaqui I would never wish to see disturbed."[11]

Having exposed natural rights arguments as foolish and dangerous, Bentham had to reconstruct a defense of property rights on utilitarian grounds. To do this he was led to posit his own state of nature, though perhaps he more than any of his predecessors understood this state to be purely hypothetical. He described "the first day of political creation": "As yet there is no law in the land. The legislator has not yet entered upon his office. As yet he hath neither commanded nor prohibited any act. As yet all acts therefore are free. . . . Restraint, constraint, compulsion, coercion, duty, obligation . . . are things unknown."[12]

The liberty of this state was the liberty to be free from the constraints of the law. But it did not include the liberty to be free from the constraints that could be imposed by other individuals. "You and your neighbor, suppose, are at variance: he has bound you hand and foot, or has fastened you to a tree: in this case you are certainly not at liberty as against him" (p. 253). If legal restraint was unknown before government, Bentham insisted his readers understand that so was legal protection.

Without government and law the goods of nature would be open for all to use. Since all would have the power to use the land, it was appropriate to say that the land was "the common property of all," or that all "have a property in it in common with the rest" (p. 255). This formulation was certainly close to what others meant by a positive community of goods. And in Bentham as in Hobbes a positive community was synonymous with chaos. According to Bentham, all property rights in land were the result of the law permitting some or one to act on the land while others were restrained from acting. When all but one person was constrained by law from meddling with something, an individual exclusive property right had been created. For Bentham, then, property rights occurred when the law created duties on the part of others by prohibiting them from interfering. In this way law turned the temporary physical act of occupation into the legal, moral, and permanent act of possession (pp.

272–76). The basically conservative purpose of this discussion is seen in Bentham's injunction to the magistrate to act so that all de facto occupations were made secure through legal possession. To Bentham the world the individual shared with nature and with other people was dangerous, potentially chaotic, and painful. In such a world, happiness demanded most of all protection and security. Only a sovereign legislator able to make and enforce prohibitions or negative duties could create the stability necessary for people to master the natural world and provide more comfortable lives for themselves.

In the *Principles of the Civil Code* Bentham provided the legislator with general rules for the creation of property rights. Achieving the supreme goal of the greatest happiness for the greatest number could be accomplished by pursuing four subordinate but specific goals: subsistence, abundance, equality, and security. The economic nature of the four subordinate goals illustrates the extent to which he measured happiness in material terms.[13] Bentham's use of money as the equivalent of happiness also had the advantage of providing a measure for happiness that could be calculated and manipulated by a legislator.

Bentham's deep interest in economics and the close ties that quickly developed between utilitarianism and political economy are easily understandable. His attack on natural law and natural rights cleared an intellectual space for appeals to the facts and "future facts" of human happiness. If happiness was measured in money, it was political economy that claimed to know the laws of behavior that tied the present facts of economic activity and happiness to the "future facts" that were sure to flow from them. The greatest happiness of the greatest number is an empty phrase without a "science" of happiness, which was precisely what political economy provided.

Bentham wasted little time in the *Civil Code* making his way to the preeminent goal of law—security. Subsistence and abundance might be more important, but there was little the law could do to increase the power of the motives nature had given to people to pursue them. Presumably the fear of starvation was sufficient to move people to work for their subsistence. And since with each desire people satisfied, a new desire was born, the desire for subsistence was soon replaced with the desire for abundance. "Desires extend themselves with the means of gratification; the horizon is enlarged in proportion as we advance; and each new want, equally accompanied by its pleasure and its pain, becomes a new principle of action" (1:304). But law did play a crucial indirect role in achieving the goals of subsistence and abundance, and it did so by promoting security. For unless individuals believed they would be able to use the fruits of their labor, the link between the motive and the accomplishment of the goal would be much weakened. In promoting security, seen by Bentham as "always tottering, always threatened" (1:309), the law did all it could to promote subsistence and abundance. And the way to promote security was to create and protect rights to property. Bentham saw in property rights, then, "security for the labourer—security for the fruits of labour" (1:304).

The distinction in the natural law tradition between occupation as temporary and property as permanent meant that property rights had long been understood to involve a relationship to the future. Like Smith in his *Lectures on Jurisprudence*, Bentham used the idea of expectation to express this relationship. Property rights existed only if owners could expect that what they worked on today would be of use to them in the future. In the absence of a law enforced by a legislator, there could be no secure expectations. What the individual held by labor, force, or cunning today could be taken away tomorrow. "Property and law are born and must die together. Before the laws, there was no property: take away the laws, all property ceases" (1:311). Disappointing the expectations that were created by previous law or were found by the legislator would not simply cause owners pain, it would violate the very essence of the property that was largely responsible for civilized life. Even the general limits on property that Bentham acknowledged as appropriate were not based on other values or goals restricting property but were seen by him as restrictions internally required, that is, necessary to the requirements of security. Thus taxes must be paid to guarantee security against foreign enemies, domestic enemies, and natural calamities.

The greatest challenge to the security of property came from attempts to realize directly the fourth subordinate goal of the law—equality. This challenge would have been easier to meet if Bentham, like Hume, had not recognized the declining marginal utility of wealth and believed that because of it, "the more nearly the actual proportion approaches to equality the greater will be the total mass of happiness" (1:307). But precisely because he saw the link between utilitarianism and equality, he had to insist again and again that it would be a serious error to disappoint the expectations of present owners. Though Bentham's argument that legislators created property rights would seem to require a cooler relationship between owners and their property than was found in

Locke's or Kames's idea of property as an extension of the personality, the following quotation illustrates the way expectations performed for Bentham what the mixing metaphor did for Locke:[14]

> Each part of my property may possess, in my estimation, besides its intrinsic value, a value in affection—as the inheritance of my ancestors, the reward of my labours, or the future benefit of my heirs. Everything may recall to me that portion of myself which I have spent there—my cares, my industry, my economy—which put aside present pleasures, in order to extend them over the future; so that our property may become, as it were, part of ourselves, and cannot be taken from us without wounding to the quick. (P. 310)

To take from someone to give to someone else, then, causes great pain for the present owner. The uncertainty created in the minds of other present owners must also be considered painful. Because of this uncertainty, individuals would be less willing to labor with all their diligence. Meddling with any current distribution of property and violating the security of expectations that surround it threatened first the goal of abundance and, ultimately, subsistence. Moreover, since equality required large and constant transfers, it could be accomplished only through the use of violence and with "an army of inquisitors and executioners" (1:312). Even moderate attempts to increase equality through government-mandated transfers was attacked by Bentham. "Equality," he wrote, "admits not of any moderate or prudent application: . . . the principle admits not of your stopping anywhere in the application of it. . . . To stop at any one point in the career of forced equalization, would neither afford security to such of the rich as it left unplundered, nor satisfaction to the poor whom it left unenriched" (1:362).

Though Bentham insisted that in any conflict between security of possession and equality, security must always be chosen, it is important that equality of possessions had some significance for him. The problem he faced was to find a way to realize equality that was consistent with subsistence, abundance, and security. Like so many others in the eighteenth century, he looked to the transfer of property from one generation to the next as the time for law to help create a more egalitarian society. To Bentham the regulation of property at death was particularly appropriate because it was only with death that all "hopes and fears," all expectations, came to an end. Only then could property be regulated without disappointing the owner. Focusing on expectations meant that both the right to make a will and the right to inherit were particularly weak claims. At death he saw property as between owners and therefore between expectations. Increasing equality, or at least assisting in the growth of an industrious class between the opulent and the indigent, was relatively simple. If primogeniture and entails were prohibited as rules of succession, monopolies made illegal, and trade allowed to proceed more freely, large estates would be divided and greater equality achieved.

So perfect was the moment of succession to Bentham's interest in both securing property and regulating or taxing it to achieve utilitarian goals that in *Supply without Burden* (1795) he recommended inheritance taxes as the best way to fund much of government's needs. Bentham considered simply abolishing wills and inheritance, in effect levying a 100 percent tax on property at death, but rejected this plan on the grounds that it might decrease the motivation to labor, increase the motivation to spend rather than save, and provide a reason for some to transfer their wealth to another country. Instead, he decided a sliding scale would be best, based on, among other factors, whether the deceased left a will or was intestate and whether close relations were still alive. In the absence of a will and near relations, that is, in the absence of any expectations, the government could take all the property. With a will and near relations, only 50 percent could be taxed. At the end of this essay, Bentham considered arguments against his proposal, especially those based on the idea that succession should be governed by natural law. He pointed out, as Smith had, that wills were of recent origin in England and that the rules governing succession varied greatly from country to country and engaged in some of his best rhetorical attacks on natural law and rights. No doubt these attacks were occasioned by recent events in France. He contrasted the rules of utility, which required "genius to discover, strength of mind to weigh, and patience to investigate," with the use of natural law, which required only "a hard front, a hard heart, and an unblushing countenance." To use natural rights, he wrote, was to speak with "verbal daggers," for "as scissors were invented to cut up cloth, so were natural rights invented to cut up law, and legal rights."[15]

Bentham's assumption that individuals were the best judges of their own happiness was easily tied to his doctrine of respecting expectations as a way to defend the justice of economic contracts. He thought that in both commercial contracts and labor contracts individuals left alone would reach agreements that benefited both parties. There were exceptions, however. For example, his general antagonism to "forced exchanges" was not present in the praise he heaped on parliamentary enclosures in *Principles of the Civil Code*. Here his general concern for the security of property and expectation was sacrificed to the particular, calculable benefits the enclosure of a common field would bring: "Happy conquests of peaceful industry! noble aggrandizement" was the way he described enclosures (1:342). The possessors of rights to a common field who were unwilling to give them up were, he said, "obstinate" (1:322).

Bentham's praise for parliamentary enclosure demonstrates that the relationship between utility and current expectation in his thought was exceedingly complicated. On one hand, law should respect expectations, but on the other, law was one of the institutions most capable of molding expectations. A utilitarian calculation of happiness could result in respecting current expectations since every disappointment would cause some pain, but such calculations, especially if they took into account the long run, could easily end critical of current practices and the expectations that grew up around them. Bentham was aware of these complications but found it difficult to remain consistent in the face of current policy disputes. Why were the expectations of those who held common rights ignored in the case of parliamentary enclosure yet the expectations of slaveowners were respected, even though he admitted slavery was inefficient and vicious?

Among those specific policy areas in which he applied utilitarian theory, perhaps his recommendations with regard to poor relief have received the most comment. He understood that any level of prosperity that might be achieved would still leave most people with only their labor for support. As a result, accidents, disease, unemployment from the business cycle, and old age might lead to privation, perhaps starvation. Bentham pointed out that the wages of many would not be enough for them to save the money necessary to protect them from these possibilities. And though private charity might help some people, its uncertain operation meant that its collection and distribution would depend more on chance than equity. Bentham could not, of course, justify a natural right to assistance, but in *Principles of the Civil Code* he did provide a powerful argument for a legal right that would seem to have a very general application: "The title of the indigent, as indigent, is stronger than the title of the proprietor of a superfluity, as proprietor; since the pain of death, which would finally fall upon the neglected indigent, will always be a greater evil than the pain of disappointed expectation, which falls upon the rich when a limited portion of his superfluity is taken from him" (1:316).

However unpleasant the circumstances might be under which Bentham would give aid to the poor, he never was willing to let them starve. Though subject to difficulties, charitable acts toward the poor were recommended by him (as they were by Paley) as both helpful to those in need and to the long-term advantage of the charitable. "If having a crown in my pocket and, not being athirst, hesitate whether I should buy a bottle of claret with it for my own drinking, or lay it out in providing for a family I see about to perish for want of any assistance, so much the worse for me at the long run."[16]

Bentham's defense throughout his life of both public and private aid to the poor was consistent with his most deeply held values. Neither freedom, individualism, nor laissez-faire was among Bentham's primary values. Instead, he valued happiness, the absence of pain, the alleviation of suffering, and the need for security. He always thought people to be sympathetic creatures whose happiness was bound up with that of others. Only the presence of sympathy explained how people concerned to maximize their own happiness could work to create the greatest happiness for the greatest number. And though he may have counseled against government intervention in general, he had no principled objection to government activity and in many cases defended it. If to all this is added his concern for social order and his fear of revolution, it is no wonder he never questioned the legal right to assistance. The English poor had their expectations, too. His definition of security in *Leading Principles of a Constitutional Code, for Any State* (1823) conveyed these concerns. Security of the person as a proper end of government required "security against evil, in whatever shape a man's person, body, and mind included, stands exposed to it," which included calamities such as "inundation, conflagration, collapsion, explosion, pestilence, and famine."[17]

We have already seen how difficult it was to trace the moral origins of property rights to a contract without acknowledging that such a contract entailed some provision under which those in need would have some welfare rights. Doing without the contractarian apparatus and tying property rights more directly to happiness, or the absence of pain, has seemed to many a more intellectually satisfying and stronger account of the origins of property rights. But again, welfare rights followed from the same premises that were used to create property rights. Diminishing pain and increasing security required legal rights to both property and aid if an individual without sufficient property faced distress. Bentham explicitly denied that even improvident conduct on the part of the poor should result in the forfeiture of aid.[18]

Bentham's acceptance of the need to aid the poor on grounds universally applicable—the pain of death being greater than the pain of losing a luxury—has received much less attention than the institutional arrangements he thought should be used to relieve their distress. And with regard to the form and amount of aid it was not his decent and less controversial proposals for corn granaries in 1793 or for price controls on bread in 1801 that have caused comment.[19] Instead, attention has focused on his attack on Pitt's bill in 1796, *Observations on the Poor Bill Introduced by . . . William Pitt*, and his proposal for a national charity company in *Pauper Management Improved* (1798), which included plans for his panopticon.

Bentham's essay on Pitt's attempt to respond to the distress of the 1790s was almost entirely critical. Its private circulation among members of Parliament has been credited with defeating Pitt's bill, though such influence cannot be proved and has been disputed. Bentham supported the idea of a national system of public relief, as he always did, but he argued that Pitt's plan would provide levels of aid that were inconsistent with economic growth. "To guarantee to every man a subsistence is practicable and practised," he stated, but "to guarantee to every man the perpetuity of his station in the scale of opulence would be altogether impracticable, the very attempt mischievous, and perseverance ruinous" (8:451).

The proponents of generous levels of aid forgot, according to Bentham, that wealth must be produced before it could be used to alleviate suffering and that some kinds of aid discouraged industry. His general point was that the categories of recipients in Pitt's bill were so vague that too many might be included (e.g., "the poor") and that the goals, similarly vague (e.g., "maintenance" or "full wage"), could not be met with the resources actually available. Both the legal setting of wages and the legal supplementing of wages were criticized from this perspective. Providing cows to poor families and using the apprenticeship system to employ poor children ran counter to his arguments for free markets in capital and labor.

If Bentham's *Observations* displays his keen mind and concern for detail in a favorable light, his *Pauper Management Improved* has all the qualities that have led so many to dismiss him as repressive and insanely controlling. His plan for dealing with those in severe need was to use the panopticon architecture of his model prison to construct a "pauper kingdom" in which the idle would find work and the needy aid. Although his plan was based on England accepting an obligation to preserve the lives of all its members, it (like Locke's proposal for poor relief) undertook to satisfy this obligation within an authoritarian environment. Education, medical care, loans, and employment information were to be provided. But the idle could be brought to the panopticon building against their will, the conditions could be no better than those experienced by the lowest paid of the employed, and the "inmates" (which included children as young as four years old) were to be constantly monitored and kept at work. It is easy to sympathize with Charles Bahmueller's critique:

> But under Bentham's system the humiliation that began with a novel form of the ancient practice of badging continued with the jail-like contrivances of Panopticon—its cells (albeit without bars), its ubiquitous rules and punishments for their infraction, its formalized procedures for doing everything, with virtually no choice whatever left to the pauper himself. The activities of each moment of every day, with the exception of one period on Sunday (for only some of the adults) would be predetermined for the pauper by his guardians and guards. . . . Perhaps enough has been said of the repressive and exploitative nature of many of the features of Bentham's Poor Law reform to show that to call it historically "progressive" mocks any notion of progress worthy of the name.[20]

Yet the problem of interpretation remains. As we shall see, there was growing belief that government could do nothing for the poor, that property rights were violated and efficiency sacrificed if any tax money was used to alleviate their suffering. In this context, it may be that Bentham's consistent defense of relief was more influential than the bizarre and repressive panopticon he suggested be used to administer it. This assessment, at least, is supported by the words of Patrick Colquhoun, one of his disciples, in 1806: "The nation may be considered as a large family. Those who have surplus labour in store are bound to support and assist that portion of the community who become indigent, and have not the means of support; since none, according to the common law and the law of humanity, must starve outright, or gradually; and since also it is evident, beyond all doubt, that many must starve if no provision were made against the casualties incident to a state of civilization."[21]

Burke, Eden, and Malthus

Bentham dismissed all natural rights to property—inclusive and exclusive—as destructive of social order. But what his utilitarianism took away in theory, it gave back in practice, providing an extraordinarily strong defense of private property combined with a defense of a legal right to aid. In the 1790s, however, as proposals to help the poor through economic depression grew more ambitious, the call for the abolition of the Poor Law increased. The great expense of solving an enormous problem led some Poor Law critics to desire the end of government aid. But more important were the arguments that demonstrated how government aid would lead to disaster for all, including, and especially, the poor. In this view, only exclusive property rights were justified by utilitarianism because inclusive rights were causally related to poverty and misery. In part, the argument against inclusive rights was economic in nature, concerned with labor markets and population growth. But as the laws of political economy became identified with the laws of nature, a religious dimension emerged in which the right to aid became a violation of the natural processes established by God.

Edmund Burke's *Reflections on the Revolution in France* (1790) used such an argument. No other action taken by the French National Assembly seemed to him so wrong as its nationalization of church lands in November 1789. "Confiscators," "Roman confiscators," "Levellers," "Anabaptists," and "Tyrants" were the terms Burke used to describe the members of the National Assembly. He tried to explain, perhaps for the first time, the relationship between modern revolutions, the rise of tyranny, and the tendency toward the nationalization of property, or, as he put it, why "revolutions are favorable to confiscation."[22] Burke understood that neither the rational calculations of utilitarianism nor rational deductions from the abstract principles of natural law were necessarily consistent with the property arrangements that had developed through history in France or England. In revolutionary situations, during which history lost its ability to command respect, the application of either utility or natural rights would require that many current owners lose their property rights. Burke admitted that the property rights of a new nation if based on the public good would be very different from those that actually existed. To Burke, though, this did not condemn current arrangements but instead invalidated any point of view that did not take historical development into account. "If prescription be once shaken," he wrote, "no species of property is secure" (p. 133).

The property arrangements Burke wanted to defend included enormous inequalities and therefore the ability of some people to live in leisure while others labored very hard for very little. Of course, Burke tried to point out the advantages of inequality, which included political stability (p. 45) and high culture (p. 142). But his deeper argument was against calculation altogether. Thus he made certain his English readers knew that applying the utilitarian calculations being made in France to England would threaten them: "It is impossible to know under what obnoxious names the next confiscations will be authorized. I am sure that the principles predominant in France extend to very many persons and descriptions of persons in all countries who think their innoxious indolence their security. This kind of innocence in proprietors may be argued into inutility; and inutility into an unfitness for their estates" (pp. 136–37). Natural rights arguments were even more dangerous to an unequal distribution of property. Not only did they begin with the idea that "men are equal" and that the earth was the "equal mother of all" but they required, according to Burke, that ownership be based on labor. Since "by the laws of nature the occupant and subduer of the soil is the true proprietor," natural rights recognized "no difference between an idler with a hat and a national cockade, and an idler in a cowl or in a rochet" (p. 196).

Abstract reason of either the utilitarian or natural rights kind placed too heavy a burden on current property rights. Unequal property, passed from generation to generation by primogeniture and entail, required foundations in religion, prejudice, and history:

The means of acquisition are prior in time and in arrangement [to government]. Good order is the foundation of all good things. To be enabled to acquire, the people, without being servile, must be tractable and obedient. The magistrate must have his reverence, the laws their authority. The body of the people must not find the principles of natural subordination by art rooted out of their minds. They must respect that property of which they cannot partake. They must labour to obtain what by labour can be obtained; and when they find, as they commonly do, the success disproportioned to the endeavour, they must be taught their consolation in the final proportions of eternal justice. Of this consolation, whoever deprives them, deadens their industry, and strikes at the root of all acquisition as of all conservation. He that does this is the cruel oppressor, the merciless enemy of the poor and wretched; at the same time that by his wicked speculations he exposes the fruits of successful industry, and the accumulations of fortune, to the plunder of the negligent, the disappointed, and the unprosperous. (P. 215)

To guarantee that the property arrangements given by history and God were not disturbed in England, Burke argued that the English Parliament had never been understood as able to "violate" or "overrule" the property rights currently in existence (p. 134).

The rural crises created by poor harvests in 1794 and 1795 led to two attempts in England to raise the wages of agricultural laborers. In the Speenhamland system local government attempted to supplement market wages through local tax funds, and in Whitbread's Bill Parliament would have set a minimum wage employers had to pay. It is against this background of proposals to interfere in the wage scale set by the labor market that Burke's *Thoughts and Details on Scarcity* must be understood. Written in 1795, it was sent privately to Pitt, on whom it seems to have had no influence, and was published posthumously in 1797.

In this pamphlet Burke invoked religion to defend markets in labor and the inequality that resulted from their unfettered operation. His hymn to the market is perfectly captured in his statement that "the laws of commerce, . . . are the laws of nature, and consequently the laws of God."[23] With God behind the laws of the market, it is no wonder Burke was able to believe in a natural harmony of self-interest. "The benign and wise Disposer of all things . . . obliges men, whether they will or not, in pursuing their own selfish interests, to connect the general good with their own individual success" (pp. 384–85). To seek to regulate the wages set by the market was to act against nature and providence, certain to end in disaster. No individual or government could possibly know enough to intervene with intelligence (p. 382). It simply had to be accepted that in "the nature of things" the price of labor rose and fell with the demand for labor, rather than according to the price of food. As a result, wages would sometimes be too low to alleviate the hunger of the aged, disabled, or children (p. 379).

Burke did not see the agricultural labor market as an arena in which equals reached agreements with one another. He understood the relationship between the laborer and the farmer as part of a hierarchy or chain of subordination. It was not the equality of the contractual relationship that interventions unjustly violated, it was the just inequality that was disturbed by government. "The whole of agriculture is in a natural and just order; the beast is as an informing principle to the plough and cart; the laborer is as reason to the beast; and the farmer is as a thinking and presiding principle to the laborer" (p. 384). Many of the contradictions that are supposed to exist between the *Reflections* and the *Thoughts* are based on importing into Burke's defense of the market egalitarian and dynamic qualities he never saw. In rural England the labor market operated within and served to justify the inequality that Burke believed was the basis of the social hierarchy. Protecting exclusive rights to property, the primary function of government, was to protect the order established by God. To redistribute even the amount of wealth that would be necessary to stop starvation was a violation of property rights (p. 391), an affront to providence, and perhaps a step on the road to confiscation he feared England might take in imitation of France. Behind his arguments in both the *Reflections* and *Thoughts* was his belief that it was "pernicious to disturb the natural course of things, and to impede, in any degree, the great wheel of circulation" (*Reflections*, p. 141). Only private charity was compatible with Burke's notion of property rights, though he was reluctant to recommend even this very strongly. "Patience, labour, sobriety, frugality and religion should be recommended to them [the poor]; all the rest is downright fraud" (*Thoughts*, p. 370).

Sir Frederick Morton Eden's influential and massive three-volume *State of the Poor* (1797) was written in a much more subdued tone than the work of Burke. Eden presented himself as an impartial observer collecting as much information as he could about the condition of the poor and the actual operation of the Poor Law. His genuine concern for the suffering of the poor was evident in his admonitions to the wealthy to relieve those in distress, in his argument that government had a responsibility to the infant, sick, and aged poor, as well as in his belief that government should increase its funds for the education of the poor.[24] Thus, even after expressing strong doubts about the efficacy of the Poor Law, he did not argue that it ought to be abolished. Instead, he suggested that prudence required revising the law while more information was gathered (pp. 489–90).

The combined effect of Eden's obvious social concern and intellectual modesty was to make his critique of subsistence rights extremely powerful. He accurately reproduced the argument made by Woodward in support of the rights position, paying special attention to the point that the poor could not be expected to obey the laws of civil society if they lacked land or jobs (pp. 413–14). Yet Eden concluded, "It is one, and not the least, of the mistaken principles on which a national provision for the relief of the indigent classes is supported, that every individual of the community has not only a claim, but a right, founded on the very essence and constitution of human society, to the active and direct interference of the legislature, to supply him with employment while able to work, and with a maintenance when incapacitated from labour" (p. 447).

Eden had many arguments against the idea of a welfare right. Acknowledging the rights of the poor seemed to him to mean accepting the inevitability of poverty, rather than trying to find measures to eradicate it. He argued that granting relief as a right would make it harder to end poverty, for it would provide incentives to idleness and actually increase the number of poor. Also, aid required taxation, which ran the risk of decreasing the private charity that would always be the largest amount of money given to end distress. Like Burke, he saw welfare rights as inconsistent with the hierarchy and deference so essential to social organization.

Though Eden denied that the poor had rights to aid, he did not deny that the wealthy had obligations to the poor. The problem for him was whether these obligations were best satisfied through the legal system or through "unrestrained charity." He considered, then, not only the Poor Law but also Whitbread's proposals and Pitt's bill. Whitbread's desire to raise wages seemed to Eden an unwarranted intervention that was likely to end in the mischief that accompanied all government attempts to direct the course of the economy. Pitt's plan was too complicated, would ask justices of the peace to perform too many tasks, and was injurious to agriculture through its use of a land tax. Eden used the works of both Kames and Smith to support his argument. But he cited and quoted Burke's *Reflections* more than anything else. Eden found in Burke's statement (which he quoted) that it was "pernicious to disturb the natural course of things" (p. 417) the guiding principle of a defense of current property rights and of the laws of supply and demand, especially in the labor market.

By far the most famous (and infamous) attack on the Poor Law and the idea of a welfare right that was written in this period was *An Essay on the Principle of Population, as It Affects the Future Improvement of Society* (1798) by the Reverend Thomas Malthus. Like Burke's *Reflections*, it too was written to defend English institutions from the dangerous principles and utopian visions of the French Revolution. Against the arguments of William Godwin and the marquis de Condorcet that placed the cause for many social problems in private property and marriage, Malthus attempted to demonstrate that both of those institutions and the social problems they were supposed to cause were inevitable responses to natural events largely outside the control of man.

> The great error under which Mr. Godwin labours throughout his whole work is the attributing almost all vices and misery that are seen in civil society to human institutions. . . . But the truth is, that though human institutions appear to be the obvious causes of much mischief to mankind, yet in reality they are light and superficial, they are mere feathers that float on the surface, in comparison with those deeper seated causes of impurity that corrupt the springs and render turbid the whole stream of human life.[25]

Instead of blaming private property for the suffering and misery of the world, Malthus pointed to the unequal relationship between the production of food and the growth in population. Since Malthus posited that the power of population to increase was "indefinitely greater" than the ability of the earth to produce food, he could argue, against all utopian schemes, that misery and vice were inevitable. In the second edition in 1803, Malthus added substantially to his work and in the process changed it from a polemic to a more scholarly treatise. He also moderated its pessimism by suggesting that "moral restraint" (by which he meant chastity and later marriages) might mitigate the misery and vice resulting from population outrunning food. But as the second edition was revised and reprinted over the next twenty-three years, the turbulent nature of British economic and political life guaranteed that its conservative political message remained foremost. Malthus never gave up hope that the laboring classes enlightened by his ideas would understand that their distress was "to a certain extent and for a certain time, irremediable" and should be borne "with patience," as he wrote in a section added in 1817.[26]

We saw in Burke that political economy could be assimilated into a conservative political philosophy through the idea that the laws of supply and demand were part of a natural world that individuals should approach with reverence because it had been created by a benevolent, if mysterious, God. In this way aid to the poor could be presented as a violation of the laws of nature and God's providence. Though Malthus recommended that aid be abolished only gradually and thought of himself as a moderate, his population argument became the primary vehicle for the popularization of this emerging conservative attitude.[27] Malthus provided an alternative to the "cosmic optimism" of Paley. His view of nature as less bountiful and human existence as more of a struggle must have seemed to his contemporaries a more realistic response to the revolution, war, and depression of the early nineteenth century.[28]

When Malthus read "the book of nature" (p. 6) he learned "that from the inevitable laws of our nature some human beings will be exposed to want" (p. 20). The extent to which Malthus relied on the rhetorical power of "natural" and "law of nature" to make his points is evident in the paragraph that followed and justified his proposal slowly to abolish the Poor Law. Here he referred to some variant of "natural" five different times (p. 202). As the way to know what was natural he proposed a broadly utilitarian standard. "Utility," he argued, "is the test by which alone we can know, independently of the revealed will of God, whether [a passion] ought or ought not to be indulged; and is therefore the surest criterion of moral rules which can be collected from the light of nature" (p. 217). From utility flowed the moral obligations to restrain from early marriages and to curb indiscriminate benevolence (pp. 168, 217), both of which, he believed, created more poor and more suffering. When Malthus defended alternatives that would have seemed to his readers particularly hard-hearted, he invoked God more directly, rather than through utility. Thus, when he explained why a family, "a mother and her children, who have been guilty of no particular crime," should be "doomed" for the acts of the father, he used "the laws of nature, which are the laws of God" (p. 202). And he could hardly have resisted using St. Paul when considering the starvation that abolishing the Poor Law might entail. "The laws of nature say, with St. Paul, 'If a man will not work, neither shall he eat' " (p. 221).

The general, long-term tendency of the Poor Law to create poverty by increasing the number of poor without increasing the food available to feed them did not lead Malthus to conclude, as some of his followers did, that government aid was always an error or that all government policies directed at decreasing poverty were either meaningless or counterproductive. Throughout his intellectual career he identified the interests of the poor with rural prosperity and sought ways to encourage agriculture or, at least, to keep public policy from benefiting industry at agriculture's expense. Public works projects and universal education also seemed to him appropriate government responses to poverty.[29] But in the long run nothing was more important to the alleviation of poverty than for government to protect private property. Malthus showed that even if God-win's assumptions of benevolence and equality were granted, the pressure that increasing population would put on more slowly increasing food resources would result in conflict and confusion, selfishness and anxiety. As scarcity inevitably would occur, so would property rights be instituted as the only way to guarantee that people would labor. Putting a particular piece of land under the direction of one person, who would either eat or starve depending on how the land was used, had the added benefit of teaching the virtue of prudence. Since the entire point of Malthus's work can be summed up as teaching people to be prudent, to exercise restraint and patience, the relationship between property rights and prudence was crucial to him (p. 193).

If private property was the inevitable and natural consequence of the tendency of population growth to outstrip the production of food, it was just as certain that property would lead to inequality. As Malthus put it, there will be those "unhappy persons who in the great lottery of life, have drawn a blank" (p. 20). Born with only their labor for support, they must suffer from want when their labor was not purchased.

In the first edition of the *Essay* Malthus concentrated on criticizing the English Poor Law and Pitt's plans to revise it from the perspective of his new focus on population and food. In the second edition, however, he took on the idea he saw behind the Poor Law and the main obstacle to its abolition—the idea that the poor had a right to relief. "As a previous step even to any considerable alteration in the present system, which would contract or stop the increase of the relief to be given, it appears to me that we are bound in justice and honor formally to disclaim the right of the poor to support" (p. 201). Without an understanding of why this right could not exist and without its "formal retraction," all attempts to limit aid would be seen as unjust (p. 244). The grounds for Malthus's rejection of the right to support are clear enough. If utility was the foundation for our rights and the right to receive aid from the government could be shown through the laws of population to create poverty rather than to alleviate it, there could be no right to receive aid. Especially pernicious was the tendency of a belief in the right to aid to suggest that individuals could marry and have children whatever their economic circumstances, for if they could not feed their children the parish would (p. 69). Since the rich did not have the power to employ and maintain all the poor, it made no sense for the poor to think they had a right to demand it of them (p. 260).

Malthus singled out for criticism Thomas Paine's *Rights of Man* because of the way it spread among the "lower and middling classes" erroneous notions about rights and the principles of government:

> Nothing could so effectually counteract the mischiefs occasioned by Mr. Paine's Rights of Man as a general knowledge of the real rights of man. What these rights are it is not my business at present to explain; but there is one right which man has generally been thought to possess, which I am confident he neither does nor can possess—a right to subsistence when his labor will not fairly purchase it. Our laws indeed say that he has this right . . . but in so doing they attempt to reverse the laws of nature. (Pp. 190–91)

Here the natural law that Paine thought conferred on all the right to be preserved was in direct conflict with the laws of nature derived from political economy which showed that all could not be preserved. Since a right to what is impossible is absurd, it could not exist. Malthus was also particularly concerned with the way middle-class radicals used the idea of a right to assistance to suggest that government was responsible for poverty. Like Burke, he thought that from a revolution of the poor led by "turbulent and discontented men in the middle class" only tyranny could be expected (pp. 191–92).

In a short essay published in 1830, entitled *A Summary View of the Principle of Population*, Malthus made explicit the conflict he thought existed between the right to assistance and the right to property. As a utilitarian, he saw property rights as "the creatures of positive law," but like Hume and Bentham before him, he found such rights so necessary they could be "considered as the most natural as well as necessary of all positive laws." Because property rights were created by law, they could legitimately be modified under some circumstances by law. But the granting of a right to subsistence was not one of those circumstances. "The concession of such a right [to subsistence], and a right of property, are absolutely incompatible, and cannot exist together."[30]

Sumner and Chalmers

Though Burke, Eden, and Malthus differed in many of their general attitudes toward poverty, the possibility of its alleviation, and the usefulness of the Poor Law to the particular circumstances of the 1790s, they were united in rejecting the idea of a natural right to subsistence that required government relief programs and in desiring in the long run the abolition of all such programs. They were joined in these beliefs in the first half of the nineteenth century by many Christians influenced by evangelical ideas, who no longer believed, as Paley had, that nature was so bountiful that all could feast at her table. The goods of nature were scarce, they thought, and were obtained only with great effort. Nature, then, required exclusive rights to property, inequality, poverty, and deference if industry were to be undertaken and order to prevail. Government interference in labor markets or property arrangements was interference in the natural processes established by God and threatened the ultimate benefits that a benevolent Deity must have associated with those processes. The last two chapters in the first edition of Malthus's *Essay on . . . Population* contained his own attempts at a theodicy, but this enterprise was carried much further by John Bird Sumner, bishop of Chester (1828–48) and archbishop of Canterbury (1848–62), and Thomas Chalmers, theologian, urban missionary, preacher, and author. The importance of these Christian economists to popular discussion can be gathered from the comment made by Malthus that Chalmers was "my ablest and best ally"[31] and by the judgment of R. A. Soloway that "it was the Rev. John Bird Sumner who made it [Malthus's theory of population] acceptable to a generation of Churchmen absorbing and trying to reconcile the truths of political economy with their reviving concepts of a Christian society."[32]

The first edition of Sumner's *Treatise on the Records of the Creation and on the Moral Attributes of the Creator* appeared in 1816. As the title indicates, it tried to demonstrate that the characteristics of the world showed the guiding, benevolent hand of God. To keep his readers from expecting too much from this world, Sumner insisted that they understand, first, that some evil was inevitable because of the nature of man; second, that the records of God's benevolence were to be appreciated from the perspective of the next world, not this one; and third, that the purpose of their arduous preparation for the next world was to make them virtuous rather than happy or prosperous.[33] The outlook defined by these conditions was especially important with regard to appreciating poverty and inequality, for without it Sumner admitted that they would be "inexplicable" (p. 95). To make the benefits of inequality and poverty more understandable, Sumner discussed them at length. The nature of his project almost guaranteed a utilitarian perspective, or as Soloway has put it, a "utilitarian casuistry." How better to discover the divine intention in an institution than to uncover the way it benefited mankind? And what logic was better suited to do this with regard to poverty and inequality than that provided by Malthusian political economy with its emphasis on prudence and moral restraint?

Nowhere were divine intentions, utility, and political economy brought together better than in Sumner's discussion of property. Sumner relied on Malthus's argument that population increased at a faster rate than food production to show that scarcity was an inevitable part of human existence. Regardless of how a people began, soon they would find themselves unable to subsist simply by gathering the fruits of the earth. Once food became the result of industry, it was necessary to institute the conditions under which industry was undertaken most efficiently. Since people would work hardest when they knew they could keep the results of their labor and since arguments would occur over the division of a common stock between families that had contributed different amounts, it would be agreed that there should be private property. Once property was private, inequality soon followed as families had varying rates of success.

Sumner suggested that people would agree to keep what their labor had produced, but neither the labor nor the agreement was important to his justification of property. Instead, Sumner relied on the "scientific" nature of Malthus's principles and the "intentions of Providence" they revealed to uncover the way unequal property served to bring virtue to mankind. Property and inequality were useful to men, but they were not chosen because of their usefulness. In fact, they were not chosen at all but were better described as given by a benevolent God. Thus, rather than use utility to establish a standard by which people should judge their institutions, Sumner assumed the usefulness of the institutions given by God and wrote so that his readers might better appreciate the goodness of the Creator who provided them. Schemes to increase equality were not just wrong and destined to result in increased poverty, they were in some sense impossible, contrary to God's will.

It was not enough for Sumner to show that property was required for preservation; he also wanted to show that unequal property was responsible for civilization. He argued that equality was compatible only with savagery and that improvement followed necessarily upon inequality. First industry, then reason, and finally virtue were all shown to be the consequences of a society divided into a hierarchy of rank and fortune:

A complete community of goods, if it could possibly exist on a large scale, might diminish the temptations to fraud and robbery; but these constitute only a small part of the moral guilt of mankind; while, on the other hand all those virtuous habits which derive both their origin and their perfections from the varieties of the human condition, all the dispositions of mind to which the different circumstances of civilized life give play and action, would lose the occasions under which they are now formed, and the opportunities in which they are displayed. The Platonic view of moral virtue, which places it in the contemplation of ideal excellence, may be consistent with a state of perfection, but is incompatible with a state of probation. Virtue is an active and energetic habit, arising from the various relations of human life, and exercised in the practice of real duties; so that, as you increase the number and variety of those relations, you enlarge its sphere of action; and in proportion as you contract them, in proportion as you bring down the conditions of mankind towards an uniform level, you lower the standard, and reduce the degree of moral excellence. (Pp. 86–87)

Sumner saw exclusive property rights transforming physical scarcity into moral virtue. Because of property, people had to exert themselves to produce subsistence and affluence. In the course of that effort they must learn frugality, foresight, restraint, and chastity. As that effort took place within a division of labor it forced people to exchange with one another and provide for one another's welfare. It produced luxury and the opportunity for the wealthy to learn how to engage in "judicious" benevolence. It produced a class of deserving poor who learned to feel gratitude when they received assistance from the wealthy. And it produced the idle poor, whose just punishment was a lesson to all.

Sumner was asked to write the article on the Poor Law for the 1824 six-volume, *Supplement to the 4th, 5th, and 6th Edition of the Encyclopaedia Britannica*. The decision of the editor, McVey Napier, to ask David Ricardo, J. R. McCulloch, and James Mill to write so many of the essays on economics and government guaranteed that this edition would play an important role in the formation of middle-class opinion. In his *Britannica* article "Poor Laws" Sumner specifically singled out for criticism the argument that the poor had a right to aid. To support this position, he quoted extensively from the fifth edition of Malthus's *Principles*. Such a right was impossible to Sumner, for it required the "eradication of the principles of human nature" and the violation of "the known rules of political economy."[34] As a result, he called the Poor Law "an unnatural system," which contravened "the natural course of population." He affirmed the sentiment that Eden thought was central to Burke, that it was wrong "to disturb the natural course of things" (p. 296). Aid to the poor, especially as it was provided by the Speenhamland system of wage supplements, interfered with the "natural spring" by which population was adjusted downward as wages fell and upward as they increased. The right of everyone without work to subsistence threatened to reduce the entire society to poverty. It was a wonder to Sumner that the Poor Law had been in operation for over two hundred years without having this effect. Only the terrible conditions of the workhouse, which kept many from claiming the aid they thought they were legally entitled to, explained England's prosperity. But outdoor relief and a widespread belief that aid was a natural right threatened to increase the number of claimants and to change prosperity to poverty.

Even more ominous to Sumner were the implications for moral character and social order if it came to be widely believed that aid was a right. Compulsory aid to the poor was responsible, Sumner thought, for alcoholism, a decline in charity, sexual promiscuity, husbands deserting wives, and a "spirit of discontent." Sumner feared that if the poor thought they had a right to subsistence, they would blame the rich, rather than themselves, for their poverty. But as God was the author of the laws of political economy so was He responsible for the inequality of rank and fortune. This meant that the poor had to rest contented with the hard labor that characterized their position and the indigent had to understand that their problems were of their own making. It was Sumner's hope that "if the poor in this country were convinced that they had no claim of right to support, and yet . . . in distresses, were liberally relieved . . . the bonds which united the rich with the poor would be drawn much closer" (p. 300). As both an individual and a bishop Sumner was charitable and helpful to the poor. Yet his concern was always more with the moral consequences of poverty relief, especially on the wealthy, than it was with the physical benefits to the poor. If aid were a right, he feared that legal and political disputes would overwhelm Christian love.

For an analysis that seemed to demonstrate the salutary effects of private charity on both the wealthy and the indigent, Sumner relied on the work of the influential Scottish clergyman Thomas Chalmers. Chalmers undertook a fifteen-year crusade against compulsory state aid to the poor and in the process contributed greatly to the popularization of the ideas of Malthus. To the great satisfaction of Chalmers, the emphasis the political economy of Malthus placed on the need for "moral restraint" proved through science what the Christian religion had all along insisted upon—the need for morality. Thus in his *On Political Economy* (1832) Chalmers wrote of "the alliance which obtains between the economical and the moral; insomuch, that the best objects of the science cannot, by any possibility, be realized, but by dint of prudence and virtue among the common people."[35]

Throughout the Scottish Enlightenment property theory was frequently used to attack primogeniture and entail in the hope that large estates would be broken up into smaller ones. In the early nineteenth century the issue of land redistribution became politically explosive, used by radical agrarians to argue for a great deal more equality than the Scottish thinkers had in mind. Perhaps as a result, primogeniture found renewed favor with a few political economists who were more concerned with the dangers of redistribution than with inefficient landowners. Malthus, for example, defended primogeniture and entail in his *Principles of Political Economy* (1820). He still saw the landed aristocracy as England's most appropriate political leaders and feared that if great estates were broken up, power would pass to "merchants and manufacturers," whose interests were not those of the public.[36] The position held by Malthus in what has been called the glut controversy also led him to defend primogeniture and entail. His belief that investment would result in the production of more goods than could be consumed by the workers who produced them led him to view favorably the luxury spending of rich landowners and particularly their preference for hiring nonproductive servants. Because he held a basically utilitarian point of view, Malthus did not have to consider the argument that all the children had equal rights to their parents' property, the theory that had been used so skillfully by earlier writers against primogeniture.

Thomas Chalmers also defended primogeniture. To convince his readers of its benefits, he raised the possibility of land being divided and subdivided until all English farming was done on equal, subsistence-level plots. But this would decrease that class of people he called "disposable"—those who produced luxury goods, worked as servants, and were available for military service. It would be difficult, he argued, to raise an army and navy from people engaged in subsistence agriculture (as they left their farms, agricultural production would decline) or to raise from subsistence farmers the tax revenue needed to pay for the military. Not only did maintaining primogeniture and entail avoid these problems, it also allowed the aristocracy to continue to exert its beneficial influence on English society. Only a class with more than it needed could afford to uphold "philosophy," "religion," "art, and all that goes to decorate and dignify human life." "When there are nobles," Chalmers argued in *On Political Economy*, "the common people are not so ignoble" (pp. 364, 369). Neither Sumner nor Chalmers would have found Burke's allegiance both to economic markets and to a traditional social structure surprising.

For the "moral and humanizing effects" of the wealthy to be transmitted to those below them, there had to exist a system of obligation and deference (p. 371). Chalmers's attack on compulsory provision for the poor was based on his sense that it created class antagonism rather than class harmony. The reason the Poor Law had this dismaying consequence was that it suggested to the poor that the aid they received was theirs by right.

> There is in England a gulf of separation between the rich and the poor, exemplified, we believe, in no other land; where the parties regard each other as natural enemies—the one challenging what they feel to be their rightful allowances; the other resisting what they fear to be interminable, and at length ruinous demands. The barriers of property have given way before the tide of an unrestrained population; and there is now a close and fierce conflict, between a sense of rightful possession on the one side, and the unappeased urgencies and wants of an ever-increasing multitude upon the other. The poor look to the rich as hard-hearted oppressors, detaining with stern grip what nature and humanity pronounce to be theirs; the rich look to the poor as so many poachers on their domain. Compassion on the one side, and gratitude on the other, are alike unknown. (Pp. 406–7)

Chalmers did not object in principle to the taxation of the propertied to assist the poor. "We object not to any amount of taxation . . . if the produce of it shall be usefully, or even innocently applied" (p. 410). The use of tax money to fund hospitals and to create more opportunities for education he wanted increased. But compulsory relief was not useful, at least not to the spiritual development in which Chalmers was interested. The Poor Law kept the wealthy from learning compassion and the poor from learning self-denial, patience, and gratitude. Moreover, in helping both the industrious and idle poor, it shielded the idle from their just punishment. State aid was wrong to Chalmers not because it intervened in an efficient competitive economy but because it intervened in the moral government of the world as it had been established by a righteous Deity.

Utilitarians, political economists, and evangelicals were united for a while in their common antipathy to the Poor Law and the idea of a welfare right they found behind it. Yet their ultimate goals were quite different. Neither Sumner nor Chalmers thought a society of markedly greater prosperity or happiness was possible. To them "the world was merely an 'arena of moral trial', an imperfect state capable of but a limited amount of welfare."[37] They did not identify nature with economic laws that, if allowed to operate, could lead to progress and improvement for all. Rather they saw behind an unfettered economy an opportunity for scarcity and competition to teach important moral lessons. They could not assent to the existence of welfare rights because such rights violated just inequalities in wealth, power, and status. Welfare rights called into question the justice of market forces and the social hierarchy and as a result the possibility of seeing behind either the benevolent hand of God. How different was the utilitarianism of Jeremy Bentham, whose extraordinary sense of the reality of pain led to attempts to relieve it, rather than to apologetics in which suffering was incorporated into Divine intention.

Mill, McCulloch, Marcet, and Martineau

The assimilation of the Malthusian critique of the Poor Law into religious social theory through Sumner and Chalmers was of considerable importance to public debate over the rights of the poor. But the most sophisticated and lasting discussions of the relationship between property rights and welfare occurred in the more secular setting of political economy. Though David Ricardo was, after Smith, the most important of the early political economists, we need pause over his attitudes about the Poor Law for just a moment because he was, in general, so completely in agreement with the analysis of Malthus. "The pernicious tendency of these laws is no longer a mystery," Ricardo wrote in *The Principles of Political Economy and Taxation* (1817), "since it has been fully developed by the able hand of Mr. Malthus."[38] Ricardo blamed the Poor Law for providing an incentive for laborers to have "early and improvident marriages." Its effect was to increase the number of poor and to increase taxes on the industrious. Only the penury of the parishes had kept a disaster from occurring. But if relief were ever made "a matter of right and honor," as he quoted Pitt's intentions, so that everyone wanting support received it, "the principle of gravitation is not more certain than the tendency of such laws to change wealth and power into misery and weakness" (p. 63).

The denial of welfare rights ran through the articles informed by the new political economy in the 1824 *Encyclopaedia Britannica*. I have already noted Sumner's essay on the Poor Law in that volume but need now to look at the contributions of James Mill and J. R. McCulloch. James Mill's reference to Locke on the first page of his essay on government was unusual in this literature and illustrates an important point. The attack that was made throughout the early nineteenth century on the idea that the poor had a right to relief was based on religious, utilitarian, and economic considerations. The natural law discussion of property, especially as it appeared in John Locke's works, was the intellectual foundation for the defenders of welfare rights. There is no evidence from the early nineteenth century that Locke's idea of a natural right to property led to possessive individualism and a defense of the property rights of the wealthy. Thus, even though James Mill cited Locke, it was only as an early, though rather vague, utilitarian. "The end of government has been described in a great variety of expressions," Mill wrote. "By Locke it was said to be 'the public good;' by others it has been described as being 'the greatest happiness of the greatest number.' These, and equivalent expressions, are just but . . . defective."[39]

A tradition of understanding Locke and especially his theory of property as utilitarian continued among political economists throughout the nineteenth century. As late as 1896 *Palgrave's Dictionary of Political Economy* concluded that though Locke inconsistently used the ideas of consent and the public good, he "would doubtless have solved the contradiction by passing, as he constantly does, from the phraseology of the law of nature to utilitarian considerations. Locke is only concerned to prove the advantage of fixed and determinate laws, which may be changed for the common good, against arbitrary government. . . . In any given country, the property rights of individuals depend upon the law of the land."[40] Although the utilitarian reading of Locke's property theory is correct for most kinds of economic regulation, it seriously misses the extent to which he thought natural law required welfare rights. The paucity of citations to Locke among the utilitarian critics of the Poor

Law was not, then, an oversight but reflected the incompatibility of Locke's ideas with their own.

Mill applied to the question of property the utilitarian perspective under which public institutions were justified to the extent that they increased pleasure and/or diminished pain. Mill thought that in the absence of abundance, disputes over subsistence goods would be endless. Government was brought into existence because of these disputes and had as its purpose the distribution of goods in a way that increased pleasure. At the same time, government had to protect that distribution against individuals or groups who wanted to upset it for their own advantage. Mill concluded that the distribution that resulted in the greatest quantity of "the objects of desire" occurred when the laborer was guaranteed "the whole of the product of labour" (p. 49). Mill believed that property rights preceded labor because people would not work if they were not reasonably sure it would be to their advantage (p. 54).

The close ties Mill saw between exclusive property rights, labor, and "the greatest part of our pleasures" help explain why he showed such considerable interest in those who seemed to live without laboring— beggars. His article on this subject in the *Britannica* was broken into sections on the kinds of beggars, number of beggars, deceptive practices of beggars, causes of begging, effects of begging, and expedients for the suppression of begging. The tone was generally that of a social scientist presenting the scholarly consensus regarding these questions. But the one-third of the article that was given over to a detailed description of the way beggars cheated the charitable who gave to them certainly would have left a strong impression on the reader. Mill suggested that virtually all male beggars did so by choice rather than necessity and that many women beggars did so too. He argued that the Poor Law, because of its settlement provisions, was "the most prolific of all the causes of begging."[41] His view that only education held out the promise of reducing mendicancy was consistent with the mainstream of classical political economy.

The long article on "Political Economy" in the *Britannica* was written by J. R. McCulloch. McCulloch's careers as journalist (he wrote seventy-eight articles for the *Edinburgh Review*), academic (professor of political economy at London University from 1828 to 1837), and civil servant (comptroller of the Stationary Office from 1838 to 1864), along with his genuine contributions to the economic theory of his day, place him just behind the first rank in the development and dissemination of the ideas of political economy. Though McCulloch shared with Chalmers an antipathy to the Poor Law, the distance between Chalmers's economics of virtue and McCulloch's concern with prosperity is indicated by McCulloch's characterization of Chalmers's work as "a tissue of abominable absurdities . . . a . . . piece of quackery."[42]

As McCulloch laid out the logical structure of political economy for the *Britannica*'s readers, he could hardly have given private property a more important position. After explaining why labor was the only source of wealth, he listed the three means by which the productive power of labor could be augmented. "The first, and most indispensable, is the security of property, or a well founded conviction in the mind of every individual that he will be allowed to dispose at pleasure of the fruits of his labor."[43] In general, McCulloch's justification of private property was a utilitarian one. The "utility" of making property secure was "obvious and striking," he argued, and was recognized almost universally. Moreover, utility justified property not only in the land cultivated and in the fruits of industry but also in the "faculties of the mind" and the "powers of the body" (p. 238).

Paley, Bentham, and James Mill believed that property did not exist in its most secure form, was not yet fully property, until it was protected by municipal law. But it seemed to McCulloch more important to emphasize that positive law came at the end of a long process of securing property, rather than to focus on it as making an indispensable contribution. McCulloch probably was wary of basing property too much on the often shifting statutes of municipal law and was eager to hold law itself to higher standards, to the rules that utility required of all governments. In both his *Britannica* article and the textbook he wrote a few years later, *The Principles of Political Economy* (1825), another effort to spread the ideas of political economy to a wider audience, he wrote, "The law of the land is not, as Dr. Paley has affirmed, the real foundations of the right of property. It rests on a more remote and a more solid basis" (p. 238). Laws, then, were not the foundation of property rights. Instead, property rights, because they made social progress possible, were the foundations of all other institutions, including government and law. By arguing that property rights arose from utilitarian calculations made prior to government, he was able to invoke property rights against an array of government regulations he wanted to end. "The right of property is violated," he asserted, "whenever any regulation is made to force an individual to employ his labor or capital in a particular way. The property of a landlord is violated when he is compelled to adopt any system of cultivation, even supposing it to be really preferable to that which he was previously following. The property of the capitalist is violated when he is obliged to accept a particular rate of interest for his stock, and the property of the laborer is violated whenever he is obliged to betake himself to any particular occupation" (p. 239). Yet however much McCulloch wanted theoretically to protect property rights by placing their utilitarian foundations deeply in the past, he never stopped paying attention to their practical consequences. To appeal to laissez-faire on all occasions, he wrote, "savours more of the policy of a parrot than of a statesman or philosopher."[44] As a result of this attitude, later in the 1820s McCulloch changed his mind about the efficacy of the Poor Law.

McCulloch confronted the criticism that private property was advantageous only to those who possessed it and against the interests of "the poor and the destitute." His response was to argue that only property made prosperity possible. Before property or without property, poverty was universal. Nor did he accept the charge that private property rights simply protected the fortunate few. "The institution of the right of property gives no advantage to any man over any other man. It deals out justice impartially to all. . . . It is not, as it has been sometimes ignorantly or knavishly represented, a bulwark thrown up to protect and secure the property of a few favorites of fortune. It is a rampart raised by society against its common enemies—against rapine and violence, plunder and oppression" (p. 240). Not surprisingly, McCulloch ended this essay with a quotation from Bentham, "a profound writer," that tied the security of property to the triumph of humanity.

The wide dissemination of the ideas of political economy was furthered by the work of two exceptional women, Jane Marcet and Harriet Martineau. The range and popularity of Marcet's work were extraordinary. Her *Conversations on Chemistry, intended more especially for the Female Sex*, published in 1806, went through sixteen editions by 1853; her *Conversations on Natural Philosophy*, published in 1819, ultimately had fourteen editions; and her *Conversations on Political Economy* went through five editions in the first seven years after it was published in 1817. This last book was her most famous and was praised by McCulloch and J. B. Say, the French economist. Even more prolific than Marcet was Harriet Martineau. Her *Illustrations of Political Economy*, a small part of her literary production, consisted of twelve short novels, each of which was meant to teach through their fictional characters and plots the truths of a particular branch of political economy. Martineau described the origin of the *Illustrations* as follows:

> It was in the autumn of 1827, I think, that a neighbour lent my sister Mrs. Marcet's "Conversations on Political Economy." I took up the book, chiefly to see what Political Economy precisely was; and great was my surprise to find that I had been teaching it un- awares, in my stories about Machinery and Wages. It struck me at once that the principles of the whole science might be advanta- geously conveyed in the same way,—not by being smothered up in a story, but by being exhibited in their natural workings in selected passages of social life. . . . I mentioned my notion, I remember, when we were sitting at work, one bright afternoon at home. Brother James nodded assent; my mother said "do it;" and we went to tea, unconscious what a great thing we had done since dinner.[45]

Marcet's *Conversations on Political Economy* opened with a young woman, Caroline, defending government regulations that would force farmers to bring their grain to the market, proportion wages to the cost of food, and regulate the use of new machinery that created unemploy- ment. Caroline's interlocutor, Mrs. B., had the task of explaining why these interventions in the economy would result in long-run suffering. Her answer, in short, was that they would make property insecure.

She began by asserting as Bentham and James Mill had that property rights made labor possible and by rejecting the idea that labor conferred property rights. Security of property, then, was a prior condition that must be met before labor could result in wealth. Thus Mrs. B. adopted a straightforwardly utilitarian derivation of property rights that stressed the role of municipal law:

> When a man has produced any thing by his labour, he has, no doubt, in equity the fairest claim to it; but his right to separate it from the common stock of nature, and appropriate it to his own use, depends entirely upon the law of the land.
>
> In the case of property in land, for instance, it is the law which decrees that such a piece of ground shall belong to Thomas, such another to John, and a third to James; that these men shall have an exclusive right to the possession of the land and of its produce; that they may keep, sell, or exchange it; give it away during their lives, or bequeath it after their deaths. And, in order that this law should be

respected, punishments are enacted for those who should transgress it. It is not until such laws have been made for the institution and protection of property, of whatever description it be, that the right of property is established.[46]

Mrs. B.'s mention of an original "common stock" allowed Caroline to voice an element in the radical critique of property rights. How could the law legitimately take land that was common and divide it into private plots that would soon become dramatically unequal in size? Mrs. B. pointed out that attempts to maintain equality—such as agrarian laws— were failures and that unless men could work on their own land they would not work. Moreover, once they had their own land it was impossible to keep plots equal. "The laborious, the intelligent, and skillful, will raise plentify harvests, nature then rewards their exertions. The possessions of the idle, the careless, and the ignorant, will, on the contrary, gradually degenerate" (pp. 40–41). And as for "the vicissitudes of human life" caused by inequality, Mrs. B. echoed Sumner in arguing that they were responsible for such useful human characteristics as "patience, resignation, fortitude . . . benevolence" (p. 41). Like McCulloch she believed individual property rights were responsible for whatever wealth existed and not for the poverty that remained (p. 51).

Marcet's criticism of the Poor Law as well as her defense of enclosures were based entirely on her assessment of their consequences. "It is by the test of general utility that the justice of all laws should be tried," she wrote (p. 45). Enclosures increased productivity and thus passed the test of utility. The Poor Law increased the number of poor, diminished the demand for their labor, and as a result decreased wages, and so it did not. But Marcet's utilitarianism did keep her from recommending the immediate abolition of the Poor Law. Because immediate abolition would occasion "the most cruel distress" among the poor, they should be weaned from it through the "gradual effect of education" (p. 176).

The lessons Harriet Martineau meant to teach her enormous following of readers about property and the poor can be seen in her novels *Decamera* (1832) and *Cousin Marshall* (1834), both in the Illustrations of Political Economy series. Though Martineau's blatantly didactic stories are easy to caricature, her life and views are much more interesting and complicated. Her defense of political economy had nothing in common with Malthusian pessimism or with insulting attitudes toward laborers. In fact, later in the 1830s she flirted with socialist ideas.[47] In the Preface to her *Poor Laws and Paupers Illustrated* she made clear that the faults she found in laborers were entirely created by institutions and capable of amelioration.

Decamera was an attack on slavery, and so it had to consider the issue of whether human beings could become property. The son and daughter of a plantation owner in Guiana returned to the plantation—named Decamera—after being educated in England for fourteen years. As the father and son toured the island, the father lamented the lack of economic improvements since the son had left and suggested that the solution was for government to use its power to create monopolies and bounties. The son had been well educated in the universal principles of economic activity, and he disagreed with his father, arguing that the first requirement of improvement was for property to be made secure on just foundations. To his father's question, "Do you think we do not know what property is?" the son replied, "I do: because I think we hold a great deal that does not belong to us."[48]

Martineau used the son to put forward the argument that the origin of property rights in the land and in the productions of the earth could not be extended to justify property rights in people. Property rights were conventional. At first, they were the result of people simply not interfering with one another's plots and thereby giving tacit consent. Later they were the result of more formal agreements, and finally they were the creation of municipal laws that were backed by punishment. Since no one would agree, tacitly or expressly, to rules that might make them slaves, the way conventional property rights arose could not be used to justify slavery. But though agreement seemed at first the act that legitimated property rights, Martineau quickly moved to a utilitarian explanation. For agreements carried moral weight because they were "essential to the public good" (p. 21). Thus "the general good is not only the origin, but ought to be the end and aim of the institution of property; and if ever there should come a time when the institution may be proved inconsistent with the general good, it will be abolished" (p. 21). The real reason, then, that slavery was wrong and would not be agreed to was that "its increase adds to the sum of human misery," and the reason it should be abolished was that "its diminution brings a proportionate relief" (p. 22). Martineau's thoroughly utilitarian perspective was explicit in the last words of this novel. She described the "ultimate aim" of society as "the greatest happiness of the greatest number" (p. 140).

In *Cousin Marshall* Martineau employed her considerable pedagogic skills against the Poor Law. The fictional format allowed her to create dishonest beggars, drunken workers, and suffering children. Most of all, her targets were simple-minded, sentimental, misguided humanitarians.

"No, no, dear. It is a deeper matter than any of these. The greatest question now moving in the world is, 'What is charity?' "

"Alas, yes! And who can answer it? Johnson gave a deficient answer, and Paley a wrong one; and who can wonder that multitudes make mistakes after them?"

"A clergyman, Louisa, a wise clergyman who discerns times and seasons, may set many right; and God knows how many need it! He will not follow up a text from Paul with a definition from Johnson and an exhortation from Paley. He will not suppose because charity once meant alms-giving, that it means it still; or that a kind-hearted man must be right in thinking kindness of heart all-sufficient, whether its manifestation be injurious or beneficial. He will not recommend keeping the heart soft by giving green gooseberries to a griped child,—as he might fairly do if he carried out Paley's principle to its extent."[49]

Martineau suggested abolishing virtually all private charity, especially gifts to pregnant women and orphans, because these were nothing but premiums on population (p. 37). Only education and hospitals for those injured on the job escaped her denunciation. It hardly needs to be said that she also attacked the public relief given by the Poor Law. She recommended the plan of Malthus for its gradual abolition.

One of her characters suggested that these recommendations would violate the rights of the poor. Martineau maintained that the idea of such a right was based on a false analogy between the family and the state, as if the state had an obligation to take care of its members as parents take care of children. The error was to forget that though a family could control its size and income, "the state cannot control the numbers of its members, nor increase, at its will, the subsistence fund" (p. 45). The seriousness of the error was in its apocalyptic consequences, for "in a few more years the profits of all kinds of property will be absorbed by the increasing rates, and capital will cease to be invested" (p. 49).

Martineau, like Malthus in his short pamphlet *A Summary View . . .*, insisted that the right to relief and the right to property were incompatible. Some of the poor, she worried, might think the right to relief made it legitimate to steal from the propertied (p. 71). More important was her argument that the state could enforce only one or the other of these rights. And where the right to relief existed and was met through a poor-law system financed by taxes, it was the poor who were secure in their right and the propertied who lacked security for their possessions:

> At present . . . the security of property is to the pauper, and not to the proprietor, however rich he may be. The proprietor is compelled, as in the case before us, to pay more and more to the rate till his profits are absorbed, and he is obliged to relinquish his undertakings one after another; field after field goes out of cultivation, his capital is gradually transferred to his wages-fund, which is paid away without bringing an adequate return; and when all but his fixed capital is gone, that becomes liable to seizure, and the ruin is complete. There is no more security of property, under such a system, than there is security of life to a poor wretch in a quicksand, who feels himself swallowed up inch by inch. The paupers meanwhile are sure of their relief as long as the law subsists. They are to be provided for at all events, let what will become of other people. (Pp. 111–12)

To Martineau the result of the Poor Law was just the opposite of that recommended by utility. The rights of the poor had only pernicious consequences which impoverished the community. The rights of property had only beneficial consequences. Utility, then, required that property be secure and the poor to work or suffer.

Black, Senior, and Lloyd

Utilitarian reflections on property and welfare always seem to begin with a strong affirmation of the need for exclusive property rights. Welfare, on the other hand, is suspect because it may act as an incentive to laziness. But utilitarian suspicions concerning government aid can be overcome, and insofar as utilitarians were strongly disposed to minimize suffering, they usually were. Only when market forces were made sacred by a divine author, or present suffering more than offset by the promise of pleasure in the next life, or appeals to history used to protect social institutions from reason could utilitarians keep from making the calculations that demonstrated that order and prosperity were not in danger from the taxes necessary to fund aid. In the 1820s, especially as the issue of whether a poor law should be introduced into Ireland became widely debated, utilitarian discussions led to a reevaluation of government assistance.

At least according to John Stuart Mill, it was John Black, editor of the *Morning Chronicle*, "a vehicle of the opinions of the utilitarian radicals," who played an important role in this process of reevaluation. "Black, as I well remember, changed the opinion of some of the leading political economists, particularly my father's, respecting the poor laws, by the articles he wrote in the Chronicle in favour of a poor law for Ireland. He met their objections by maintaining that a poor law did not necessarily encourage overpopulation but might be so worked as to be a considerable check to it and he convinced them that he was in the rights."[50] Black also seems to have influenced McCulloch, for in the *Edinburgh Review* article in which McCulloch announced his support for the Poor Law, Black's *Chronicle* articles were praised and liberally cited.

In 1822, five years before his most important article on the introduction of a poor law into Ireland, Black considered the status of property rights in a discussion of the legitimacy of the Irish tithe, which he defended against the attack that it threatened the institution of property: "Is a people to be considered subordinate to property, or property to a people? . . . The appropriation of land, or any thing else, to individuals, has its sanction in the superior utility and benefit of which it is productive to the Community at large; and a property which threatens to burst the bonds that hold the Community together, ought no more to be allowed to exist, than a right ought to be allowed to any one to set fire to a city." In 1826 he repeated the argument that private rights to property were subordinate to the public welfare. "Property," he wrote, "is allowed for the benefit of the community, but still the lands of a country belong, in the abstract, to all its inhabitants."[51] Black's willingness to treat any current distribution of property rights as problematic was exactly what McCulloch tried to prevent with his emphasis (at least in the early 1820s) on the growth of property rights for utilitarian reasons long before the establishment of government and his assertion that some of those rights should be respected even if they were inconsistent with immediate benefits.

Black's innovation was to turn the population argument in favor of a poor law. He argued that a poor law in Ireland might have helped to keep the population down and might do so in the future if one were enacted. The mechanism for this effect was that a poor law would interest the landlords and gentry in the number and condition of the poor and provide them with an incentive to restrain the population growth of the poor in their parishes. Black praised the laws of settlement, suggesting that the threat of removal would keep young men who were working outside their parishes from marrying and on their best behavior. Black never argued that the poor had a right to aid, but neither did he think property holders had a right to their property. Both property and aid had to be judged solely on whether they served the benefit of the community.

To defend the laws of settlement required confronting not only the argument about their consequences given authoritatively by Adam Smith but also his argument that they violated the natural rights of the laborer. Black's answer was straightforwardly Benthamite: "As to violations of natural liberty and justice, all men, both poor and rich, must reconcile themselves to them, as the price of their enjoying the advantages of the social union. . . . From our childhood to our grave, we are in constant subjection to restraints of various kinds. The question is, are the restraints necessary, with reference to the general good? If necessary, they are justifiable."[52] Black's influence can be seen in the following quotation taken from McCulloch's widely read 1828 *Edinburgh Review* article defending the Poor Law:

> It is idle to talk about a violation of natural liberty; for that has long ceased to exist. Society, in fact, originates in its annihilation, or, at least, in the restraints imposed upon it; and the real and only question, with respect to any given restraint that either has been or may be imposed, is, whether it is advantageous or not. If it not be for the public benefit, it ought as certainly to be repealed. If we refer to any other standard than this, it is impossible we should ever arrive, except by the merest accident, at any sound conclusion, in any department of political science.[53]

McCulloch, then, perhaps under the influence of Black, came to believe that there were good reasons for government to aid some people if it were done in certain ways. McCulloch began his defense of the Poor Law by pointing out that there were problems with reconciling the logic of the deductive argument against aid with what had actually occurred. His task was to find the countervailing tendencies that kept the Poor Law as it actually operated from causing economic decline. McCulloch thought the explanation was found in the way aid had been given. The workhouse, the difficulty of obtaining a legal settlement, and local control and financing all worked to create barriers to the wide and easy availability of aid. To McCulloch, the virtue of the Poor Law was less that it helped poor people who were unable to work than that it provided strong incentives to local landowners "to oppose themselves to the increase of the laboring population" (p. 309). Cottages were not built, farms were not divided, legal settlements were not given, and marriages were not undertaken because of the interests of the landowners. Given this perspective, it is easy to understand why he worried that English workhouses had been "too comfortable" (p. 308).

McCulloch adopted Black's arguments defending the Poor Law because its harshness kept the laboring population from increasing. His effort was aimed against the proponents of outdoor relief and those who favored centralized administration. He argued that both of these methods of providing aid would end in treatment of the poor that was too kind and would thereby encourage rather than discourage the growth of their population. He believed the widespread acceptance of the right to relief would cause similar problems. McCulloch, then, like many utilitarians of this period, defended some aid to the poor, but only if it were given under the harshest circumstances. And it must be admitted that in this early utilitarian defense, McCulloch's goal was as much to limit the number of poor as it was to relieve their privation.

The link that was thought to exist between aid and increased population was crucial to the critics of the Poor Law and had to be rethought before a utilitarian defense of aid could become widespread. Black's work was important for this reason, and McCulloch's willingness to defend the Poor Law depended on it. It is not surprising, then, that the most prominent economist among the commissioners who proposed the 1834 changes that continued government aid in the New Poor Law, William Nassau Senior, was skeptical of Malthus's population theory. As McCulloch had appealed to the idea that aid had not caused poverty in England, Senior pointed out that population had not outrun food production in England or any other civilized country. Knowledge, security of property, and the ambition to better one's condition that comes with free markets and equal opportunities all motivated people to limit their family size and increase their productivity.[54] Though one consequence of this view was to emphasize once again the need for the security of private property, so thoroughly a utilitarian as Senior never assumed what the particular effects of particular regulations would be on that security. His position is nicely summarized in his disagreement with Smith's use of the natural law vocabulary to attack apprenticeship laws. "I have already proved," Senior wrote, "that it is the duty, and therefore the right, of a government to take any measures, however they may interfere with the will of individuals, which are conducive to the general welfare of the community."[55] Only this general perspective legitimated Senior's recommendations for legislation to improve sanitation, housing, the conditions of children's employment, and education.[56]

Senior thought government had a duty to improve the welfare of the people. Neither the holders of property under the law nor the recipients of government aid could argue that their legal rights were required by something called natural justice. Both had to bring their arguments before the bar of utility. In general, utility validated both the existence of private property and some intervention in its affairs by government, including regulations that would provide aid to the poor under the proper circumstances. Senior was certain of the probable harmful consequences of government aid, especially as aid was administered before 1834. But his fear was not that aid increased the future poor through a population mechanism so much as it was that aid had a detrimental affect on the work habits of the present laborers. "The mass of mankind will not work for themselves, save for themselves, or even think for themselves, if they can get others to do it for them; many will give up, and almost all will relax, their industry, activity, and forethought, if they believe that a substitute for their results is to be obtained from charity."[57]

Although increased idleness would result in declining economic productivity, equally important to Senior was the effect aid could have on the character of laborers. For though English history since feudalism had been characterized by the growth of individual freedom and responsibility, the effects of the Poor Law were in the opposite direction. His description of the English Poor Law as beginning in "selfishness, ignorance, and pride" and as an attempt "to revive the expiring system of slavery" captures his fear that laborers would trade their freedom for dependence. And slavery, he argued, "destroys all the nobler virtues, both moral and intellectual; it leaves the slave without energy, without truth, without honesty, without industry, without providence."[58]

These consequences did not accompany private aid, but they did result when laborers had a legal right to relief. The Speenhamland system of wage subsidies was particularly dangerous because it suggested that wages were a matter of right rather than private contract. His sense that there were no obvious limits to the resources that might be required to satisfy the exercise of this right led him (like Bentham in his criticism of Sieyès's proposal) to portray it as "the most dangerous of all principles, the principle that the poor are in fact the owners of the land, and that to the extent of their wants."[59] It was to make clear that aid was not based on a right to the ultimate ownership of the land that Senior at one point suggested that relief be given in the form of a loan.

Senior's objections to the Poor Law as it existed before 1834 were primarily based on the way it was administered. He seems to have always recognized the benefits of government aid but thought that the disadvantages that accompanied the Old Poor Law's method of giving aid outweighed the benefits. His concern was to find a different form of administration, one that would allow the benefits to operate unimpeded. Thus he wrote in 1836 after his plan had been enacted, "I now believe that in England, or in any country in which the standard of subsistence is high, a provision for the able bodied in strictly managed workhouses in which their condition shall be inferior to that of the independent laborer, may be safely and even advantageously made."[60]

The main benefit he found in government relief programs was their ability to lessen the fear felt by large parts of the population that a calamity would reduce them to starvation: "A man who has no property and who relies for his own bread and that of his family on his share in producing a commodity which is to be sold perhaps in another hemisphere, or which depends on mere fashion for its utility, can never quite banish from his mind the fear, that the day may come when his services will be no longer wanted. . . . Now this cause of unhappiness can be removed. It is in the power of a government to say that not one of its subjects shall perish by want."[61] Senior seems never to have questioned the provision of aid to the sick and aged. The question was always whether government aid should be given to the able-bodied. But since aid administered efficiently by a central board, confined to an unpleasant workhouse, and limited to an amount less than that earned by the lowest paid laborer (the terms of the New Poor Law) guaranteed that aid would be sought only by those truly in need, the advantages of government aid which reduced fear and ended starvation could be realized.

Between 1832 and 1837 William Forster Lloyd occupied the Drummond Chair in Political Economy at Oxford University. If Lloyd appears in histories of economic thought it is usually as an early contributor to the theory of marginal utility. But of his twelve published lectures, eight were directly on the subject of the Poor Law and three others (two on population, one on rent) were closely related to issues involving the poor. Lloyd's work contains a particularly sophisticated utilitarian argument for government assistance to the poor.

In his 1834 lectures at Oxford, published the next year as *Four Lectures on Poor Laws*, Lloyd acknowledged the Malthusian criticism that since poor laws could not increase the food supply, they could result in shifting hardship from one laboring class to another. As Lloyd pointed out, this result occurred only when a country suffered from an aggregate food supply that was inadequate or barely adequate for its population, conditions that did not exist in England. When the problems of the poor stemmed from the distribution of a more than adequate food supply or from the vicissitudes the laborer was subject to, a poor law could mitigate suffering even if it could not guarantee employment or a comfortable provision to all.[62] Unemployment caused by the use of new machinery seemed to Lloyd a particularly easy case for the use of government aid. If the laborers could be fed before the machinery made their labor unnecessary, and the machines were adopted because they increased productivity, it followed that more resources would be available after their use than before. Thus it could not be argued that newly redundant workers could not be fed because the total supply of food was inadequate (pp. 84–88). A poor law that provided subsistence provisions to those unemployed because of the business cycle or changes in fashion also could not be criticized by population arguments. Moreover, so long as relief was modest in amount he believed it would not promote idleness.

More central to this study were Lloyd's comments on the justice of poor laws. Lloyd specifically considered Malthus's attack on the right to relief found in Paine. Lloyd saw that the argument of Malthus (and of Eden as well) was based on the impossibility of feeding everyone and amounted to little more than saying that no one could have a right to food if the exercise of such a right was impossible. But such an argument was irrelevant to a situation in which enough food was available to feed all possible claimants. To hold in that situation that

> none, whose labor is not wanted, have any claim of right to the smallest portion of food, involves a monstrous consequence. It implies, that the right of the possessors of the world, to do with it as they please, is absolute and uncontrollable. . . . In short, it implies the tacit assumption that the interests of society ought to be subordinate to the supposed rights of property; as if such rights could exist as rights, or be defended on any other grounds than their

tendency to promote the happiness of society, by a reference to which they ought at all times to be defined and modified. (P. 48)

In this passage, so much like Black's quoted earlier, Lloyd made clear that a utilitarian defense of property rights did not allow property holders simply to invoke their legal rights against people in need. Only the happiness of all—including the poor—could justify rights of any kind.

So easy was it to use an inappropriate mental image of the relationship between the rich and the poor that Lloyd had his readers compare three different situations (pp. 50–51). In the first, two people begin with equal resources but become unequal through the idleness of one and the hard work of the other. This situation, Lloyd suggested, would call for the wealthy to show pity on the poor. In the second image, an accident such as a flood caused someone previously equal to his neighbor to become needy. Charity was the proper response here, argued Lloyd. But he insisted that neither of these two images accurately depicted the problem England faced. A more appropriate way to visualize the rich and the poor in England would be to compare one person born with land and able to live without working with another born without land and required to work hard for even a subsistence. This inequality, Lloyd emphasized, was the creation of human institutions, not of idleness or calamity, and could be justified only to the extent that it furthered the common good. When the laboring poor were deprived of their ability to work through forces beyond their control, those human institutions that were ultimately responsible for the poor's precarious situation should be arranged to mitigate their suffering. Without government aid to the poor it could not be held that unequal property satisfied the utilitarian requirement of furthering the greatest happiness of the greatest number. Since government assistance increased the happiness of society, Lloyd argued that transfers from the rich to the poor were a matter of justice.

Lloyd's analysis was entirely within the utilitarian framework summarized by Nassau Senior—that the government had the right and duty to do whatever was in the common good. In a way reminiscent of Bentham, Lloyd admitted that he did not like discussions of rights because of the "obscurity which frequently attends them" (p. 40). For that reason he adopted the perspective of "general utility" (p. 96), which meant in this case that if poor laws benefited society, justice required that those in need have a legal right to relief (p. 41).

In his *Two Lectures on the Justice of the Poor Laws*, delivered in 1837, Lloyd considered the argument that the only obligation the rich had to the poor was to employ them at a fair wage (not below the market rate) and that any aid given beyond that was charity. Lloyd saw that this argument depended on the assumption that wages constituted an equivalent for the labor performed and in that sense discharged the obligations that employers had. He agreed that in "so far as an exchange of equal values in the markets is an exchange of equivalents," wages were an equal exchange for labor.[63] But this was to say no more than that the laborer had received as much as the current state of labor market competition allowed. The exchange of equivalents here was simply a matter of definition. It was not to say that the laborer received a "reasonable share of the produce of his labor" or an amount proportioned to the quantity of labor he gave in exchange. The question was not, then, whether the laborer received wages equivalent to his labor; by definition, he did. The question was "whether the law, under particular circumstances, ought not to interpose to secure him something more" (p. 11). In effect, Lloyd denied moral meaning to the labor market and insisted that it, like all other institutions, was subject to the judgment of utility.

To drive his point home, Lloyd compared the situation in which English landowners allowed aged or ill laborers to die of starvation with one in which slaveowners allowed aged or ill slaves to die. The slaveowners would in such a case be guilty of murder, according to Lloyd, and a magistrate would be required by justice to intervene, feed, and save the slave. The argument that the slaves had been given subsistence while they worked and could not in old age be expected to be maintained while idle was illegitimately used with regard to slaves as well as with laborers. In both cases, the lives of the aged should be understood to be more important "to the general welfare of the human family" than the luxuries of the rich who had employed them (p. 26).

Lloyd also considered the argument that granting a legal right to relief violated the property rights of landholders. He compared the view that "the title of the appropriators of the soil [is] clear and unquestionable" (i.e., unconditional) with the belief that the land was "the common inheritance of all the inhabitants of the earth" (pp. 37–38). Lloyd's conclusion that "all the writers on the theory of property" had held the latter position is more or less the point of view of this book. Private property, he argued, could only be defended because of its contribution to maintaining first the lives and then the comforts of a civilized people. Neither equal property nor an unconditional exclusive right to property could pass this test. Lloyd could find justification for considerable inequalities but only if a mechanism existed to ensure that everyone shared in the benefits created by inequality. He thought that the need for government programs was increasing with economic development. Not only were the distinctions between landlords, capitalists, and laborers becoming more rigid, but the number of those living on their labor alone and subject to the instability of the labor market was increasing proportionately (p. 74).

Read, Scrope, and Longfield

Though Lloyd thought of himself as a thoroughgoing utilitarian, his concern that national wealth might grow at the cost of increased misery for the poor would seem more directly addressed through a theory of the rights of the least advantaged. Not surprisingly, between 1829 and 1837 another group of political economists, all of whom wanted to make a strong case for a poor law in England and Ireland, resurrected the language of natural jurisprudence as the proper basis for a legally required welfare provision. That the situation in Ireland became part of the Poor Law debate was particularly important because no one could claim that its unemployment resulted from individual improvidence or laziness. Although these writers remained utilitarian in their fear that aid could act as a disincentive to labor, they thought aid to the poor outside the labor market was best understood as a natural right. The rural disturbances and violent urban union activity of this period may have had a particularly strong impact on these writers. They were certainly responding to the development (chronicled in the next chapter) of a radical or working-class political economy that defended the interests of the laboring population. Their project, at least in part, was to fashion a political economy that defended the major economic institutions and practices of their society against radical criticism. But they also recognized that this defense was best accomplished if those institutions were also made responsible for people left out of or harmed by economic progress. Though their fears of social upheaval can be used to reduce them to ideologues interested primarily in making political economy more palatable to laborers, this makes it too easy to reject their noteworthy attempts to find institutional ways to realize both the exclusive and inclusive nature of property rights.

Samuel Read, whose *Inquiry into the Natural Grounds of Right to Vendible Property or Wealth* was published in Edinburgh in 1829, wrote to counter the radical interpretation of Ricardo that since all wealth came from labor there should be no return to capital. To sort out the relative positions of labor and capital Read returned to the work of Smith, specifically to its natural law justification for property rights. According to Read, the four-stage theory of economic development explained why the rights to property in land, capital, and welfare coexisted as natural rights. He began with the earth as originally a common to which all had access. Over time individual labor and common agreement legitimately resulted in private holdings. Since neither industry nor frugality was found in equal amounts, private holdings became unequal. The inheritance by one generation of another generation's honestly acquired property meant that inequality would be perpetuated. And from this just inequality emerged capital. Read saw capital as originating first in the forgone consumption of people who had more than their subsistence required and as receiving a return when it was used by others as an incentive to further saving and investing.[64] Second, he saw a return to capital as derived from contracts under which labor agreed to pay a return because of the added efficiency capital made possible (p. 125). The return to capital, then, was not something taken from the laborer. "The claim and right of the capitalist to share in the produce to which his capital contributes rests partly upon compact and agreement with the labourer, to whom he pays his wages in virtue of that agreement, . . . partly upon the comparative degree in which labour can produce with and without capital, and partly upon the cost and difficulty or privation which the particular contribution of capital requires" (p. 128). In fact, "capitalists are in reality the greatest of all benefactors to the community" since it was their saving that made wages possible (p. 56). Read did not distinguish capitalists from landlords and seems to have collapsed the two groups together as nonlaborers, both living off the contracts made with laborers to farm the land or work with the machinery of the "capitalists."

But Read attached to this defense of common land becoming private and unequal the condition that when all the land was occupied those without land or a job had a right to relief. Property rights and welfare rights were two sides of the same coin. Neither property rights nor a government to protect them would have been agreed to unless they were thought to be to everyone's advantage. Because private property increased productivity, it was to everyone's advantage. Many might become landless, but they could prosper through their labor in an advancing economy. Nothing in this argument works, however, for someone without land or a job. Such a group would be better off in the state of nature and could not be thought to have agreed to property or government (p. 366). He cited a number of cases in English law in which starving people were acquitted when found taking others' property to substantiate his belief in the right of necessity (pp. 368–69). He concluded that property and government were legitimate only if they included a welfare right. "The right of the poor to support, and the right of the rich to engross and accumulate, are relative and reciprocal privileges, the former being the condition in which the latter is enjoyed" (p. 375). Not surprisingly, Read used two long quotations from the "approved and popular" Paley to help convince his readers.

Read's explanation of welfare rights was based on a consent theory of landed property. Labor was entitled only to the value it added to land; the land itself, given by God, could be divided only by a contract under the terms discussed above. Read used this distinction between the original gift and the value added by labor (or capital) to explain how a welfare right should be funded. He noted that rents rose in part because of a general increase in social prosperity rather than from individual effort. This part of rent belonged to everyone and could be taxed to fund payments to the poor without violating the individual rights of landowners. In Read's estimation, the social part of rent was between one-eighth and one-quarter of total rent. At the end of his book, perhaps building on his sense that exclusive rights to land were responsible for commerce and manufacturing as well as agriculture, he suggested that welfare rights should be financed by a graduated tax on all property, not only on land (p. 360).

Like other defenders of government-funded aid in this period, Read had to confront Malthus. Read noted that insofar as the objections to aid were based on the way it provided incentives to idleness and to early marriages, it left untouched arguments for helping children, the aged, and the disabled. Only help to the able-bodied poor was actually called into question by Malthus, and aid to that group was easily justified as long as it was less than the "ordinary" rate of wages. Because he believed the poor had a right to welfare, he objected to the settlement laws and urged that welfare be recognized as a national responsibility. No doubt it was also because aid was a right and had to be given in a way that respected the people who claimed it that his plan for providing relief did not mention the workhouse.

The most important political economist to defend the Old Poor Law on the grounds that the poor had a right to support was G. Poulet Scrope. Scrope wrote several articles on the Poor Law for the Tory *Quarterly Review* and also considered them in his *Principles of Political Economy* (1833). Like Read, Scrope wrote to defend a return to capital and used a Smithian framework to do it. Scrope was a member of Parliament, a geologist, and a "model landowner," as well as an accomplished economist.

Scrope's journal articles were concerned primarily with questions of immediate policy and were not fertile ground for philosophic discussions. But as he made clear in an 1832 article attacking the plan of Chalmers to rely entirely on private charity to help the poor, his analysis was always based on the idea that the poor had a right to support from organized political society. "The truth . . . is, that the poor have a decided claim, in justice, to a support from the land on which Providence has placed them. . . . Such a provision, therefore, instead of being a matter of charity and benevolence . . . is but the legal concession of a right antecedent even to that of the owners of the soil—a divine right—a right based on the external and immutable principles of intuitive justice."[65]

Scrope singled out Harriet Martineau's *Illustrations of Political Economy* for criticism in another essay he wrote for *Quarterly Review*. "It is . . . impossible not to laugh," he wrote, "at the absurd trash which is seriously propounded by some of her characters, in dull didactic dialogues, introduced here and there in the most clumsy manner."[66] Scrope criticized Martineau's use of Ricardo's theory of rent and her defense of enclosures, but his main targets were her ideas about social welfare and the poor. He exposed the errors in her wild projections of population increase, doubted that hospitals were incentives to the poor falling ill, and denied that education was an appropriate solution to the immediate physical suffering of the poor. Scrope was particularly scathing in his comments on Martineau's treatment of the problem of Irish poverty. Her refusal to acknowledge the harmful effects of absentee landlords and the need for government to compel them to use some of their rents to maintain their peasants outraged Scrope. Simply waiting for economic forces "spontaneously" to work, he pointed out, would condemn large numbers of Irish peasants to starvation.

When Scrope tried to explain in his *Principles of Political Economy* (1833) what he meant by a "natural right," a "divine right," or a "sacred right" of the poor to support, he usually referred to a right to use one's labor on "the common gifts of nature."[67] Only if work was not available did the right take the form of a right to subsistence. Poor Law payments, then, were seen as given in lieu of the opportunity to work. Understanding this reasoning behind Scrope's argument helps to make clear why he suggested that public work projects were the best way to satisfy welfare rights of the able-bodied who were without employment. Especially in his argument for a poor law in Ireland, he urged that the unemployed be used to build bridges, roads, canals, and ports and to reclaim waste land. If the poor were without work and not given aid, their right to work on "the common gifts of nature" became the right of necessity. It was a happy combination of justice and prudence to respect the rights of the poor, for not to do so created both injustice and chaos. Scrope reiterated the same point that was at the center of Read's argument: "There can be no security for property where the body of the people have no security for life" (p. 330).

Asserting a natural right to relief did not immediately settle arguments about the way relief should be given or about the amount of aid the poor should receive. Yet if aid was a right, it must be given in ways that showed respect for the people receiving it. To Scrope, like Read, this meant that aid could not be given in a workhouse setting, which he described as causing "humiliation and debasement" (p. 321). Scrope also insisted that subsistence must be understood historically, that is, that it must be based on "the natural wants of the pauper, taking into consideration the habitual standard of necessaries among the population."[68]

Scrope's most innovative discussion of how to pay for poor relief occurred in his *Principles of Political Economy*. There he constructed what amounts to a social security insurance system. All employers would be required to put a set amount for each employee in a fund that the unemployed, aged, and disabled would be able to draw upon when needed (p. 316). By including capitalists as well as landlords among those responsible for payments to the poor, he recognized the new realities of British economic life. Scrope and Read are often labeled paternalists, as if concern for the lives of laborers could be based only on sentiments of superiority derived from a style of thought rooted in the past. But to think of them this way misses the contribution their work made to funding and delivering a welfare right.

Mountifort Longfield was the first occupant of the chair in political economy at the University of Dublin and author of *Four Essays on Poor Laws* (1834). Like Read and Scrope, he wrote, at least in part, to defend a return to capital against the arguments that such a return cheated labor. He praised Senior and the New Poor Law for its tough-minded treatment of the able-bodied poor and attacked the Speenhamland allowance system in hope that it would not be adopted in Ireland. But unlike Senior and the other authors of the New Poor Law, he suggested that aid to the aged and infirm should be generous and understood as satisfying a right.

Longfield followed the logic of incentives most rigorously. That is, he understood (as Read and Scrope also did) that any demonstration that aid given above market levels created disincentives to industry left untouched arguments for aid to those who could not work or aid in amounts below prevailing wages. Longfield developed his defense of aid against Say's objection that any government aid was illegitimate because it involved compelling one person to labor for another and, in that sense, made the industrious slaves to the idle.[69] Longfield accepted this argument for property earned through labor or purchased from the proceeds of labor. He referred to "the property a man has in the fruits of his own industry" as "the most sacred right of property" (p. 17). But, he added, "a great part of the property of the country owes its existence to the gratuitous gift of nature" (p. 18). Since people did not create land, labor could not explain why land was privately owned. Thus, Longfield stated, "society distributes this land among certain persons, and protects it as private property" (p. 18). But though society distributed property to some, it expected obedience from all. According to Longfield, obedience could be expected from those who could no longer exercise their rights to common land only if they received aid when they were unable to find work. In a way reminiscent of Woodward, he likened the division of land to an enclosure bill under which those deprived of their common pasture received some compensation from those who gained private property. Without aid to those who had lost their "right to commonage," the regulations of society would require that some starve (p. 20). Only if aid were available could the destitute be fairly expected to obey the laws against stealing.

To make sure his acknowledgment of a natural right to aid remained consistent with the good of the community, Longfield, like the other political economists who defended public assistance, was at pains to explain its limits. It applied only to subsistence and could not be claimed by those destitute because of their idleness or overindulgence. Moreover, though the destitute had a right to aid, they did not have the right to specify the amount or circumstances under which it would be given.

Longfield acknowledged that most of the able-bodied unemployed in Ireland were without jobs through no fault of their own and thus had not forfeited their right to subsistence. Unlike Read and Scrope, however, he recommended the use of workhouses, which would offer wages under the prevailing wage and that only in exchange for a "severe, or . . . disagreeable labor" (p. 35). Stonebreaking seemed to him an appropriate task for the able-bodied recipients of assistance. Moral and religious education was also recommended. Aid given under these circumstances ran no risk of decreasing the exertions of laborers. Although Longfield's approach to the able-bodied was harsh, he had nothing in common with those who saw the poor as deserving their fate or as part of a system of providential punishment. Thus, when he dealt with those who were disabled or too old to work, those outside an economy based on incentives, he suggested they "should be *liberally* assisted by the state." Hospitals for the sick and pensions for the elderly were "productive of unmixed good," he concluded (p. 32).

In 1872, thirty-eight years after Longfield gave these lectures, he published another entitled "The Limits of State Interference with the Distribution of Wealth in Applying Taxation to the Assistance of the Public." Longfield again began with the problem of incentives and its relationship to state aid. It was possible, he acknowledged, that those taxed might work less if they found their wages went more to the government than to themselves. Similarly, those given aid might work less if they found government would provide them an acceptable standard of living without their own exertions. But he thought neither outcome was likely. The first objection to redistribution through taxation Longfield dismissed as not relevant to Great Britain in the late nineteenth century. Since "the disposition to accumulate depends more upon habit and temperament, than upon any calculations of reason . . . and in Great Britain is greater than is necessary," he argued that the relationship between taxation and effort was highly elastic (p. 135). In short, taxation had shown no tendency to diminish the labor of taxpayers. Longfield considered the problem of decreasing incentives in those who received aid in more detail. The aged, disabled, and ill were not subject to incentives and could, therefore, be liberally helped without fear (pp. 136–40). Longfield also found good economic reasons for the state to provide free education, to provide parks "for health and recreation," and to enforce food, sanitary, and housing regulations (pp. 142–46). A better-educated and healthier work force, he maintained, would strive to better its condition and to work hard to achieve its goals. In all of these cases, taxes could be collected from the wealthy and safely spent in ways that especially benefited the least advantaged members of society without harm to industry. Longfield argued that in these cases the relationship between incentive and government interference was precisely the opposite of what those opposed to assisting the poor thought it was.

Longfield's modern editor has concluded that this last essay "anticipated most features of the modern welfare state."[70] But the same could be said of some of the ideas found in Read and Scrope. In fact, both private property and government-funded aid to the disabled and unemployed were deeply embedded in the political economy of the 1820s and 1830s. It may be, then, that there was a logic to the recognition of a welfare right in these primarily utilitarian political economists that was similar to that in Bentham. A derivation of property rights from the need for security, the fear of pain, and the desire to promote happiness led almost ineluctably to a justification of some welfare provision to those whose economic insecurity threatened them with considerable suffering. But there were limits to a welfare right developed within this tradition. Not just Bentham's bizarre panopticon but also the workhouse terms of the New Poor Law, Read's insistence that the right to aid for the unemployed was satisfied with payments one-half that of the lowest wage, and Longfield's praise in the 1830s for stonebreaking illustrate these limits.

SIX

Welfare Rights and Radical Politics

Paine to the *Poor Man's Guardian*

To the self-conscious defenders of "the poor," "the people," or, to use Burke's phrase, "the swinish multitude," it mattered little that political economy in the 1820s and 1830s finally came to recognize some forms of government aid as a right or as consistent with utility. They had opposed from the start all attempts to abolish or limit aid as violations of the rights of the poor, and they were outraged at the conditions under which aid was given in the New Poor Law. To make their case, these writers relied heavily on the natural law tradition regarding property. If they were right, the natural right to property was more appropriately invoked by those who wanted to share in economic resources than it was by those who wanted to protect the resources they already controlled.

This chapter will follow the ideas of property rights and welfare rights from their use in the attacks on Burke in the 1790s; through their role in the agrarianism of William Ogilvie, Thomas Spence, and Thomas Skidmore; to the defense of the Old Poor Law in the early 1830s by William Cobbett; and ultimately to their place in the working-class political economy of the Ricardian Socialists. These groups used property theory both for an early defense of a welfare state and for a critique of inequality that required, along with payments to the poor, the redistribution of productive resources. Almost all of these theorists adopted the idea that labor provided the only legitimate title to property. This chapter will document the widespread use of that Lockean assumption among more or less left-wing critics and follow the implications these critics thought it had for the institutions and social relations of their society.

Wollstonecraft, Paine, Barlow, and Thelwall

From Mary Wollstonecraft's initial attack on Burke's *Reflections* in 1790 to John Thelwall's critique of his *Regicide Peace* in 1796, Burke's defense of political inequality was seen as inseparable from his defense of the economic disparities of late eighteenth-century England. As a result, his critics almost always added to their arguments for greater political equality proposals for increasing economic equality. To make these arguments, the natural law discussion of property rights, especially its Lockean variation, was indispensable. Its assumption of an original common to which people had rights that could never be completely given up and its derivation of property from labor were perfect tools for criticizing large, inherited, absentee-owned property holdings. A deep sympathy for the poor, a refusal to blame them for their poverty, a defense of their right to public assistance, and an attack on the unequal property relations of late eighteenth-century England were themes common to the books and essays written against Burke's *Reflections*.

Although Burke's critics defended private property and recognized the inevitability of inequality, their praise for property had limits. Mary Wollstonecraft explicitly expressed this acceptance of and uneasiness with property. "The demon of property," she wrote in *A Vindication of the Rights of Man*, "has ever been at hand to encroach on the sacred rights of men, and to fence round with awful pomp laws that war with justice. But that it [property] results from the eternal foundations of right—from immutable truth—who will presume to deny, that pretends to rationality."[1] Later, she likened property to a "golden image" that had drawn people away from liberty. Wollstonecraft's enemy was history, found concretely in "hereditary property," and against it she hurled reason and the rights that it gave to all people. Only if property reflected the talent and industry of the people who held it, instead of the "demon" laws of primogeniture, would it correspond to "the eternal foundations of right."

Wollstonecraft thought the property of the French Catholic church had been acquired by force and fraud and was used to support "idle tyrants," and she had no sympathy for Burke's outrage at the confiscation of church lands. She saved her "indignation" for what she saw as Burke's "contempt for the poor," especially as it was expressed in his statement that they had to respect property they could never have, labor for what they could not obtain, and be taught that their consolation would come in the next world. Wollstonecraft called this "contemptible hard-hearted sophistry" and insisted that the poor "have a right to more comfort than they at present enjoy" (pp. 142–44). She suggested that wastes be reclaimed and distributed to the poor and that large estates owned by religious orders or used as hunting preserves be divided into small farms (p. 148).

Though Wollstonecraft invoked the rights of the poor, she did not pause long enough in her attack on Burke to provide an account of these rights. To find such an account it is necessary to turn to Thomas Paine. Like Wollstonecraft, he tried to discredit Burke by drawing attention to the great disparity that existed between the rich and the poor in the world given by history and by contrasting it to the equality of rights required by natural justice. Thus, in his first criticism of Burke, a resolution that he drafted for a meeting of the London Revolution Society, he criticized the court for its luxury, compared it to the suffering of the poor, and argued that "the moral obligation of providing for old age, helpless infancy, and poverty, is far superior to that of supplying the invented wants of courtly extravagance, ambition and intrigue."[2]

Paine continued to defend the poor in his widely read *Rights of Man, Part Second* (1792). The last chapter, in particular, was almost entirely concerned with their condition and put forward a strikingly modern welfare system to improve it. Paine's proposals for poor relief were meant to deal with the situations under which people with no savings faced considerable hardship because they could not work. The young, the old, and those unemployed because of the business cycle ("thrown off from the revolutions of that wheel, which no man can stop") were the groups whose plight he addressed.[3] He began by suggesting that taxes on the goods people consumed should be lowered. But he added to this common complaint a plan to abolish the Poor Law and replace it with a welfare program more generous and less humiliating. His plan to guarantee "comfort" to the aged who could not support themselves was based on their rights and denied that public assistance to them should be thought of as granting a "favor" or "charity" (1:427).[4] The rest of his program included grants to families for the education of children, payments to women on the birth of children, and employment for the "casual poor" in London. The extent of his proposal is evident from the summary he provided:

First, Abolition of two millions poor-rates.
Secondly, Provision for two hundred and fifty-two thousand poor families.

Thirdly, Education for one million and thirty thousand children.

Fourthly, Comfortable provision for one hundred and forty thousand aged persons.

Fifthly, Donation of twenty shillings each for fifty thousand births.

Sixthly, Donation of twenty shillings each for twenty thousand marriages.

Seventhly, Allowance of twenty thousand pounds for the funeral expenses of persons traveling for work, and dying at a distance from their friends.

Eighthly, Employment, at all times, for the casual poor in the cities of London and Westminster. (1:431)

The purpose of these payments was to alleviate suffering and provide opportunity. Paine was quick to defend private property and to deny that he wanted to level it. But at the same time, it is clear that the only property he thought legitimately acquired by natural law was that acquired by the individual's industry and labor. The identification of property with labor enabled him to criticize laws that regulated the wages of workmen as infringing on their property (1:439). Later in his career, he used the same identification to argue that if the franchise were given to all those with property, it had to be given to anyone who performed work or a service, for they had property in their labor (2:581). His concern, though, was not just to praise those who worked but was also to increase the opportunity everyone would have to labor. To that end, he proposed a progressive tax on land to motivate wealthy individuals who had inherited large estates to sell their unfarmed land rather than pay taxes on it (1:434–39). He also hoped that such a tax would convince the rich to divide their estates among all their children in their wills. Property that was so large that it could not have been acquired by the labor of the owner had no special protection from state regulation (1:434). In fact, he recommended his plan for progressive taxation not only because it would raise revenue but because it was required by justice to take from the rich wealth they had taken from others (1:436). The distinctions implicit here between property acquired by industry and property inherited, as well as the correlative distinction between the classes that produced and those that lived off inherited property, were central to the radical political philosophy of the late eighteenth and early nineteenth centuries.

Although *The Rights of Man, Part Second*, set out a nascent welfare state with more detail than can be found in any other book at this time, its invocation of welfare rights was short on philosophical justification. It may even seem contradictory for Paine to have denigrated government, praised Adam Smith, attacked monopolies, and linked the laws of free trade to the laws of nature in the same book in which he set forth his welfare proposals. This is in some ways the mirror image of the Burke problem, for as the conservative Burke should not, some think, have embraced the market, the "bourgeois" Paine should not have produced a plan for a welfare state. Certainly it is important to remember that Paine thought his welfare proposals would cost less and be less intrusive than the Poor Law and to that extent were consistent with his overall view. But the key to understanding his defense of natural rights, including welfare rights, is in his attitudes toward history and individualism.

Paine defended use of the rights language for precisely the same reason that Burke opposed it. Only natural rights, held by everyone equally and available to everyone's understanding, provided a perspective from which to argue that the inequality in both hereditary political power and hereditary property holdings was wrong. Both were examples to Paine of "governing beyond the grave," which he called vain, presumptuous, ridiculous, insolent, and tyrannical (1:251). Paine simply took the natural law commonplace that had been used so effectively against primogeniture, that no generation could legislate for another, and applied it rigorously to both political and economic power. Paine insisted that every law continued to have force only because it was consented to by a current generation, if not explicitly, then implicitly, because it had not been repealed (1:254). Paine's argument that "every age and generation must be as free to act for itself, in all cases, as the ages and generations that preceded it" (1:251) was behind his defense of revolution and of representative institutions that embodied the principle of one man, one vote. But these sentiments were also behind his attack on the distribution of property in his time. Just as hereditary political power failed because, as Paine pointed out, wisdom was not inherited, hereditary property failed because talent and industry were not inherited. Primogeniture, entails, charters, and monopolies were all ways that the past exerted its power over the present and violated the rights of individuals who were excluded from their benefits. Abolishing these restrictions and putting in their place free markets would help to end the tyranny of history.

But Paine did not want only to destroy the past he found, he wanted to diminish the importance of any past and protect the rights of every future generation. "Every child born into the world must be considered as deriving its existence from God. The world is as new to him as it was to the first man that existed, and his natural right in it is of the same kind" (1:274). Paine understood that even distributions at first based on labor could degenerate into corrupt inheritance. Thus he made certain through his grants to mothers at childbirth that all children would start life with their physical needs met and through his education grants that every child would have the ability to labor with skill. These provisions would ensure that not even the history of a parent could overwhelm the rights of children to their natural inheritance. Similarly, Paine's proposals to provide aid or work to those in "temporary distress" and benefits to the aged might be thought of as protection against those aspects of individuals' own history that were beyond their control. Only welfare rights could guarantee that distributions of property created in a past generation, even if created justly, would not violate the rights of new members of society to act for their own "comfort and happiness" (1:275).

In his years in France during the Revolution, Paine continued to affirm welfare rights and to look for their foundations in justice, as can be seen in the *Declaration of Rights* he drafted with Condorcet in late 1792. After asserting that the purpose of civil society was to defend natural rights, he listed these rights as liberty, equality, security, property, social protection, and resistance to oppression. The next thirty-two articles of the *Declaration* explained the content of these rights. Thus liberty included free speech, free press, and the free exercise of religion. Equality entailed that everyone have the same rights and that public employment should be open to all with preference given only for "talents and virtues." Security consisted in the protection of "person, property, and rights." Paine filled in the content of the property rights that were to be protected in articles eighteen to twenty-four. The first five of these were rights to exclude others. They included the ability to dispose of "goods, capital, income, and industry," the right to engage in any trade or profession, and the right to representation in taxation and to compensation for public use of individual property. But the last two property rights in Paine's list demonstrate that he understood that property rights were also inclusive and required that some part of the nation's wealth be shared by all. Article twenty-three stated that education was owed to all members of society, and in article twenty-four he wrote, "To aid the needy is a sacred debt of society; and it is for the law to determine its extent and application" (2:540).

Paine clearly thought that individuals had a right to assistance and that this was part of their property right. But it was not until *Agrarian Justice* (1796) that Paine worked out a plausible derivation of inclusive property rights. There he made clear why society owed a debt to individuals that they had a right to collect in the form of education and public assistance. *Agrarian Justice* is sometimes considered a dramatic departure from Paine's earlier work, a retreat from his devotion to private property that was forced upon him by the Conspiracy of the Equals of François-Noël ("Gracchus") Babeuf. In fact, it only explained more completely the right to assistance that Paine seems to have believed in since *The Rights of Man, Part Second.*[5]

Paine began with individuals in the state of nature as "joint life proprietors" in the earth (1:611). He called the earth, air, animals, and water natural property, gifts from the Creator to all people. In the course of civilization, individuals improved the land through cultivation. Through individual labor some property justly became private or, in Paine's words, "artificial." Because of the legitimacy of artificial property— property that was the invention of man—Paine opposed Babeuf and all agrarian laws. "Nothing could be more unjust," he wrote, "than an agrarian law in a country improved by cultivations; for though everyman, as an inhabitant of the earth, is a joint proprietor of it in its natural state, it does not follow that he is a joint proprietor of cultivated earth. The additional value made by cultivation, after the system was admitted, became the property of those who did it, or who inherited it from them, or who purchased it" (1:612).

But the crux of Paine's argument was that though the value added by cultivation was justly private, the earth itself, because it was given to people and not made by any or all of them, must remain common. Unfortunately for posterity, "the common right of all became confounded into the cultivated right of the individual" (1:612). Paine argued that under these circumstances the landless had been "dispossessed" of their "natural inheritance" and had a right to receive an "equivalent" for the loss of their share of the common earth (1:612). As in *The Rights of Man, Part Second*, Paine counterpoised to the exclusive property rights inherited by a few the inclusive rights to property that all were entitled to inherit. The plan Paine proposed in *Agrarian Justice* to satisfy the rights of the landless differed from the proposals of the *Rights of Man, Part Second*. Payments still went to the aged and the disabled. But instead of a public employment scheme, Paine advanced the idea of cash payments to all individuals on their twenty-first birthday. "With this aid they could buy a cow, and implements to cultivate a few acres of land; and instead of becoming burdens upon society, which is always the case where children are produced faster than they can be fed, would be put in the way of becoming useful and profitable citizens" (1:618). Paine hoped that providing people with resources when they were young would prevent poverty and to that extent would be an improvement over programs that tried to mitigate its effects.

Paine wanted compensation given in forms that enhanced the opportunities and independence of the recipients. His inclusion of education in the list of property rights drawn up with Condorcet is evidence of this as was his hope in *Agrarian Justice* that some recipients would buy land and reclaim directly their common right to the earth. Because Paine suggested that people might buy land with their payments, he is often listed among agrarian reformers such as William Ogilvie and Thomas Spence. But as we shall see in Spence's criticism of Paine, on the question of whether one had an inalienable right to land or whether common rights could be given in an equivalent form, Paine's use of the equivalent formulation requires that he be placed in a welfare rights rather than an agrarian tradition.

The sources of the funds needed to make payments to the old, disabled, and newly adult followed from the distinctions Paine made between natural and artificial property. Since the cultivator could claim as his own only the value created by his work, he owed society a "ground-rent" for use of the earth that was owned by all (1:611). The same principle was applied to personal property. "All accumulation ... of personal property, beyond what a man's own hands produce, is derived to him by living in society; and he owes on every principle of justice, of gratitude, and of civilization, a part of that accumulation back again to society from whence the whole came" (1:620). His sense that personal wealth was often accumulated by cheating others—"paying too little for the labor that produced it" (1:620)—rather than by labor added to the justifications for taxation. That he regarded the underpayment of labor as a form of cheating, instead of intrinsic to the labor contract, illustrates his distance from later labor theorists and his primarily political explanation of inequality. Paine's plan to raise money was to levy a 10 to 22 percent tax on all inheritances, supposing that this amount would correspond to the social portion of property (1:616). An inheritance tax was the fairest way to collect money, Paine said: "The bequeather gives nothing: the receiver pays nothing" (1:614).

It is not unusual to find in histories of British radicalism of this period an implicit teleology in which the sophistication of a critique is judged by how closely it resembled Marx's analysis. According to this standard, Paine's work suffered (was bourgeois) not only because it was based on rights and markets but also because it emphasized political corruption rather than the inherently exploitive relations of capitalist production. And it cannot be denied that Paine understood too little about the emerging world of the industrial revolution. But it does seem to me to be an open question whether the agrarian, artisan, and cooperative movements considered in the rest of this chapter, all of which were more far-reaching in their criticisms, provided more intelligent responses than Paine did to economic growth and the dislocations it caused.

Paine's use of the rights tradition to criticize both Burke and Babeuf, his defense of a free market and of protection from its cycles, his recognition that property rights were legitimately exclusive and inclusive, his belief that inclusive rights should be given in ways that would produce opportunity and independence, and his search for administratively plausible ways to satisfy inclusive rights all constitute an important moment in the history of liberal political thought. Nor did his defense of welfare rights go unnoticed. As we have seen, it was Paine whom Malthus singled out for attack in his criticism of welfare rights in the second edition of the *Essay on Population*. But Paine was not alone in drawing these conclusions from the natural law discussion of property and deploying them against Burke especially.

Joel Barlow is most famous as the "poet laureate" of the American Revolution for his epic poem *The Vision of Columbia* (1787, revised as *The Columbiad* in 1807). But his attack on Burke, *Advice to the Privileged Orders* (Part 1, 1792; Part 2, 1795) was widely read in both England and America. Barlow graduated from Yale College in 1778, served as a chaplain in the revolutionary army, went to France in 1788 as an agent for an Ohio land company, so fervently supported the French Revolution that he was made a French citizen, became friends with Paine, and later undertook diplomatic duties for the American government.

Like Paine, he was, to some extent, a bourgeois radical. He self-consciously identified with the middle class and their fight against aristocratic oppressions; he blamed government for the creation of poverty and inequality; and he saw commerce as bringing virtue and peace to social relations.[6] There was, however, also a communitarian, millennialist side to Barlow, a vision of the future in which individualism and private property would be unnecessary to the order and prosperity of society. "Perhaps, in a more improved state of society, the time will come when a different system may be introduced; when it shall be found more congenial to the social nature of man to exclude the idea of separate property" (p. 81).

Although this radical vision gave Barlow a perspective that was more critical of "the idol Property" (p. 7) than anything found in Paine (and reminds us of the "demon property" of Wollstonecraft), neither his vision nor his critique led to proposals that were significantly different from Paine's. In fact, Barlow specifically praised that part of *The Rights of Man, Part Second*, in which Paine laid out his poor relief policy (p. 81). He, too, thought that every person had a "birth-right" to property, that is, "an imprescriptible claim to a portion of the elements" (p. 56). And like Paine he did not think fulfilling this right required land redistribution, for though the birthright was inalienable, it could take a variety of forms. In a society in which land was already private the first new form this birthright took was an education, at least in part, in political philosophy:

> The general stock of elements, from which the lives of men are to be supported, has undergone a new modification; and his portion among the rest. He is told that he cannot claim it in its present form, as an independent inheritance; that he must draw on the stock of society, instead of the stock of nature . . . but knowledge is a part of the stock of society; and an indispensable part to be allotted in the portion of the claimant, is instruction relative to the new arrangement of natural right. To withhold this instruction therefore would be, not merely the omission of a duty, but the commission of a crime. (P. 56)

All individuals, then, had a right to know their rights. Those who were born "of poor parents" and without the means of subsistence would have an additional right to a vocational education and the opportunity to use it—the means by which they could provide for their own subsistence. Society, he argued, "is bound by justice as well as policy, to give him some art or trade. For the reason of his incapacity is, that she has usurped his birth-right" (pp. 56–57). An education and a trade, both providing opportunity and independence, seemed to Barlow to be the proper equivalents to a birthright in the common earth. Barlow's general point, that individuals had a right to the means necessary for happiness, led him to add that individuals with "defective" faculties, no doubt the disabled and aged, also had a right to support (p. 60).

That funding these policies would necessitate taxes and transfers was not a problem for Barlow. He believed that "society is the first proprietor" of all landed property and that individuals could have as private only what was not required by their political community (pp. 59–60). Both primogeniture and entail were invalidated, he thought, by this argument. Even the justification for individuals enjoying the fruits of their labors was utilitarian in Barlow (pp. 81, 99). In effect, he argued that only inclusive rights were natural rights or birthrights, whereas rights to exclude could be given by society only for utilitarian reasons. But since Barlow followed Paine in believing that private property, commerce, and free trade tended to spread property more equally and that governments caused poverty, his belief in the social nature of property did not end in a call for its extensive social regulation. The assumption that a free market would increase equality enabled bourgeois radicals to reconcile their economic egalitarianism with their moderate interpretation of what an equal right to the earth required.

Barlow's insistence that labor was a just title to property only because it passed the test of usefulness was unusual among Burke's critics, most of whom relied on Lockean arguments. Locke's labor argument was deployed time and again to argue for increasing access to both political power and economic resources. In *Review of the Constitution of Great Britain* (1792), James Oswald considered the link that Burke had insisted upon between owning property and political participation. But if people had property in their labor, Oswald asked, should not those who labored be allowed to vote? If labor were the only legitimate title to property, the British political system was grossly unfair. Those who took part in it were idle inheritors without a just title to property while those who labored and created property were disfranchised.

> But what if we should prove that, so far from representing property, the Parliament of England have overturned all property.—What is property? Property is something which a man makes his, by communicating to it the sweat of his brow, or the forms of his genius; it is something that belongs to a man, that is, lies alongside of him: and this, in all languages, is the natural sense, and the true etymology of the word property. According to this definition, the monopolists of great masses of property, who also arrogate to themselves the exclusive monopoly of making laws, are men of no property whatever.

They neither plow nor sow, and yet they reap
The fat of all the land, and suck the poor.
The poor, who are the true proprietors, the oppressed poor, who
communicate to matter the sweat of their brow, are the forms of
their genius; without which matter is not peculiar to any, but common to all.[7]

George Dyer in *The Complaints of the Poor People of England* (1793)
used the labor argument to criticize a favorite target of the radicals, the
game laws. Dyer footnoted Locke's *Second Treatise* when he argued,
"The air and the water, and the creatures that live in them, are the
common gifts of providence: and till a man has, by his own industry,
acquired some right in what nature has left common, they are as much
one man's as another's . . . God has never said, the squire may shoot a
partridge or a pheasant, though the labourer shall not."[8] He also cited
Paine against primogeniture and Barlow on the need for a free public
school system.

At the end of his pamphlet, Dyer applauded Major John Cartwright
and the London Corresponding Society as well as the corresponding
societies in Sheffield and Norwich. The members of these societies,
mostly artisans, believed in "absolute political democracy; root and
branch opposition to monarchy and the aristocracy, to the State and to
taxation."[9] Their most significant theorist was John Thelwall, and his
most important work, written against Burke's *Regicide Peace*, was *The
Rights of Nature* (1796). Thelwall's respect for Paine is well illustrated by
his remark that one Paine was worth twelve Aristotles or twelve Gib-
bons. In part, Thelwall argued for an extension of the suffrage by using
the same labor argument found in Paine and Dyer. But tied to his concern for political reform was a critique of the economic disparities and
conditions under which many in England were forced to live.

To make his case that the economic inequality that characterized England in the 1790s was illegitimate, Thelwall used the natural law discussion of property and the idea of inclusive rights that came with it.
Thelwall explicitly maintained that the welfare rights people had entitled
them to more than mere subsistence and could not be met in the "full
crammed, noxious workhouses of Britain."[10] He announced this intention on the second page of his book: "I shall show hereafter, that, in the
present state of society, the laborer has a right to something more than
meat, drink, sleep, and clothing, in return for his productive toil" (p. 2).
He argued that "comforts and enjoyments," some leisure, and education

were required by such a right and later described its content as guaranteeing "decency and plenty." Since he maintained that these "sacred and inviolable" claims grew out of "that fundamental maxim upon which alone all property can be supported," it is clear that he thought a welfare right was a form of property right (pp. 18–19; 2:92).

The natural rights vocabulary and the idea of a state of nature which it contained did not imply to Thelwall any more than it did to Paine that individuals were to be thought of as originally or fundamentally solitary or egoistic creatures. As Paine had affirmed the existence of "social affections" (1:357), Thelwall believed that people always lived together in associations and were by nature "social and communicative" (p. 21). Thelwall used a state of nature to express the basic characteristics of the human personality and natural rights to express the moral equality of all human beings. Neither he nor Paine would have thought their use of rights led to a society of "atomistic" individuals.

Because individuals were morally equal, Thelwall thought of them as beginning with equal rights to the earth and its productions. Among these rights were those to the air, light, and water, none of which could ever be given up. "The actual produce of individual labor" could legitimately become private, Thelwall argued, but he insisted that labor be defined strictly and limited to physical exertion (2:28). Land also could become subject to exclusive rights but only through contracts to which reasonable people would have attached conditions. Thelwall argued that there were two conditions that would be attached to any agreement under which people would have given up their right to equal access to the land. The first would require that any system of private and unequal holdings serve the public interest. The second condition would be that individuals receive something in return for giving up their common rights. "Society," he wrote, "is responsible . . . for an equivalent for that which society has taken away" (2:77). Thelwall's rights to decency, plenty, and education were, then, the equivalents individuals should receive in an organized social setting for giving up the common rights to property they had in the state of nature. But Thelwall repeatedly insisted that he opposed leveling or a community of goods (p. 67; 2:70). Thus, once these two conditions were met, the inequality that developed was legitimate.

Thelwall added a historical dimension to his argument, at least in part, to break the hold of present property rules over the minds of his contemporaries. He began with a savage state in which people were primarily hunters and the earth was a common from which everyone took what was needed. The savage could be said to have a claim based on first possession in the deer he killed or fruit he picked. In this stage there was a virtual equality between men, though women were in a kind of slavery. The earth remained common in the pastoral stage, but the sheep people reared and cared for were legitimately owned by them. In this stage property could be accumulated, and therefore laws (or agreements) were needed to protect property. Thelwall did not give high praise to these early periods. Instead, he saw both the hunting and the pastoral stages as characterized by almost incessant wars as tribes fought to expand the land they controlled and used for hunting, fishing, and grazing. His unrelenting denigration of the second stage was meant to be a reply to Burke's praise of the German tribes from which English liberty was supposed to have derived (2:57–60).

Thelwall's history of the third stage, cultivation, was the center of his discussion. It was likely, he thought, that farming was at first a tribal activity in which land was owned by the tribe and was cultivated by all. Soon it was discovered that production would be increased if the land was divided and farmed by individuals who were allowed to keep what they produced (and presumably barter or sell any surplus). "Common expendiency" was the justification for dividing the land into shares, though it was understood that the land remained ultimately owned by the community (2:76). Shares were first divided equally, and as long as waste land existed, equality was preserved. For as children came of age they left the family share and began to farm reclaimed waste land. His assertion that originally the father's share was inherited by the youngest son because older brothers would have left the family for their own farms was certainly meant to deny any special status to primogeniture. With the disappearance of easily reclaimable waste, the father's property was inherited equally by all the children, male and female, old and young. So strong was the spirit of equality that the father would not have been allowed by the community to vary equal inheritance by more than a set amount. Thelwall mentioned the Swiss practice of allowing the father to choose one child to inherit half of the property, if reasons were given in the will, with the rest of the children splitting the other half equally. But since family sizes would differ, inequality was inevitable under any inheritance rules. And from these inequalities came even more disparities, as economic power was translated into political power. Corporations, charters, patents, and "the hideous—the barbarous—the unnatural law of primogeniture" (2:73) enabled so few to monopolize so much that the distinction between those who owned property and laborers who owned neither land nor tools came to dominate society. In setting out the depths to which his society had sunk, Thelwall moved close to a recognizably working-class critique:

> Machines would be invented and improvements made; not indeed, with the benevolent view of diminishing the toil of the labourer; but to furnish a cheaper substitute for manual industry, and thus increase, at once, the dependence of the cultivator, and the wasteful enjoyments of the employer. These arts and inventions as they threw advantages into the hands of the Capitalists would, of course, accelerate the progress of accumulation, till the labourers became so many and their wants so urgent, that mere competition must reduce them to absolute subjection, and destroy all chance of adequate compensation. (2:89)

Linking all attacks on privilege in this period was the idea of monopoly and the way education, political power, and productive resources were used by the few for their own benefit. But as monopoly robbed those who labored, the recognition of the "rights of labourers" would restore justice. Thelwall derived inclusive rights from three sources. The first was a birthright to an "equivalent" to what society had taken away through exclusive property rights in land. The second was derived from the mutual need of capital and labor for each other. Employers could not appeal to wage contracts entered into by propertyless laborers who had no alternative but starvation. Since it was precisely this situation of propertylessness that was illegitimate and in need of reform, contracts drawn up under its influence were "extortion" and not valid (2:79). Thus the laborer had a right, Thelwall argued, "to a share of the produce, not merely equal to his support, but, proportionate to the profits of the employer" (2:80). The third right he invoked was based on the conditions implied by civil association. Only if the institutions sanctioned by law benefited everyone could people be thought of as having agreed to join and obey the rules of the nation (2:80–81). A system of exclusive property rights in which many were landless, without work, and without government assistance violated the right all people had to be included in the wealth of the nation.

Though private property and some inequality could be made legitimate, Thelwall joined Wollstonecraft and Barlow in believing that property was held in too high esteem. Too easily, Thelwall wrote, did a veneration for property become "destructive to the morals and intellects of society [and] the source of all that oppressive rapacity and unfeeling avarice which produce so many vices in one description of men, and so much misery in another" (p. 42).

Although all the rights theories deployed against Burke defended private property, they did so in ways that made possible strong criticisms of many existing property rules and distributions. And though they were mostly concerned with large landholdings, their arguments were easily accommodated to emerging concentrations of capital. Theories of inclusive rights to property were not incidental to the rights theories of Paine, Barlow, and Thelwall. They were at the center of their attack on Burke and their understanding of the injustice of British society.[11] Though Thelwall and some of the other radicals of the 1790s became, or were seen as, increasingly moderate by the 1820s, their use against Burke of both the labor and consent arguments for inclusive property rights had a history independent of their intentions. Tenant farmers, agricultural laborers, artisans, and industrial workers could all insist that their labor was a property that entitled them to vote, that large concentrations of land or capital deprived others of the opportunity to labor, that the idle owners of land and capital were living off their efforts, and that no one could be understood to have agreed to obey laws that might require starvation or a life of abject poverty.

Ogilvie, Spence, and Skidmore

The position that common rights to the land could be legitimately resigned as long as they were returned in an equivalent form was not acceptable to all of the social critics of this period. The extent to which access to land remained central to ideas of freedom and independence into the nineteenth century can be seen in the agrarian radicalism of William Ogilvie, Thomas Spence, and Thomas Skidmore. But at the same time, the obvious improbability of their schemes for redistributing land illustrates the difficulty of using landownership to achieve increasing access to economic and political resources.

In 1764, when Adam Smith resigned his position at the University of Glasgow and Thomas Reid was hired to replace him, William Ogilvie (1736–1813) was given Reid's vacant position at the University of Aberdeen. After a year as the professor of philosophy, Ogilvie switched to the chair in humanities, where he remained until his retirement. Ogilvie had been a student at Glasgow when both Smith and Adam Ferguson were lecturing there and can be presumed to have heard them. For three years he and Reid, the Scottish philosopher most sympathetic to the idea of welfare rights, were colleagues at Aberdeen and for the rest of their lives they were good friends. His most famous student was James Mackintosh, author of the anti-Burke tract *Vindiciae Gallicae*. In 1781 Ogilvie published anonymously *The Rights of Property in Land*. James Mackintosh accurately described this book when he wrote that it was "full of benevolence and ingenuity, but not the work of a man experienced in the difficult art of realising projects for the good of mankind."[12]

The agrarianism of William Ogilvie is another indication that interpretations of Locke developed just as Rutherforth feared they would. Ogilvie understood Locke's comment about the "industrious and rational" to be directed against landlords who owned land but did not cultivate it, not the poor whose idleness was forced on them by the distribution of property. It was wrong, Ogilvie wrote, for the land to be "appropriated in such a manner as that, when not more than half cultivated, the further cultivation and improvement should be stopped short, and the industry of millions willing to employ themselves in rendering the earth more fertile should be excluded from its proper field, and denied any parcel of the soil, on which it could be exercised, with security of reaping its full produce and just reward" (p. 9). Not surprisingly, Ogilvie had a special enmity for absentee landlords who had inherited their estates. Ogilvie adopted both the idea that the earth was given to mankind in common and the argument that individuals can come to have property rights in land only through their labor. But according to Ogilvie, the common grant of the earth limited the labor argument and could not completely give way to it. Thus no individual through his labor could come to hold by natural right any more land than all others could also own. Land held in excess of the equal share was held by municipal law, not natural law (pp. 7–8). Ogilvie's goal was not to divide the land into equal shares but to guarantee to everyone a share (once specified by him as forty acres) to farm as an independent owner. He also seemed to have had no interest in limiting inequalities of movable property. He did make provision for individuals to alienate their right to land, but he explicitly denied that this alienation could occur through tacit consent. Only an express contract entered into at "a mature age, after having been in actual possession, or having had a free opportunity of entering into the possession of his equal share" would be valid (p. 9). Even then Ogilvie insisted that governments should make it possible for people who alienated their share to reclaim their birthright.

To defend the power of the public authority that this plan required, he pointed to many current English practices, including eminent domain, land taxes, and the Poor Law. According to Ogilvie, "England virtually acknowledges, by the system of its poor laws, that right of common occupation of the territory of the state which belongs to every individual citizen" (p. 36). But Ogilvie believed that the Poor Law recognized this right in an ineffective form. The poor, he asserted, wanted a farm, not relief.

Perhaps because of his years with Smith and Ferguson at Glasgow, Ogilvie constructed his own theory about the development of property. He distinguished between three stages of property owning—"the domestic, the feudal, and the commercial." But instead of a progressive history, Ogilvie presented each stage as worse than the one before. The situation of small farmers had become increasingly desperate, he believed, because of a decline in paternalism. In the first and second stages "the affectionate sympathy of the chief" protected the cultivators, whereas in the commercial state the chief "has hardly any obvious interest but to squeeze his industry as much as he can" (p. 44). Thus in a commercial society the small cultivator was especially in need of legislative protection.

The paternalist nature of Ogilvie's work is just as evident in the way he envisioned the enactment of an agrarian law. He listed as occasions that would be favorable to reforming property laws "conquering princes," "heros," "new colonies," "a wise and benevolent sovereign," and a "great monarch" (pp. 43–50). Aside from the unlikelihood of such heroes emerging, it is striking that almost all of these occasions were based on a revolution from above. Ogilvie insisted that those whose property was taken to be redistributed to the poor should "receive rents from the new owner" and, even more astonishing in a writer included in histories of socialism, he wrote that "every person who has acquired an allotment of land in this manner shall to the lord of the manor owe certain aids and services of a feudal nature, so regulated as to produce that degree of connection and dependence which may be expedient for preserving order and subordination" (p. 100). The closest (though not only) descendants of William Ogilvie were the Tory paternalists of the early nineteenth century, whose concern for the poor led them to champion allotment schemes in which the uncultivated land of large landowners was rented to families.

William Ogilvie's book did not reach a large audience, as was noted by Thomas Spence in his description of it as "a very important book too little noticed."[13] Spence is often paired with Ogilvie in discussions of early socialism, though neither had any interest in nationalizing property. Ogilvie's goal was to spread private property to more small farmers, and Spence's was to assert local or parish control over land so that it could be rented in parcels appropriate for single families to farm. Both were self-conscious proponents of an agrarian law, which they expressed as a moral requirement by using the language of inclusive property rights.

Spence's pamphleteering on behalf of land reform spanned the period from 1775 to 1814 and included *The Real Rights of Man* (1775), *Pig's Meat* (1793–96), *The Rights of Infants* (1797), and *Restorer of Society to Its Natural State* (1799). He was arrested more than once for his activities as a writer and publisher, spending seven months in jail in 1794 and twelve months in jail in 1801. In the 1790s he was a member of the London Corresponding Society, the most important radical democratic movement of the time. Spence was also interested in the reform of the alphabet and in 1803 published an account of his trial in a phonetic alphabet of his own creation.[14] A recent appraisal of him as a "radical crank" captures some of his eccentricities but not the wide interest in his schemes by both fellow radicals and the authorities that lasted well into the nineteenth century.[15]

The relationship between the enclosure of common land, at its height in the 1760s and 1770s, and the discussion of property rights was clearly expressed in Spence's work. In fact, his entire corpus may have been based on a single event that occurred in 1771, the Newcastle Town Moor Act, under which part of the town moor was enclosed and cultivated. The passions aroused by this event and the way a vocabulary of common property was essential to its interpretation can be seen in the words of Spence's mentor, the Reverend James Murray:

> In the land of Moab . . . every inch of ground was claimed by some engrosser, and the cautious surveyor marked out every common, which formerly was as free as the light of the sun and the air. . . . From a pretence of improving waste and common lands, the grandees of Moab obtained laws to have them divided; but then those

who had no estates joining to those commons, received no dividend, and were deprived of the means of support which naturally belonged to them. The idea of a common suggests at once, that it belongs to all within the district, and cannot be divided, without giving every one his proper share. The original design of a commons was, that those who had no separate lands of their own, might have a common estate with so many others; and formerly, it is highly probable that every township had a common which was the poor man's estate, as well as that of the rich. Moab never had a day to do well after the covetous landlords monopolized the common lands. The legislature in Moab might as well have made a law for the rich to divide their estates with the poor, as to have made acts of parliament to oblige the poor to part with a privilege, to which they had a prescriptive right. The claims of freedom and liberty ended with the division of the common.[16]

Spence read widely, if not deeply, and drew on the biblical and commonwealth traditions (James Harrington, in particular), as well as the work of Locke. Thus he made use of the Jubilee described in Leviticus 25:10 and of Deuteronomy 15:1–2 in which debts were forgiven every seven years. In a sense, the argument of Spence and all the agrarians was much like the one Filmer made 125 years earlier, though of course they drew opposite conclusions. Filmer had argued that if the earth was given to man as a common to which all had equal rights, private property could not justly be introduced. Since private property was beyond question for Filmer, the conclusion had to be that the original grant was not in the form of a common. Spence also used the apparent contradiction between an original common and private property, but to him it was the original common that was beyond question and private property that was illegitimate. Thus, assuming that "the country of any people, in a native state, is properly their common, in which each has an equal property," Spence asked if it were "lawful, reasonable and just, for this people to sell, or make a present even, of the whole of their country, or common, to whom they will, to be held by them and their heirs for ever."[17] Spence argued that the natural right to preservation held by everyone precluded land (as the means to preservation) from becoming the private property of a few. Consent could not legitimate private property because the living had no power to give away what was not entirely theirs. "For the right to deprive anything of the means of living, supposes a right to deprive it of life; and this right ancestors are not supposed to have over their posterity" (p. 6). Nor could labor be used to justify private property in land because labor did not create land. Only arrogance prompted the first people who claimed land to act "as if they had manufactured it and it had been the work of their own hands" (p. 7). Land, then, like rights to air, light, and the heat of the sun, was among the "common gifts of nature" to which all had an equal claim (p. 10).

In the 1790s Spence expanded his critique and began to investigate in more depth the link between private property and political power. His plea for a freer press, wider franchise, and lower taxes, as well as his antipathy to war, were all part of the radical politics of this period. Spence was unique, however, in finding the source of all corruption in the private and unequal ownership of land. From their monopoly of land the rich were able to control government, to raise taxes, to fund places and pensions, to prohibit the publication of ideas they found dangerous, and to fight wars that were to their advantage. The public debt and the standing army were easily added to this list. The government's indictment against Spence in 1801 was certainly correct in saying that his intention was "to cause the subjects to think and believe that the ownership and enjoyment of land in the country by the present owners and proprietors . . . are the causes of great evil and oppression to the People of this Realm."[18]

Spence's solution to England's problems varied as little as the other parts of his philosophy throughout his life. It too was formed and given expression in his 1775 pamphlet *The Real Rights of Man*. Spence suggested that each parish constitute itself as a corporation and as the sole owner of all the land contained within its boundaries. The most important consequence of this act would be to turn present owners into renters who would pay their rent to the parish, which would then spend it according to the votes of all the adults. As the owner of all the land, the parish could let out its land in "very small farms" to increase employment. With the rent it collected Spence expected the parish to relieve its poor (who would be few under his scheme), build and repair bridges and highways, reclaim waste land, pay the salaries of public officials, and arm a militia. In *The Right of Infants* (1797) he envisioned that after all these activities were funded there would be an "overplus" that should be "divided fairly and equally among all the living souls in the parish."[19] And in the *Restorer of Society to Its Natural State* he added that part of the rent should go to fund schools and to purchase grain for a public granary to guard against famine.[20]

There are two important points in Spence's plan. The first is that it was not a land nationalization scheme. "I would not have the land national, nor provincial," he wrote in the *Restorer of Society*, "but parochial property, that the people might be as interested as possible, both in the improvements of their estates, which thus would be always under their eye, and in the expenditure of all public monies" (p. 40). Spence was a critic of individually owned private property, but he was just as antagonistic to the idea of property owned by the nation and administered by a national institution. Like so many radicals of this period, Spence could not help but identify national power with oppression. The second point is that this scheme left a great deal of inequality untouched. Though he was prepared in the *Restorer* simply to confiscate land (the people should not pay compensation when they were simply taking back what was theirs), he left the wealthy "their money, plates, jewels, furniture, apparel, cattle, and moveable effects of every kind" (p. 44). The right to property, according to Spence, was a right to land or to the rent derived from the land; it was not a more general right to economic equality. Spence still saw land standing in a special relationship to self-preservation and to independence.

Spence was no more successful than Ogilvie in explaining how "Spensonia" (as he sometimes called his utopia, situated between "Utopia and Osheana") would be achieved. Whereas Ogilvie put his misplaced hopes in a revolution from above, Spence put his in a peaceful and spontaneous uprising from below. "But how is this mighty work to be done?" he asked in *Restorer of Society*. "I answer it must be done at once. For it will be sooner done at once than at twice or a hundred times. For the public mind being suitably prepared by reading my little tracts and conversing on the subject, a few contiguous parishes have only to declare the land to be theirs and form a convention of parochial delegates" (p. 29). Only in a single passage written in 1795 did he note the possibility that force would be needed to defend the parishes that carried out these changes.[21]

In the turbulent years between 1816 and 1820 Spence's ideas were revived by his friend and former London Corresponding Society member Thomas Evans. Like Spence, Evans had been imprisoned, first in 1796 and again in 1817. His *Christian Policy, the Salvation of the Empire* was published and went through two editions in 1816. According to Evans, the solution to the economic problems England was experiencing in the aftermath of the Napoleonic Wars was to declare England "the People's Farm" (the Spenceans' favorite phrase). He advanced Spence's plan for each parish to declare itself the owner of its land and to convert all titles to leaseholds with the parish the recipient of all rents. Evans did not envision the redistribution of property so much as he thought rents paid to the parish would result in annual dividends paid to every individual in England.[22]

Although Spence and Evans showed a great deal of respect for Paine, a considerable distance separated their demands from Paine's more moderate reforms. The first confrontation between these traditions was instigated by Spence in his pamphlet *The Rights of Infants*, to which he added comments on Paine's *Agrarian Justice*. Though Spence began by praising Paine for joining Locke and the Bible in acknowledging that "God hath given the earth ... to mankind in common," he quickly added that the conclusions that Paine drew from this premise were completely unsatisfactory. He called the payments Paine wanted to provide to the poor "contemptible and insulting" and characterized Paine's plan as an "execrable fabric of comprimissory expediency." Paine had argued that only 10 to 20 percent of the value of the land was appropriately public, with the rest justifiably private because of the improvements made by individual owners. Spence denied this division of the value of the land. Who actually did the improving, he asked? Was it the proprietor alone or was he aided by laborers? And were not improvements made because of the demand for agricultural products by the laborers and their families? In at least one area Spence thought Paine's plan was a step backward. With some prescience Spence understood that Paine's hope to create a kind of welfare state and, at the same time, to diminish the size and influence of the national government was impossible. "All the complexities of the present public establishments, which support such hosts of placemen, will not only still continue, but also the evils of them will be greatly enhanced by the very system of Agrarian Justice." Spence saw Paine's plan as reforming, rather than destroying, the present system. Thus Spence argued that under Paine's proposals taxes and monopolies would continue, the poor would still exist, and the aristocracy would stay in place.[23]

The radical politics of the 1840s in England gave birth to a more practical attempt at land reform. But the Chartist Land Company under Feargus O'Connor was never able to overcome the problems of his personality or the difficulties of raising enough money from working-class people to buy land that could be farmed economically.[24] Although it may seem that agrarianism was inevitably a critique rooted in the past and bound to fail in the industrial society of the nineteenth century, this was not altogether so. In America agrarianism and the work of Thomas Spence were not just influential but in a way victorious, which can be seen by a quick excursion (or detour) through the work of Thomas Skidmore and George Henry Evans.

Thomas Skidmore's *Rights of Man to Property* (1829) is one of the most comprehensive defenses agrarianism ever received. Skidmore was a machinist who helped start the New York Working Men's party in the year his book was published. He came very close to being elected to the state assembly on the Working Men's ticket that year. Hostility to the inequalities of private property was widespread among the mechanics of New York City during this period. Cornelius Blatchly expressed the opinion of many when he criticized "that selfish system of exclusive rights to property, power, and respect" and argued for its replacement by "a system of social, equal, and inclusive rights, interests, liberties, and priviledges to all real and personal property."[25]

The debate in America was in part shaped by its own natural law tradition, with its affirmation of inalienable rights to "life, liberty, and the pursuit of happiness." Needless to say, artisan radicals had no difficulty turning that last phrase to their own purposes. "If each be entitled to pursue his own happiness," one critic wrote, "whatever institutions or systems, that do not freely admit of equal participation, and equal access to equal exertions, must be at variance with the incontrovertible truth of the foregoing proposition."[26] Skidmore praised Thomas Jefferson, but so sure was he that property theory provided the structure of thought most likely to lead to the redistribution of land that he wanted property to take the place of "pursuit of happiness" in the Declaration of Independence.[27] Skidmore also had lavish praise for Paine but found fault with his attempt to construct a social contract that would be acceptable to both rich and poor. He asked how "so sagacious a writer as Paine" could err so greatly as to attempt "to erect an equal government, upon a foundation where inequality had already found an existence" (p. 67).

Skidmore maintained that rights to exclude could come only from the consent of others. In organized society people had property rights only because government and law—the legal expression of the people's consent—made them possible. Exclusive property rights were never simply natural facts that had to be accepted, he argued; they were social creations that reflected choice and decision. To maintain that consent alone could give title required that Skidmore confront the arguments that derived property from labor, possession, or occupancy. Against all these he used the idea that a positive community could be divided only by consent. Considering the example of a savage making a bow, Skidmore argued that "the material, of which the bow is made, is the property of mankind. It is a property, too, which, previous to the existence of government, has never been alienated to anyone. If it has not been alienated, it cannot belong to another . . . what right then had that other, to bestow his labor upon it. . . . Instead of acquiring a right, thereby, to the bow, he has rather committed a trespass upon the great community of which he is a member" (p. 33). Skidmore pushed his argument to its conclusion by maintaining that the savage should be punished for his act rather than gaining title to a new bow by it. By the same logic, he denied that cultivating a field conferred title to the field or to any of its productions.

Whereas the consent of others was the basis for the right to exclude, the right to be included was required by the common ownership of the earth. For as a co-owner in a positive community each person had an equal right to the benefits of the land. Skidmore's position was perfectly summarized in his revision of Descartes: "I am; therefore, property is mine" (p. 357). Individuals were no more capable of alienating this right than they would be of alienating their right to life or to parts of their body. It was "the Creator of the Universe" who furnished the earth and "ordered it to be distributed equally" (p. 43). Society stood as a trustee guarding the common estate and seeing that all legatees received the share to which they were entitled.

But nothing was further from Skidmore's mind than the amount of social control we associate with a government capable of redistributing property on a grand scale. Thus, though property was legally owned by the nation, it was administered through individual shares. Skidmore's most deeply held values were individualism, the dignity of labor, and fear of large economic and public institutions. In his mind, individuals would be able to protect themselves and to reap the benefits of their labor only if they had their own property: "I take it to be a truth not to be controverted, that each individual knows better how to apply his own industry, his own facilities, advantages, opportunities, property, etc. than government can possibly do" (p. 80).

Skidmore's plan for the redistribution of property currently held was extremely complicated, in its own way as strange as Ogilvie's hero worship or Spence's Jubilee. But agrarianism in America was saved by the existence of public lands, legally owned by all, that could be distributed, instead of having to be redistributed. George Henry Evans became the major spokesman for the view that these lands should be open to settlers free of charge. Evans became editor of the *Working Man's Advocate* in 1829 and dedicated it for a short time to spreading Skidmore's ideas of land reform. After its collapse, Evans continued at the center of radical political activity through the publication of his daily *Man* in the 1830s and the *Radical* in 1841. Not only would opening public lands to settlement benefit the many who would farm the land, he argued it would also enable eastern workingmen, who would be no longer in oversupply, to strike bargains with their employers that would more accurately reflect the value of the work they did.[28] "Vote Yourself a Farm" became his slogan. His position was summarized in the first issue of the *Radical*.

> That the use of the LAND is the equal natural right of all the citizens of this and all future generations, and therefore that the land should not be a matter of traffic, gift, or will. In other words, that the land is not transferable like the products of man's labor. From which it will be inferred that I consider the institution of property in land to be the great error . . . which makes labor subject to the landlords, contracts the sphere of its operation, and deprives it of its just reward.[29]

Evans drew heavily on the work of Thomas Spence, whom he was reported to have met in England before he traveled to America. The July 1841 *Radical*, for example, was given over almost entirely to a reprint of Spence's *Real Rights of Man*.

So important did the movement for the free settlement of public lands become that the 1852 Free Democratic party platform stated, "That all men have a natural right to a portion of the soil; and that, as the use of the soil is indispensable to life, the right of all men to the soil is as sacred as their right to life itself."[30] The agrarian tradition finally achieved success in America with the Homestead Act. Though it is a historical oversimplification to move from Spence to the Homestead Act, one American historian has concluded, "Out of these reflections inspired by Skidmore, came the land reform movement of the 1840s and 1850s that played so great a role in winning passage of the Homestead Act during the Civil War."[31]

Carlile and Cobbett

A little over twenty years after Spence's criticism of Paine, another encounter took place between these two strands of the radical tradition. One of the most important of the radical papers in the period around 1820 was Richard Carlile's *Republican*. Carlile championed the usual list of demands—universal suffrage, annual parliaments, lower taxes, free speech, and the repudiation of the debt to fundholders. But in considering the question of taxes and in recommending a single tax on land as the most just and efficient way to raise money, he came to compliment the Spenceans and, in particular, Evans's *Christian Policy*. He gave a brief outline of their plan (erroneously neglecting to differentiate between nationalizing the land and putting it in the hands of the parish) and concluded that though it could not be introduced in a country that already had private property, the same ends could be achieved through a land tax.[32] He developed his views on a single land tax in more detail in 1822. Property in land, he held, was different from movable property because the latter resulted wholly from individual industry. But "land . . . is a public property which the public or people can never justly suffer to be monopolized." Since not everyone can own land in a populous country, the revenues from a land tax "must be considered as a rental, or a payment from those who hold to those who do not hold." The productions of industry were necessarily private, according to Carlile, and could not be taxed, but land, ultimately public, was held only conditionally, by the law of the land, and should bear the public's expenses (vol. 6, December 1822).

In 1824 Carlile published an exchange between himself and another Spencean, Allan Davenport. But this time conflict rather than compliments surfaced. Carlile, the deist and staunch supporter of Paine's *Age of Reason*, objected to Davenport's invocation of God's intentions that there should be "an absolute equality in land." Carlile responded, "It ranks among the class of absurdities, to be ever saying that an almighty power intends that which is never brought about" (vol. 10, October 1824). Radical Christianity was always a powerful element in Spence and his followers and anathema to the deist Carlile. But their real disagreement was over the justice of unequal private property holdings in land. Davenport echoed Spence's belief that Paine did not go far enough in recognizing the completely public nature of land and therefore did not take equality seriously enough. Equality, for Davenport, did not mean that everyone should own a plot of the same size. Rather, it required that individual ownership be abolished, that rent from the land be spent in ways that benefited the public, and that all persons receive an equal cash payment as their share of joint ownership. "Why should not every child that is born in the country be entitled at its birth, to a revenue from the state, from the common farm, from the productions of the earth." It was especially important to Davenport's argument against Carlile that freedom required this economic equality. Thus he denied that universal suffrage by itself, within a system of great economic inequality, could guarantee liberty.

Throughout Davenport's essay Carlile provided footnotes indicating his objections. In general, Carlile maintained that all the advantages of the Spencean system would be achieved in a system of private property, universal suffrage, and a single tax on land. If the people controlled government, its expenses would be greatly reduced and all the money necessary could be easily raised through a small tax on those who owned land. Such a system also would better respect labor and industry. Moreover, it escaped the charge he leveled against Davenport of creating a nation of "Royal Families," that is, of fostering idleness through the payments to which everyone would be entitled. Carlile, then, adopted the idea that some of the value of the land was independent of individual exertion and for that reason properly belonged to the community, but he did not accept either Paine's idea of making small cash payments to the poor or Davenport's idea of distributing revenues to everyone as joint owners of the land.

By far the most important carrier of Paine's critique of corruption and taxation into the volatile period after the end of the Napoleonic Wars was William Cobbett. So enormous was his impact that E. P. Thompson has written, "It was Cobbett who created radical intellectual culture" in England.[33] In the winter of 1816–17 his paper the *Two Penny Register* had a weekly circulation of between forty and sixty thousand. Throughout the 1820s his books and pamphlets sold between fifty and two hundred thousand copies. Though his relationship to Paine was complicated, in the period of Cobbett's life and work with which we are concerned, his veneration for Paine is nicely captured in the fact that he brought Paine's bones back to England when he returned from America in 1819.

The question of whether Cobbett was nostalgic or prophetic, Tory or democrat is not of concern here. It is beyond doubt that he failed to assimilate the new language of political economy into his work and that his targets remained roughly similar to those of Paine. His champions were "artisans," "laborers," "shopkeepers," and "coal miners,"[34] and his most deeply held values were individualism and independence. It is not surprising, given the tradition from which he emerged, his supporters, and his values, that he did not call into question the legitimacy of private property. But it is the purpose of this short discussion of his work from 1817 to 1834 to demonstrate the extent to which he used the natural law discussion of property to attack the large holdings of the rich and defend the right of the poor to relief. Cobbett is often portrayed as basing his arguments entirely on his sense of custom and constitutional rights, but so pervasive and powerful was the language of natural rights in discussions of property that their use could not be avoided even by someone self-consciously attempting to defend England from the dangerous innovations of political economy and industry. The importance of Cobbett's argument can be gathered from Herbert Spencer's comment later in the century that it was Cobbett who had "popularized" the idea that the Poor Law was based on a "right" which "everyone has . . . to a maintenance out of the soil."[35]

Cobbett's primary concern with property in his *Weekly Political Register* of 1818–20 was to identify it with the labor of those who worked with their hands so that all the respect and privileges traditionally given to landed property in English political life would be extended to those who were excluded. Of course, this was one of the major themes of the tradition from Paine to Cobbett and it was one of the most important legacies of Locke's identification of property with labor in the *Second Treatise*. Aside from making the laboring class more respectable, Cobbett was able to use this position to score some specific points. For example, if labor was "an absolute possession; an ownership complete and unlimited," then it, like all other forms of property, should be taxable only with the owner's consent. Taxing laborers, whose property was not represented, especially to pay interest on the debt, was stealing from the poor to give to the rich (vol. 34, January 1819). Seeing labor as property was also central to defending the rights of labor to strike, a situation understood by Cobbett as one in which people chose to keep rather than to sell their property at a price they thought was too low. "You have labour to sell," he wrote to laborers. "You demand a certain price for it. Those who are in the practice of buying your labour think this price is too high. They refuse to purchase at your price, you keep your labour unsold. Well! What is there in all this contrary to the principles either of natural equity, or of law" (vol. 34, December 1818)? Cobbett's insistence that the sole foundation of property was labor easily led to a criticism of absentee landlords and ultimately to his recommendation that those who rented and worked small farms should be made their owners (vol. 34, March 1819).

Of all the objects of Cobbett's scorn, "Parson Malthus," to use Cobbett's phrase, occupied a special place. That no one else represented so completely the forces against which Cobbett fought can be seen in his comment to Malthus: "I have, during my life, detested many men; but never any one as much as you" (vol. 34, May 1819). Cobbett used these words to open an essay in his *Register* entitled "To Parson Malthus, On the Rights of the Poor." This topic did not consume him as much in the *Register* as it would later, but it was nevertheless present. He refused to blame the poor for their poverty and attacked those who did. He opposed workhouses and declared that poor relief was neither a gift nor a favor (vol. 36, February 1820). He asserted that the right to relief would have been insisted upon at the creation of the social contract (vol. 34, March 1819) and hinted that revolution or at least legitimate taking was justified if the just claims to relief were not met (vol. 35, October 1819).

In the late 1820s and early 1830s, when Poor Law reform became a pressing political issue, Cobbett returned to these themes in more detail. In his *History of the Protestant Reformation* (1829) he argued that the Poor Law was a necessary response to the destruction of the English Catholic church and its system of poor relief. His nostalgic view of English history is evident from his statement that before the Reformation England was "the happiest country that the world has ever seen."[36] But that was ended when "those great estates [managed by the Catholic church] which of right belonged to the poorer classes, had been taken from them" (1:para. 331). When large amounts of land were owned by the church, the revenues it produced were spent on people in the parish. Absentee ownership was unknown, leases were on easy terms, and land never passed into the hands of "squandering heirs." In short, "titles, and every other species of income of the clergy, were looked upon, and were, in fact and in practice, more the property of the poor than of the Monk, nuns, priests, and bishops" (2:para. 18).

As landed property fell into the hands of private individuals and families, the revenues produced by the land were used less to maintain the people than to buy luxuries for the rich. The number of beggars and vagabonds increased dramatically, and they required government assistance. The Reformation "despoiled the working classes of their patrimony; it tore from them that which nature and reason had assigned them; it robbed them of that relief for the necessitous, which was theirs by right imprescriptable, and which had been confirmed to them by the law of God and the law of the land" (1:para. 127). That the government assistance that began with Elizabeth was paid for out of a land tax seemed appropriate to Cobbett, for it was because the poor were excluded from the land that they needed relief. Cobbett surveyed the state of the poor from Elizabeth to his own time with a special interest in the proposals put forward to control or help them. Most of these recommendations for change seemed to him to have involved attempts by the wealthy to punish the poor and to escape their own obligations. Cobbett's strategy was obviously to link the current effort to change the Poor Law with these past efforts and to characterize them all as violations of the rights of the poor. The poor, he wrote against Hume, did not receive alms but "what they have a right to by the laws of nature" (2:para. 19).

Cobbett's defense of the Old Poor Law rested at least as much on the idea of a natural right as on an ancient English legal claim. It is important, then, that the natural law discussion of property had developed in such a way that he and others could use it as a powerful (even indispensable) weapon in defense of Old Poor Law and the welfare rights of the poor. Thus in Cobbett's most sustained discussion of welfare rights, *The Poor Man's Friend* (1829), he relied heavily on the contract justification of property found in Grotius and Pufendorf. "Now let us hear what that Grotius and that Pufendorf say; let us hear what these great writers on the laws of nature and nations say," Cobbett announced as he began his refutation of Blackstone.[37] And he proceeded to quote two pages from Grotius and three from Pufendorf on the origin of property and the right of necessity.

In *The Poor Man's Friend*, Cobbett argued that a poor law was neither a prudential measure nor an act of social charity; it was required by the rights that people would have insisted upon at the origin of society. Cobbett used the idea that the earth was originally a common and that private property was instituted through a contract to maintain that those about to give up their rights to use the common would have insisted on the right of necessity. Cobbett seemed to suggest that the creation of civil society required another contract. In this contract those with as well as those without property (but with the right of necessity) would have agreed to obey the laws of civil society and to fight for it in time of war only if it were guaranteed that anyone who became destitute would have a right to be supported by the others. The first contract established rights to property and to necessity, while the second established government and changed the right of necessity from a liberty to a claim on the wealth of others that the state would enforce:

> No man will contend, that the main body of the people, in any country upon earth, and, of course, in England, would have consented to abandon the rights of nature; to give up their right to enjoy all things in common; no one will believe, that the main body of the people would ever have given their assent to the establishing of a state of things which should make all the lands, and all the trees, and all the goods and cattle of every sort, private property; which should have shut out a large part of the people from having such property, and which would, at the same time, not have provided the means of preventing those of them, who might fall into indigence, from being actually starved to death! It is impossible to believe this. Men never gave their assent to enter into society on terms like these. (Para. 47)

If the right of necessity was central to the legitimacy of private property and if state-supported aid was central to the legitimacy of civil society, Cobbett argued that the abolition of government aid would first free the destitute from any obligation to obey the law (and serve in the armed forces, for example) and then, if they were unable to obtain private assistance, from any obligation to respect others' property. The specter raised by Cobbett was that of morally lawful looting of the rich by the poor if the Poor Law was not maintained:

> Now I beg you to mark well what I say, if civil society get into such a state, that men cannot, by their labour, provide themselves and families with a sufficiency of food and of raiment; if, at the same time, there be no magistrate, or other person, having authority to take from the rich and to give to the suffering poor, a sufficiency to preserve them against the natural effects of hunger and of cold: if (mark well what I say) civil society get into this state, then the law of nature, as far as regards the destitute person, returns in its full force. My loaf is no longer exclusively mine: it is yours, as much as it is mine; and you, if you be amongst the destitute persons, are held to have a right to take as much of my loaf as you want to relieve yourself, so that you do not expose me to suffer from want. (Para. 34)

The power of Cobbett's analysis here can be appreciated only by realizing that this discussion of the right of necessity was no longer merely theoretical as it had been for so long in the modern natural law tradition. In the English countryside machines were being destroyed, barns and houses were being burned.[38]

In one of Cobbett's last works, *Legacy to Labourers* (1834), he made it clear that in his view the only absolute and inalienable right to property was the inclusive right to subsistence. All exclusive rights to property were established by government and were subject to limits. His assertion that landlords did not have the right to do whatever they wanted with their land was part of his criticism of enclosures and a justification for a land tax to support the Poor Law. The property rights of landlords, he insisted, were limited by the rights of others to subsistence. The rhetorical questions he posed at the beginning of his chapters (or letters as he called them) capture his argument:

—Letter IV. Have the landlords dominion in their lands? Or, do they lawfully possess only the use of them?
—Letter V. Can the landlords use their lands so as to drive the natives from them?
—Letter VI. Can the landlords rightfully use the land so as to cause the natives to perish of hunger or cold?

Not surprisingly, Grotius and Pufendorf (on the right of necessity), Locke ("God has not left one man so to the mercy"), and Paley ("The poor have a claim") were cited extensively. Even though the New Poor Law would not abolish aid, its attempt to make it more difficult to receive was incompatible with Cobbett's sense that the rights of the poor required that relief be given in a manner that showed them respect. The radical tradition may not have thought well of the Old Poor Law, but when its abolition became a possibility, and when its replacement by the workhouse of the New Poor Law became likely, radicals of all kinds came to its defense by linking aid to the requirements of natural law.

The emphasis on industry in the tradition from Paine to Cobbett was directed against the idle rich. And though it may have been possible to direct similar criticism toward the unemployed poor, in general this did not happen. Not only was there little political reason to turn the critique downward, but there seems to have been no sense that any substantial group existed that was destitute by choice. Vagrants, beggars, and drunks were the concerns (or symbols) of Mill and Martineau, not Thelwall or Cobbett. The idle poor were unemployed, Cobbett and his predecessors argued, because the economic resources of the nation—land, machines, wealth, and education—were monopolized by too few. And these monopolies, they argued, violated the inclusive property rights of others.

Hall, Hodgskin, Thompson, and the Poor Man's Guardian

In moving from analysis of Paine and Cobbett to that of Charles Hall, William Thompson, and Thomas Hodgskin we are supposed to be crossing an important divide in the history of social criticism. That these three are often referred to as Ricardian Socialists captures the argument that their critique was based on the categories of political economy and for that reason better understood the capitalist society growing around them. Patricia Hollis has aptly noted that their critique was of exploitation rather than land theft or corruption.[39] They located the cause of working-class misery within economic activity and no longer thought of political corruption (the debt and taxes) as the cause of poverty and inequality. Their attention was less on the owner of land than on the owner of capital, less on the farm, the landless, and the unemployed than on the factory and the working poor.

Without denying the historical importance of their attempt to find a radically critical edge to classical political economy, it is wrong to ignore the crucial role that the natural right to property played in the thought of these writers. Only a property theory that contained an explanation of legitimate and illegitimate appropriation could provide the reason why the term *exploitation* was appropriately used to describe working for an employer. That is, a theory of property first had to explain why laborers were rightfully entitled to the complete product of their labor before moral outrage could be expressed because they did not receive it.[40]

The first step toward a theory of exploitation is often credited to Charles Hall. His book *The Effects of Civilization on the People in European States* first published in 1805, was reprinted in 1813, 1820, and 1850.[41] A rural medical practice brought him into contact with the poor, and he witnessed firsthand the conditions of their poverty. In 1807 Hall engaged in a short correspondence with Thomas Spence, each of them sending two letters to the other. In addition to the personal information contained in his two letters, Hall provided information about his social views. Hall, like so many others in the early nineteenth century, exhibited an odd combination of nostalgia and criticism. He wrote to

Spence that "I think that what we should aim at should be to go back a good way towards our ancestral state: to that point from which we strayed." He defined the point before England strayed as one in which property was divided so that no one had more than another. Thus Hall criticized Spence for wanting to equalize only the land and not all forms of wealth. Although his own vision was more egalitarian than Spence's, he had no suggestion for how to bring it about other than to convince "both the rich and the poor." Spence, on the other hand, accused Hall of following Thomas More in wanting to nationalize all property, which would lead, Spence argued, to putting everyone "to work under guard masters."[42]

The self-conscious nostalgia expressed by Hall in these letters seems infertile ground in which to find new forms of social criticism. And a great many of the themes expressed in *The Effects of Civilization* exhibit his veneration for a previous period. He was antagonistic to manufacturing and foreign trade. His ideal was a nation of small farmers, he placed his hope for reform in the wealthy, and he seemed to have found more inspiration from the Old Testament than any other source.[43] Like Spence, he wrote approvingly of the Jubilee.

But it was precisely because he was so antagonistic to manufacturing that he attempted to demonstrate that it and international trade were largely responsible for the dire circumstances of the poor. His analysis of the contracts that were entered into between those who provided materials and those who labored began with the denial that these contracts were voluntary or that they served the interests of both parties. Instead, he characterized them as entered into by the laborer because of "an absolute necessity." "The manufacturer," Hall wrote, "forces his workmen to work for him and to give him a share of what the work produces . . . for the poor are under a necessity of working for him on terms held out, or go without the things on which they subsist" (p. 72). Because the laborer must work or starve, the capitalist obtains the goods produced "for less than their full value" and therefore "takes part of the fruits of the labor of the poor" (p. 70). Profits occurred because the capitalist sold goods made by the laborer for much more than he had to pay the laborer to produce them. With the profits extracted from these forced contracts the capitalist was able to hire more laborers and extract more profit. By Hall's various reckonings, the poor spent only one day in a workweek producing goods that equaled the value of their weekly wages; the rest of the time they produced for the capitalist. Could the capitalist be said to provide anything to the laborer? Hall said no. "The poor produces by his labor almost everything that the rich man eats, drinks, and wears. . . . Now, what does the rich man produce for the use of the poor man? Precisely none of all the things mentioned" (pp. 100–101). But not only did the capitalist extract more labor from the workers than he paid for, he did so by employing them in the production of luxury goods. Manufacturing, then, took people who could be producing the necessities they needed and diverted their labor to producing luxury goods they could not use and the rich did not need. His nostalgia is again evident in his belief that the absence of manufacturing during feudalism meant that during that period the poor enjoyed a higher standard of living than they did in the early nineteenth century. International trade seemed to him to involve mostly sending out of the country what the poor needed and importing consumption goods for the wealthy. To all this can be added his argument that the wealthy controlled government and used it to maintain their domination.

That the contracts entered into by labor and capital resulted in inequality may be admitted without obvious moral embarrassment. Hall understood this and confronted directly the utilitarian argument that inequalities of wealth were necessary to move indolent people to exertion (p. 50). His target was the utilitarian defense of private property he identified with Hume and Paley, whose famous pigeon statement he nevertheless quoted in its entirety and with approval. Hall first denied the conclusions of the utilitarian argument:

> Does the husbandman, who works for his shilling a day, without having any interest in the produce of his work, and knowing that eight-tenths of it will go to other people; does he, I say, work so cheerfully and industriously as he would do, if he worked on his own land, and would be entitled to the whole produce, the corn, the wine, and the oil, that come from it? In the present system, the people of landed property being few in number, few only receive encouragement to industry on it, from the possession of it. The people of no property being the many, the many receive discouragement, from being deprived of it. (P. 60)

Hall's other tack was to use a rights argument. From this perspective, inequality in land and in the contracts that left the laborer with less than the full produce of his work violated the rights of the laborer.

Hall traced the historical origin of property rights to conquest. After one tribe had conquered another, the victorious warriors seized the lands of the vanquished. Among a people who did not suffer an invasion Hall believed the primal act of dispossession occurred when "some daring spirits arose [who] seized certain parts to themselves" (p. 57). The origins of "exclusive property" in land were, then, from unlawful takings or seizures. Even if it were possible that the first grants of land were from the community to reward virtuous individuals, exclusive property could not have continued legitimately for more than a generation, for "every succeeding generation [has] an equal right to the use of the land, with the preceding" (p. 58). Only communal ownership was consistent with God's intention that the earth provide for the sustenance of everyone. To demonstrate this point, he used the following argument. If "the principle of exclusive and perpetual property in land" was legitimate, he wrote, an owner could let his land lie idle. If one owner could do that, they all could. The consequence, of course, would be mass starvation. Hall concluded that "this consequence being absurd, the premises must be false" (p. 59). Individuals have "clear, natural rights" that the land remain common and that they have the use of what they produce to preserve themselves. Like Ogilvie, whom Hall seems to resemble more than anyone else, he suggested that families be given an "allotment" of a size necessary for the production of their necessities.

The radical political economists of the 1820s discussed with a good deal more detail and sophistication the idea that only labor created wealth, that employment contracts were unequal and unfair to labor, and that returns to capital in the form of rent and interest were unjust. But to use the language of fairness and justness they had to continue to consider the problem of property rights. Unless labor had a right to the wealth it created, there was no necessary wrong in it receiving less in wages than it produced.

The most thorough application of the labor argument to the increasingly industrial economy of early nineteenth-century England is found in Thomas Hodgskin's *Natural and Artificial Right of Property Contrasted* (1832). Hodgskin wrote to counter the utilitarian position he identified with James Mill and Jeremy Bentham that rights depended for their existence entirely on law. It was not enough for Hodgskin to criticize British political and economic life for not having calculated properly what would bring the greatest good to the greatest number. British law, he insisted, violated the natural rights of the laborer. Without natural rights, man "may be experimented on, imprisoned, expatriated or even exterminated, as the legislator pleases. Life and property being his gift, he may refuse them at pleasure; and hence he never classes the executions and wholesale slaughters, he continually commands, with murder—nor the forcible appropriations of property he sanctions, under the name of taxes, titles, etc. with larceny or high-way robbery."[44]

To support this view, he relied heavily on the argument of John Locke that rights preceded government and included the right to property. Understanding the basis of property rights was also important for Hodgskin because he saw them as the cause of social conflict. "The right of property, which is now arming the land owner and the capitalist against the peasant and the artisan, will, in truth, be the one great subject of contention for this and the next generation; before which, it needs no prophetic vision to foretell, the squabbles of party politicians, and the ravings of intolerant fanatics will die away unnoticed and unheard" (p. 15).

Though Hodgskin's first target was the utilitarian justification of unequal property, he also worked to dissociate himself from the belief in communal ownership. He listed the Moravians and Saint Simonians among the sects who believed in common ownership, but his real antagonists were "Mr. Owen's cooperative societies" (p. 24). In many ways, Hodgskin was a radical individualist or anarchist more than he was an early socialist. "A complete community of goods . . . never has existed, and never could exist. . . . The approximations to a community of goods among some religious, and some political societies, have always been the constrained and unhappy results of positive institutions" (p. 41). Thus, against both utilitarians and communitarians Hodgskin deployed Locke's argument for a natural right to property. "I heartily and cordially concur with Mr. Locke, in his view of the origin and foundation of a right of property" (p. 25). Hodgskin accepted fully the mixing labor argument, and to make sure his readers knew it, he provided them with long quotations from chapter 5 of the *Second Treatise*. Only Bentham seems to have stressed as much as Hodgskin did the differences between utilitarian and natural right theories and to have believed that great political consequences followed from choosing one or the other justification for property rights.

In Locke's labor theory the moral content of the mixing metaphor, the reason why laboring on something made it private independently of the acts of others, was dependent on an argument from God's ownership and intention. Hodgskin understood this, for he often invoked God or, more in keeping with his deism, "nature," in discussing the origins of property in labor. It was nature, he wrote, that "gives to each individual his body and his labor" (p. 26) and nature that "creates man with . . . wants and conjoins with them the power to gratify them" (p. 27). Hodgskin argued that the desire to labor, the ability to labor, the expectation that one would be able to use what labor created, the enjoyment of using goods one produced, and the motives for respecting the property rights of others all existed naturally and independently of contracts or consent, legislatures, or laws. To Hodgskin the idea of private property was an extension of the idea of personal identity and a "necessary consequence of existence" (p. 29). Only the insane lacked the idea of private property. It is not surprising, then, to find Hodgskin engaging in short anthropological excursions in which both the "Esquimaux" and Australian aborigine were shown to recognize property rights from labor.

Hodgskin interpreted the labor argument to mean that individuals could own the agricultural produce that resulted from their labor, but the land itself could never be made private property. Hodgskin misquoted Locke to defend this view: "As much land as a man tills, plants, and improves, cultivates, and can use, the product of so much is his property" (p. 61). Notice how the meaning of this sentence changes if the last comma is moved from after "use" to after "of," as Locke had it. According to Hodgskin, the farming of land conferred on the laborer a use right to the land cultivated and a property right to the produce of the land. But an individual could use only as much land as he could cultivate by his labor to produce the conveniences of life. Hodgskin used a short discussion of the stages of property to point out that in moving from hunter to shepherd to farmer the amount of land needed to sustain an individual decreased and that with the application of science to agriculture this amount decreased still more. Thus "the right of each individual to own land, on Mr. Locke's principle, ought to be gradually limited to an ever narrowing, ever decreasing space" (p. 67). He concluded that both enclosures and primogeniture, since one increased individual holdings and the other maintained farms larger than anyone could cultivate, violated natural rights to property. Hodgskin seemed to make room for farms as agricultural businesses by suggesting that they might require different standards than family farms, though even here he thought that as managing became more complicated the extent of land that could be managed efficiently by an owner would decrease in size (p. 67). Absentee owners and titles to land that was not farmed (and kept for game preserves, for example) were obvious targets for him.

If it were the rule of nature that individuals could claim as their own only what they had made or freely exchanged with others, how did it happen that priests, landowners, and stockholders had so much property? Hodgskin's answer was contained in his class analysis of state power. Only those groups were politically represented and therefore only they had the political power to pass legislation. Not surprisingly, the laws they enacted protected their interests. Municipal law, then, had created artificial rights to property, rights that violated the laws of nature.

At first, Hodgskin identified the class that monopolized power as the landed aristocracy, which explained why land could lie uncultivated and why wild animals were protected from hunting by the hungry. More interesting was his analysis of the political allegiance of the middle class. Though he recognized the possibility of disagreements between capitalists and landowners over, for example, the corn laws, he concluded that both "willingly support the government and the church; and both side against the labourer to oppress him; one lending his aid to enforce combination laws, while the other upholds game laws, and both enforce the exaction of tithes and of the revenue. Capitalists have in general formed a most intimate union with the landowners" (p. 53). But his attitude toward the middle class was ambivalent. In part, they were laborers, but they often were also the recipients of rent and dividends (pp. 97–98). He tried to enlist the sympathy of the middle class for his distinction between "natural" and "artificial" property by reminding them that they once represented the rule of nature that wealth should go to labor and that they were opposed by the artificial laws of the landed aristocracy. He was also eager to remind them that they came to power under the banner of equality and freedom (p. 101).

To James Mill and McCulloch, two of Hodgskin's favorite targets, the right to own property stood between civilization and barbarism. Only if people's property rights included the ability to consume, accumulate, or invest the proceeds of their labor would they undertake industry. Capital to them was made up of virtually all the goods, machines, and wealth that were available to assist production. But Hodgskin insisted that this understanding of capital hid an important point. He defined capital as that which was employed by the owner not to produce goods for his own use or enjoyment but only "to procure its owner a revenue."[45] Wages were paid to laborers and machines made available to them only so "that they . . . may produce [for owners] something of greater value than their wages" (p. 242).

Hodgskin's understanding of capital was a mirror image of his labor theory of property. Capital provided a return to an owner who had done no labor. Moreover, as it was invested only to bring the owner a profit, many projects that could have provided people with labor were not undertaken. The reclaiming of marshland, for instance, would provide subsistence to many but did not occur because its rate of return was not high enough. Capital, then, committed two sins against labor. It robbed labor first of part of its product and, second, of its opportunity to be employed. In fact, insofar as wages were in reality the subsistence goods that allowed laborers to survive, it could be said that the capitalist only paid wages, and allowed laborers to live, to the extent that they returned a profit to the capitalist (p. 249). Both the machine and the laborer were, then, merely means to a nonlaborer's profit.

Hodgskin, of course, denied that capital deserved a return because it was productive. Capital was produced by labor, and any return to it would have also been produced by labor. "We speak," he wrote, "in a vague manner, of a windmill grinding corn, and of steam engines doing the work of several millions of people. This gives a very incorrect view of the phenomena. It is not the instruments which grind corn, and spin cotton, but the labor of those who make, and the labor of those who use them" (p. 250). The capitalist or "the mere owner of the instruments" contributed nothing, Hodgskin declared. The artificial rights to property, those based on law and ultimately class power, did not guard civilization from barbarism by guarding labor from thievery. Instead, they represented thievery against labor, idleness against industry.

Though Hodgskin's labor theory was used to argue that the owners of capital did not deserve a return because they were not productive, it also had to confront the argument that a return to capital could be justified on the utilitarian grounds that it was a "motive to save" and a "spur to industry" (p. 254). His labor theory was somewhat beside the point in this argument, and as a result he seemed less certain of himself. He warned his readers that he "will not hastily and dogmatically decide concerning it" (p. 254). Hodgskin noted that when the accumulation of wealth was accomplished through a process that relied on private individuals, a great deal was wasted in the form of their conspicuous consumption. And insofar as it was believed that the liberal reward of labor brought forth the greatest effort, Hodgskin could argue that a return to capital decreased labor's share and its incentive to work. Neither of these comments exactly got to the problem of saving, nor did Hodgskin's assertions that individual laborers would save to provide for their children and to pay for consumer goods seem an adequate response (p. 255). Hodgskin's artisan radicalism, his strong sense of the relationship that should exist between skilled labor and property, was unable to provide a mechanism for the saving and pooling of capital necessary to the production of large modern factories and machines. His opposition to the accumulation and investment of capital through private mechanisms and his equal opposition to a state powerful enough to undertake saving distance him from both capitalist and socialist traditions. Perhaps he knew that without the pooling of capital, neither the factories nor the industrial proletariat of modern industry would be able to displace the system of artisan production that he so admired.

Though Hodgskin's work quickly fell into obscurity and was not rescued until 1899, when Adolph Menger wrote *The Right to the Whole Produce of Labor*, he exercised considerable influence at the time. Not only did he provide a criticism of capital that other radicals used, he also had an impact on more traditional political economists. It was partly in a reaction to his work that Read and Scrope, for example, made provision for welfare rights in their theories.

Hall's sympathy for the rural poor and Hodgskin's allegiance to artisan ideals led them both to view the newly developing industrial world with antipathy and to use a theory of exploitation to attack what they saw growing around them. That labor provided the only just title to property and was the only source of wealth, that capital was only stored-up or past labor, that the owners of capital were able to extract a price for its use because propertyless laborers must work or starve, and that this element of compulsion resulted in contracts in which the unproductive took from the productive can be found in the writings of both. Hodgskin especially hurled Locke's theories against the unproductive owners of capital and argued that the natural property rights of laborers were being violated.

But though the language of natural rights to land and/or labor was used by most radicals to criticize political and economic inequality, it was possible to reconstruct this argument on utilitarian grounds. Those critics who became enamored of the cooperative communities inspired by Robert Owen were especially important to the attempt to turn the greatest happiness principle into a radical critique. The best examples of such an analysis were William Thompson's *Inquiry into the Principles of the Distribution of Wealth Most Conducive to Human Happiness* (1824) and John Gray's, *Lecture on Human Happiness* (1825). Thompson self-consciously worked within the boundaries established by Bentham's utilitarianism, especially its categories of security and equality. His opening sentence announced his commitment. "Utility," he stated, "calculating all effects, good and evil, immediate and remote, in the pursuit of the greatest possible sum of human happiness, is the leading principle constantly kept in view, to which all others are but subsidiary."[46] Gray was just as certain that the conflicts and difficulties of moral and political life were susceptible to resolution if people remembered that good and evil were "only distinguishable by the former promoting and the latter injuring the happiness of our species."[47]

The reason that Thompson and Gray are appropriately discussed with Hall and Hodgskin is that they both quickly moved from the happiness of society to the conditions under which labor would produce the conveniences and comforts that happiness required. As Thompson pointed out, happiness depended, at least in part, on a standard of living possible only in an economy in which people labored with diligence. Thus it was a psychological fact of some importance to him that people expected to use what they produced. "The industrious, whose time has been occupied, whose mental and corporeal powers have been respectively on the stretch, to produce these articles with the view of adding to their own comforts, stand forth and claim as their own, as their property, what their labor alone has made. . . . To take from them what their arm guided by their mind has produced, is like taking from them a part of themselves" (p. 94). This claim to own what labor produced had to be validated by the greatest happiness principle before it could attain moral status. But both the disappointment or pain that would result from its abrogation and the negative effect it would have on economic motivation led him to demand that society "secure to the producer the free use of whatever his labor has produced" (p. 95). Here, then, is the radical twist that Thompson gave to Bentham. Whereas Bentham thought security required upholding any current distribution of property holdings, Thompson turned security into a defense of the industrious and a criticism of the unproductive wealthy. He called the interpretation of security "spurious" which was "slavishly and ignorantly worshipped by political economists" because it allowed a few to command the products of others (p. 585). Thompson's discussion of the ways laborers were forced to part with what they had produced was primarily political. Game laws, apprenticeship regulations, monopolies, anticombination laws, primogeniture, entails, taxes, and limited educational opportunities were the mechanisms he listed as forced exchanges (pp. 364–65).

Gray relied on the research of one of Bentham's most devoted followers, Patrick Colquhoun, to measure the amount of property that was taken every year from the laborers of England. According to his estimates, the productive classes retained only about one-fifth of the produce of their labor (p. 16). His explanation of this theft focused on the injustice of rents and interest. Landlords contributed nothing, he argued, toward agricultural production but collected rent from the people who did because they were unjustly allowed to own land (p. 30). Nor did the lender of money contribute to manufacturing. Only contracts in which equal quantities of labor were exchanged were just, Gray wrote, and by that standard neither the landlord nor the shareholder was entitled to receive part of the produce of the laborer.

Thompson and Gray moved so quickly from the greatest happiness principle to the need to secure to laborers the full produce of their labor or its equivalent that there are long stretches in their discussions that are indistinguishable from the works of Hall and Hodgskin. Gray, in fact, frequently invoked laborers' "natural and unquestionable right to the produce of their own labor," no doubt meaning to emphasize that according to the nature all people shared they could not be happy unless they could use or exchange all that they had made. But the utilitarian foundations of their thought did turn out to have important consequences. For though they thought that a productive system made up of small units, as Hodgskin had imagined, would return more to the laborer than the present system did, they were critical of all economic competition, even if it were between laborers whose rights were protected.

When confronted with the increasing importance of the division of labor in modern industry and the difficulty it seemed to pose to disentangling the products of individual labor, Hodgskin simply maintained that fair individual contracts within the enterprise would reflect individual labor. Thompson, however, used the division of labor as his entry to a theory of voluntary, mutual cooperation. Since he thought that it was impossible accurately to decide how much of a product created through a complex division of labor was produced by each laborer, he argued that the psychological link between individual labor and the products of labor had weakened enough for laborers to adopt a collective point of view under which they would cooperate in production and receive approximately equal shares in return. To Thompson, then, the nature of modern industry was inconsistent with individual exclusive property rights. In *An Inquiry* he charged even fair competition with five "evils": it depended on selfishness; set individuals against one another; allowed individuals to make errors of judgment a community would not make; could not deal with sickness, old age, and unemployment; and limited the diffusion and use of knowledge (p. 369). Only the self-sufficient, communal, and egalitarian economic system of a cooperative society escaped the competition and exploitation inherent in individual ownership.

At the end of Gray's *Lecture* he appended the "Articles of Agreement" for the formation of a cooperative community to be set up outside of London. The preamble to the agreement blames the misery of the present society on "competition and private accumulation," which had resulted in "excessive inequality of wealth." To avoid these vices the economic organization of the cooperative community required first that all members be co-owners and second that all members agree to work for the common benefit. In return, everyone received free housing, medical care, food, clothing, furniture, and education. The equality granted to women and the desire to lessen the length of the workday were other features of this plan. It is possible to think of these arrangements as returning to all members an equivalent of their labor and therefore as protecting the property rights Gray invoked against capitalists and landlords. But it is probably more accurate to think of these communities as beyond the need for property rights because they no longer were subject to the conditions of scarcity that made rights necessary. The deepest commitment of Gray and Thompson was to equality because that seemed to them to be the circumstance most conducive to realizing the greatest happiness for the greatest number. If Hall and Hodgskin tied the protection of natural property rights to an artisan mode of production that was increasingly obsolete, Thompson's and Gray's attempt to do without property rights ended with the utopian communities that grew and died in the early nineteenth century in both England and America.

All of the themes of radical political culture were brought together in the early 1830s and used to interpret the extraordinary events of that period to a large popular audience in the *Poor Man's Guardian*. Published by Henry Hetherington and edited from 1832 to 1835 by Bronterre O'Brien, the *Poor Man's Guardian* has been called "the finest working class weekly" that had yet existed in England. It reached the peak of its popularity when its publication and distribution were illegal, in violation of the stamp duty it refused to pay. Between 1831 and 1834, when its circulation was close to fifteen thousand, more than five hundred people were fined, imprisoned, or both for selling the *Poor Man's Guardian*.[48] Yet seventy-six issues after Henry Hetherington was acquitted by a jury of violating the stamp duty, the *Poor Man's Guardian* ceased publication. As O'Brien's biographer has remarked, "Working men, it seems, would buy an illegal paper, for that was to give a blow at the Government, but when the paper—even the famous and gallant *Guardian*—became respectable, their support declined."[49]

Describing the *Poor Man's Guardian* as a working-class paper is doing no more than recording its image of itself. Unlike Hodgskin, for example, who was ambivalent toward the middle class and who hoped they might be enlisted in the fight against the "artificial rights" of property, the *Poor Man's Guardian* saw them as the inevitable allies of the aristocracy. Instead of seeing their middle position as enabling them to escape the vices of arrogance and weakness, O'Brien maintained that

> they insensibly contract the vices of both tyrant and slave; tyrants to those below them—sycophants to those above them—and usurers from necessity and habit—they prey on the weakness of the workmen, while they extort all they can from the vanity of the aristocrat. Indeed the middle classes are the destroyers of liberty and happiness in all countries. It is their interest (under the present form of society) that the poor should be weak, and the rich extravagant and vain; and this being the case, the man who expects from them any real opposition to despotism, from inclination, must be a fool or a madman.[50]

The economic interests of "the banker, the lawyer, the exciseman" were in pleasing or selling dear to the wealthy and buying labor cheap from the poor. The inevitable antagonism between their profits and laborers' wages meant they would work "to keep the operatives in the most dependent and degraded state" (no. 133, December 21, 1823). The aspirations of the middle class were to become rich, thus their sympathies were always with the privileged or propertied. The relatively new and unrelenting antipathy to the middle class that we find in O'Brien stemmed, at least in part, from recent disappointment over the 1832 Reform Act, which broadened the franchise only to include some parts of the middle class.

Though O'Brien drew on all parts of the radical tradition, he criticized much of it to create his own political perspective. Though generally respectful of Cobbett, for example, he gave himself credit for moving radical criticism away from the corruption and taxes argument and toward an analysis based on exploitation (no. 175, October 11, 1834). Not surprisingly, then, Richard Carlile, the most unchanging member of that tradition, was critical of the *Poor Man's Guardian* and accused it of attacking private property, promoting what he called "a common scramble for all existing property" (no. 179, November 8, 1834). Hetherington replied to these charges in a long article that upheld the legitimacy of property rights based on labor, denied the legitimacy of most current private holdings because they were not based on the labor of the owner, and used long quotations from Paine, Locke, and Hall to buttress his argument. But Hetherington stopped short of suggesting that current holdings should be declared invalid, suggesting instead that he wanted only for labor to be accorded suffrage so that the laws regulating property would guarantee that future acquisitions would be fair.

Hodgskin and Hall provided the *Poor Man's Guardian* with the substance of its economic perspective. In issues 86 and 87 O'Brien directly confronted the utilitarian defense of property put forward by the Society for the Promotion of Christian Knowledge. "Oh, property!" he began, "what recollections are associated with thy name! What wars, and crimes, and superstitions hast thou fostered among men! and what countless miseries are hourly inflected in thy name" (no. 87, February 2, 1833). To the "superstition" that current property rights must be inviolate or industry, accumulation, and prosperity would collapse, O'Brien replied by denying the link between the protection of current property and industry. Those who actually labored to produce the wealth of the country did so, he wrote, because they feared starvation or punishment. They could not be motivated by the desire to accumulate property because their property, their labor, was taken from them as they worked. At the same time, those with property were idle. O'Brien labeled the argument that the wealthy were living off their property "a wicked, damned lie" because it hid the fact they were really living off the labor of others (no. 86, January 26, 1833). Those who labored, then, had no property, while those with property did not labor. O'Brien also argued that "natural" property rights, based on labor, could not justify exclusive rights in land.

O'Brien's relationship to another wing of radical politics, the cooperative schemes of Robert Owen, was complicated. He strongly disapproved of Owen's antagonism to political reform and political activity. The minimum demand of O'Brien and most other working-class radicals was for universal manhood suffrage. His confidence in a truly representative Parliament seemed, at times, unbounded. Working with the idea that all social ills came from the laws that created "artificial" property rights, it seemed obvious that representatives from labor would change the laws and stop the robbery (no. 199, March 28, 1835).

But achieving such cooperation was a problem. O'Brien's dislike of the individual competition that was created by private rights to property led him to see cooperation as a superior moral and economic ideal. Competition, he believed, was responsible for the low wages given to laborers and, therefore, the unequal exchange with capital (no. 146, March 22, 1834). Moreover, he thought it created a kind of "civil war": "We do not, to be sure, eat one another's flesh, like cannibals or fishes, but, like cannibals, we are constantly preying upon one another, by seeking to appropriate each other's means of existence; and, like fishes, the small ones among us are made the prey of large ones" (no. 130, November 30, 1833). As a result of this view of competition, he was drawn to Owen and described himself at one point as a staunch cooperator (no. 175, October 11, 1834).

It was difficult, however, for O'Brien to find an institutional way to achieve cooperation. Though he thought some might want voluntarily to give up their property rights to a group and live in a cooperative arrangement, he doubted that many would adopt such a solution and seemed temperamentally at odds with the withdrawal this arrangement suggested. Instead, like the other "Lockean radicals" who thought labor was a just title to property, he sought reforms that would allow exclusive rights to be acquired legitimately, rather than trying to find ways to abolish them. Thus his most interesting discussion of how to achieve a situation in which "there shall be henceforward no idlers, and that each individual shall receive the full equivalent of his services, and no more" occurred in a critique of Owen's desire to abolish private property. O'Brien described his goal as introducing the "democratic principle" into all social institutions. After the franchise was extended, democracy would require placing the ownership of "commercial and manufacturing establishments" in the hands of the people who worked them. Profits generated by these businesses would be divided among the employees according to their labor, rather than going to owners who did none of the work. Parliament should appropriate "the whole soil of the country to the whole people of the country." Rents would be paid to the nation and used for national purposes out of the income farmers would justly derive from selling the produce they raised. At the same time, large estates would be divided and rented and waste land reclaimed and culti-vated (no. 199, March 28, 1835). O'Brien insisted that present owners of factories, farms, and the national debt should be compensated through bonds that would bring an income for twenty years.

O'Brien's plan to put factories under the ownership of the people who worked in them implied an acceptance of the large-scale machinery and technological innovation they required. This attitude brought him into conflict with those who wanted to restrict the introduction of machines. In April 1833, the editors of the *Poor Man's Guardian* were "accused" of using machines to print their paper. O'Brien's response was to defend machinery as laborsaving and to blame its ill effects on the system under which it was presently used. But under circumstances in which wealth went to the laborers who created it, O'Brien found the use of machinery wholly beneficial (no. 97, April 13, 1833). He even looked forward to the time when three or four hours of labor a day might provide laborers all the comforts they needed (no. 86, January 26, 1833). According to O'Brien, then, the logical result of a consistently applied labor theory of property to an economic system of large-scale industry was in its broad outlines similar to the system of producer cooperatives recommended by J. S. Mill in his *Principles of Political Economy* (1848) or to what is now referred to as market socialism.

Because the focus of the *Poor Man's Guardian* was on the way the labor of the working poor was taken from them through contracts that did not return an equivalent, and because it looked to the day when no one would be poor or without work, it did not join the battle over the New Poor Law until late. But after its passage the *Poor Man's Guardian* devoted several issues to criticizing it and urging a return to the Old Poor Law. O'Brien placed the responsibility and blame for the New Poor Law entirely on the middle class. Descriptions of the sad circumstances into which the New Poor Law forced the poor took some space, as did refer-ences to the work of Captain Swing and the number of suspicious fires that had recently occurred (no. 179, November 8, 1834). And along with these appeals to sympathy and fear went appeals to history. O'Brien used Cobbett to argue that the rights of the poor were more than two hundred years old, given to them in exchange for the confiscation of the church lands that were used to support them before the English Reformation (no. 176, October 18, 1834).

O'Brien's strongest defense of the unemployed poor's right to assistance occurred in an argument with Daniel O'Connell over the Irish poor. Without going into O'Connell's volatile career, it can be said that at this point he had reluctantly come to approve of a poor law in Ireland but specifically denied that it was required by the "abstract [natural] right of any class of men, however indigent" (no. 206, May 16, 1835). The reasons O'Connell gave for a poor law, to check the spread of disease and to give landlords an interest in the well-being of their tenants, were similar to the reluctant defense of the Old Poor Law given by McCulloch in the late 1820s. But subsistence and social control did not impress O'Brien. His first point was to insist that those who held property had only a natural right claim to what they had produced through their labor; the rest they held by "the law of the land." But because the power to make law had been "usurped" from the people and had been used to take property from the poor, the claims of the propertied to what they had were weak indeed. In fact, most of the goods possessed by the propertied belonged in justice to the poor because it was their labor and not the labor of the rich that had produced them. Poor laws, according to O'Brien, simply returned to the poor a portion of the produce of their labor which was rightfully theirs in the first place. The fact that poor relief assisted people who were not working did not invalidate the use of the labor argument. Most of these people had worked for years and were simply receiving in aid what they produced but did not receive during their employment. The able-bodied unemployed were not lazy but excluded from the use of productive resources. As O'Brien asked O'Connell, "Why does he not inquire whether the poverty of the poor is not owing to this very circumstance of exclusion" (no. 207, May 23, 1835)? Thus the monopoly in land and capital resulted in most people working for wages less than the value of what they created and in others not able to work at all. Since the laws that created the monopoly were made by the rich, the poor were not responsible for their poverty and should not suffer because of it or have to beg for relief. O'Brien ended one of his issues by demanding

> that the poor who cannot find employment shall be maintained at the expense of the rich till they can—that meanwhile they shall be admitted to the exercise of their full rights of citizenship, so as to exert a coordinate authority with the rich in making or new modeling the laws and constitution of the country—but that, until such change takes place, they shall consider themselves to have as perfect

a right to that portion of the superfluities of the rich, called the poor's rates, as the rich themselves have to the remainder. (No. 207, May 23, 1835)

The idea of a natural property right was used throughout the period between 1790 and 1834 to defend the economic interests of those people who were excluded from the benefits of English political and economic life. The development of inclusive property rights was especially important to the attempt to maintain or expand government assistance to the poor and unemployed. First in Paine and then in Cobbett this vocabulary was deployed to argue that it would be a violation of the rights of the unemployed to allow them to suffer. Other theorists thought the natural right to property required more than a welfare right. The appropriation of the land by only a few seemed to many to violate the rights of the rest and to require redistributions so that all would have an opportunity to work their own farms. The emphasis that the labor title to property seemed to some of these writers to place on physical labor did lead them to anachronistic defenses of small farms and artisan production. In Bronterre O'Brien's application of the labor argument to large-scale production, however, we can see that anachronism was not inevitable. In fact, the use of the rights language to accomplish economic ends had an extraordinarily beneficial consequence (one that is lost when Marxism becomes the main vehicle for radical criticism). Using the language of natural rights tied economic justice to the recognition of civil and political rights as well. All of these writers believed in a political system that protected rights to a free press and free speech, to religious freedom, and to equal political representation as well as to an economic system that provided opportunities to all, rewarded productive labor over ownership, and protected everyone from the suffering that can accompany unemployment.

CONCLUSION

I t has been one of the purposes of this study to pay some attention to the political and intellectual contexts that led to the modern natural law discussion of property. As we have seen, property rights were part of disputes over issues as various as international fishing rights, God's providence, political representation, revolution, primogeniture and entail, enclosure of common fields, and the justice of a return to capital.

Virtually all of the attempts to understand the nature and meaning of natural property rights that were provoked by these disputes were based on drawing meaning from the idea that the earth was a common inheritance or a general patrimony or (in the language of Adam Smith) that "the earth and the fullness of it belongs to every generation."[1] The assumption of moral equality that was behind both the rights theories derived from Grotius and the utilitarian theories indebted to Bentham required understanding the earth as a common. As everyone's preservation was equally valued, no one could be excluded from the resources necessary for preservation without good reason. Just as no generation held a privileged position that enabled it to dictate property rules to later generations, no individual or particular group of individuals could lay claim to the earth and exclude others. Private appropriations had to be justified in terms that would bring forth the respect, if not the actual approval, of others.

But though the political theorists who wrote on property rights in the seventeenth, eighteenth, and early nineteenth centuries began with common property, their goal was to finish with an argument that demonstrated the tie between property rights and the deeper, enduring requirements of human nature and human society. Preservation, order, peace, political representation, prudence, and benevolence were all claimed to depend on the recognition of individual rights to property. At times the relationship between exclusive property and these values was stressed to defend the current holdings of a particular society. But to stop at this use of natural property rights would be to miss all of those other times this way of thinking about property provided powerful intellectual weapons to the critics of current property arrangements. Filmer may have been correct from the start and Burke right later to believe that the egalitarian and rationalist assumptions of modern natural law meant that its understanding of property rights was incompatible with the strong defense of current holdings conservatives desired. To think about property as primarily, or naturally, a common inheritance or general patrimony easily led to the desire that ownership be spread throughout all of society. It almost guaranteed a suspicious attitude toward all great concentrations of property (especially when ownership was absentee and inherited), and it demanded that no arrangement of rights be thought so strong it could be upheld against the claims of life.

The path from common rights to private rights that was most frequently traveled went through consent, which is not surprising in a political tradition that relied so heavily on contracts to explain the rights and duties of political life. Consent theorists assumed that when rational individuals were faced with the conflicts and inefficiencies that came from the use of a common by an increasing population, they would consent to the introduction of private holdings to preserve themselves. In this way, rules establishing private property could be understood as legitimate for the same reason all other rules were—they would have been agreed to, expressly or tacitly, by those rational people who were subject to them.

Many of the theorists who used consent also assumed that conditions would be attached to such agreements. First, people who gave up their right to take from the common would insist on the right of necessity. This condition is similar to that of the right to rebel, which would have been required by people about to give up their natural freedom to join a civil society. In neither case would people make agreements without specifying that if their lives were threatened by tyranny or starvation the agreements would lose their binding power. This argument was taken even further by theorists who maintained that a second condition would also be insisted upon. People concerned to safeguard their preservation would likely stipulate that in need they would have a claim on the wealth of the nation that their government would have to satisfy through institutional assistance. The parallel in political argument would be to the construction of constitutional safeguards that protected liberty so that no one would ever have to use the right of rebellion. The nature and the amount of aid necessary to satisfy these welfare claims, the circumstances that would call them forth, and the conditions under which they would be given are the problems posed by this account of property rights and welfare rights.

The most important intellectual competitor to the contract theory of natural property rights was the labor argument, a variant of the idea that occupation or possession could create a property right independent of the consent of others. Since it could not have been necessary to ask the permission of others to exist, it seemed unnecessary to the labor theorists to have to ask permission to keep the fruits of one's labor, the necessary condition for continued existence. Labor and its products were so constitutive of one's being that to need the permission of others to keep what one's labor had created implied that one existed only by the permission of others. The labor argument did have problems, however. It was sometimes rejected because it seemed to rest rights, which entail the recognition of others, on individual, physical acts—mere seizures, according to Pufendorf—that were without moral content. Even if labor was accepted as a legitimate title to property before civil society, it was far from clear what status it retained after people agreed to allow public authorities to adjudicate conflicts and act in the public good. Moreover, it was always difficult to apply the labor argument to land, which was obviously not the result of human labor.

Whatever its theoretical problems, the labor argument played an important role in the politics of this period. Locke used labor to establish property rights in the state of nature to advance his argument that the only legitimate basis for the exercise of political power among people equal and independent was consent. At the end of the eighteenth and beginning of the nineteenth centuries, the labor argument again became a powerful weapon, this time in the hands of those who believed their contribution to the prosperity of the nation required that they play a greater role in its politics and share more equitably in its wealth. The labor argument threatened the property rights of absentee landlords whose land was cultivated by tenants, if it was cultivated at all, and the idle recipients of dividends and interest. Although labor could be used to defend exclusive rights to property, it was as plausibly invoked to argue that tenants should have property in the land they cultivated and wage earners in the profits they generated for the owners of capital. The thrust of the labor argument was toward the redistribution of resources to the people who actually produced them, to providing the opportunity for all people to use their labor, and to thinking of the land as the property of the nation.

Once we are aware that the natural right to property in both its consent and its labor forms was as likely to be used by the defenders of the poor and excluded as by current property rights holders, it becomes easier to explain the persistent tendency of conservative theorists to deny the validity of the natural rights vocabulary to understanding property rights. Unburdened of the need to demonstrate that the rights to unequal property that they wanted to defend were consistent with an original common and the moral equality it implied or resulted from the labor of the owners, conservatives could then rely on the legitimacy of history, the providence of God, or the contribution of the present distribution to the public good. They could point out that conflict would result from any attempt to change the distribution that already existed and that current levels of prosperity would inevitably decline in the insecurity that would accompany considerable change.

But resting property on the public good and legal rights had its own problems as a defense of strong exclusive rights. It seems almost inevitable that the calculations that characterized the utilitarian political economists of the 1830s would be made and exclusive property rights limited. People who wanted to avoid conflict, diminish suffering, and promote the happiness of all would find that the poor could be helped through government programs and their own values furthered without sacrificing the benefits of private property. Welfare programs that increased happiness or diminished pain were, then, required as a matter of justice. As current holders of property rights acknowledged no higher principles than happiness and municipal law, they had no intellectual defense against such programs and the taxes they would require.

Understanding that the property theories that were handed down to the major figures of nineteenth-century liberalism—J. S. Mill, T. H. Green, and L. T. Hobhouse—contained arguments that quickly led to the affirmation of inclusive rights suggests that the welfare provisions in their own political theories should be understood as continuing a tradition rather than as taking it in new directions.[2] For example, the argument that the special relationship between labor and exclusive property could not be applied to the land was central to John Stuart Mill's arguments in his *Principles of Political Economy* (1848). "When the 'sacredness of property' is talked of, it should always be remembered," Mill wrote, "that any sacredness does not belong in the same degree to landed property. No man made the land. It is the original inheritance of the whole species."[3] Taxes on the land, then, were not really taxes at all. They were "a rent charge in favor of the public" (p. 820). Later, T. H.

Green in *The Principles of Political Obligation* (1880) and L. T. Hobhouse in *Liberalism* (1911) continued to use the idea that the land, as a "gift of nature," was "by right communal and not personal property." Hobhouse, like Mill, used this idea to defend increasing taxes on landowners and to propose schemes whereby more land would be made available to small farmers.[4]

Even the great nineteenth-century libertarian Herbert Spencer, at least in his first edition of *Social Statics* (1850), denied that land could be made fully private. He described the land as existing in a positive community with all people as the "joint heirs." The consent of the current generation could not result in property rights because it could not bind future generations. Nor could labor, which involved only turning over the soil to the depth of a few inches, scattering a few seeds, and then gathering the fruits which "the sun, rain, and air helped the soil to produce," lead to private rights. Spencer concluded, "Equity, therefore, does not permit property in land." Instead, he thought that land should be owned by the public and rented to private citizens.[5]

The idea accepted by all of these nineteenth-century liberal theorists, that property arrangements had to include an inclusive element, was given especially succinct expression by T. H. Green: "The rationale of property, in short, requires that everyone who will conform to the positive condition of possessing it, viz. labour, and the negative condition, viz. respect for it as possessed by others, should, so far as social arrangements can make him so, be a possessor of property himself, and of such property as will at least enable him to develope a sense of responsibility, as distinct from mere property in the immediate necessaries of life" (p. 220). The desire to spread ownership to as many as possible and especially to those who presently labored led Mill to include in his proposal that landownership be extended to tenant farmers a proposal to expand producer cooperatives so that factory workers could become owners (pp. 760–94).

The belief that the property rules that were most conducive to the development of social and individual good were ones that increased the opportunities to labor and that spread ownership to as many as possible was not used by any of these later liberal theorists to justify the suffering of people who could not work or find work. Though Mill, for example, began his discussion of poor relief with the usual fears of unrestrained population growth among the poor, he did not conclude that government relief was always a mistake. A system of government relief that was "freed from its injurious effects upon the habits and minds of the people" would be justifiable. And since it had been "irrevocably established" that the New Poor Law worked just this way, "society can and therefore ought to insure every individual belonging to it against the extreme of want, . . . physical suffering or the dread of it" (p. 366). So strongly did he feel about the justice of the Poor Law that he wrote, "humanity has no worse enemies than those who lend themselves . . . to bring odium on this law" (p. 366). Like William Forster Lloyd, then, Mill believed that since a way had been found to diminish suffering without causing greater problems, justice demanded that such action be taken and "an absolute right to be supported at the cost of other people" be established (p. 366).

Hobhouse also defended government relief programs as part of a citizen's inclusive right. To do this he, too, pointed to the Poor Law, the very existence of which acknowledged that citizens had a "lien" or "claim" on public resources that could be invoked when they were unable to use their labor and were destitute. Hobhouse did not think that the level and conditions of aid established by the "principle of '34" were any longer appropriate to a country as wealthy as England. The workhouse should be abolished and the amount of aid changed from that below the lowest wage earned to that necessary to "a healthy, civilized existence" (p. 96). Hobhouse's arguments that a great deal of the property that individuals held had its origins more in social cooperation than in the unaided industry of the individual enabled him to extend the size of the "social inheritance" that was properly at the disposal of society and appropriately used to satisfy the rights of the unemployed. Taxes on this amount were not "deducted from that which the taxpayer has an unlimited right to call his own, but [were] rather a repayment of something that was all along due to society" (p. 104). Thus, though those without property could justly complain that their "rights *to* property" (p. 97) were violated, those who held property had no ground for complaint when they were taxed to provide for others.

The history of property theory that this study has examined should make us aware of the difficulties in constructing a thorough justification of exclusive property rights that does not require on its own principles a justification for a right to be included in the use of resources necessary to life and livelihood. This is not to say that there has been common agreement about the content of inclusive property rights. The right of necessity, government provision of the barest necessities, the creation of free markets that would result in the dispersion of ownership, public education, land distribution and redistribution, generous government assistance to broad categories of people who were thought unable to work, public employment, and extending property rights to workers in the goods they produced and the tools they used were some of the various ways proposed to satisfy inclusive rights. But though the proper way to satisfy the inclusive nature of property has been a matter of continuing dispute, the idea that there was an inclusive side to just property arrangements was a dominant, if not universal, theme in this discussion.

What has emerged from the intellectual history presented here is an awareness that the characteristic assumption of liberal political thought —that people have natural rights to property—has included a recognition of both inclusive and exclusive property rights. Only by making provision for the right to exclude others as well as the right to be included could a property system respect both the individual talents and the common humanity of the people subject to it. It was and is those outside the liberal tradition who think that property systems must be either entirely inclusive or exclusive. The institutions of the liberal welfare state are the latest in a long history of attempts to protect both exclusive and inclusive rights to property. The liberal welfare state may not, then, be awkwardly suspended between the two ideals of private liberty and social solidarity, nor should it be reduced merely to the results of compromise and expediency. Instead, the liberal welfare state's simultaneous protection of property and social welfare should be seen as necessary to the creation of a just property system. The attempt to construct a property system with both inclusive and exclusive elements is not a measure of confusion, it is precisely the mark of the liberal welfare state's intellectual coherence and moral superiority.

NOTES

Introduction

1. Gray, *Liberalism*, pp. 65–66.
2. Hobhouse, *Liberalism*, p. 54.
3. Tucker, *The Marx-Engels Reader*, pp. 42–43. For a short account of antiliberalism see Pocock, *Virtue, Commerce, and History*, pp. 59–61.

Chapter One

1. Pagden, *Languages of Political Theory*, p. 79.
2. Smith, *Lectures on Jurisprudence*, p. 397.
3. Krieger, *Politics of Discretion*, p. 134.
4. Grotius, *Rights of War and Peace*, p. xx. All subsequent citations are given parenthetically in the text.
5. Tuck, *Natural Rights Theories*, p. 79; Haakonssen, "Hugo Grotius and the History of Political Thought."
6. Knight, *Life and Works of Hugo Grotius*, p. 93.
7. Tuck, *Natural Rights Theories*, p. 77.
8. For a different conclusion see Tully, *Discourse on Property*, p. 70.
9. Knight, *Life and Works of Hugo Grotius*, p. 106.
10. Selden, *Of the Dominion, or, Ownership of the Sea*, p. 21. All subsequent citations are given parenthetically in the text.
11. Tuck, *Natural Rights Theories*, p. 97.
12. For contrasting views on Selden's account of political obligation see Tuck, *Natural Rights Theories*, chap. 4, and Sommerville, "John Selden, the Law of Nature, and the Origins of Government."
13. Pufendorf, *Of the Law of Nature and Nations*, p. 207. All subsequent citations are given parenthetically in the text.
14. Selden, *Table-Talk*. All subsequent citations are given parenthetically in the text.
15. Filmer, "Observations upon Hugo Grotius's *De Jure Belli ac Pacis*," in *Patriarcha and Other Political Writings*, pp. 261–72. All subsequent citations are given parenthetically in the text.
16. Wolfe, *Leveller Manifestoes*, p. 272.
17. Woodhouse, *Puritanism and Liberty*, pp. 53–59.
18. Wolfe, *Leveller Manifestoes*, pp. 288, 348, 390, 302.

19. Woodhouse, *Puritanism and Liberty*, pp. 58–69.

20. For a recent account of the "common program" of Grotius and Hobbes see Tuck, "Grotius, Canneades and Hobbes."

21. Hobbes, *Leviathan*, p. 234; *De Cive*, p. 80; *Elements of Law*, p. 279. All subsequent citations, abbreviated as *L*, *DC*, and *EL*, are given parenthetically in the text.

22. Cumberland, *Treatise of the Laws of Nature*, p. 326. All subsequent citations are given parenthetically in the text.

23. More, *Enchiridion Ethicum*, pp. 238–39. All subsequent citations are given parenthetically in the text.

24. See Laslett's "Introduction" to Locke, *Two Treatises of Government*, p. 88.

25. For more on the relationship between Grotius, Hobbes, and Pufendorf see Hont, "Language of Sociability and Commerce," and Tuck, "Modern Theory of Natural Law."

Chapter Two

1. See Schochet, *Patriarchalism in Political Thought*; Kenyon, *Revolution Principles*, esp. chap. 5; and Goldie, "John Locke and Anglican Royalism."

2. Ashcraft, *Revolutionary Politics*, p. 246.

3. Tyrrell, *Patriarcha Non Monarcha*, p. 116 (sig. M3v). All subsequent citations are given parenthetically in the text. Because of incorrect pagination, some page references to this book will be accompanied by signature numbers. For a possible explanation for the apparent late insertion of a new section by Tyrrell see Tuck, *Natural Rights Theories*, pp. 169–70.

4. The relationship between Tyrrell and Locke is discussed by Gough, "James Tyrrell."

5. See Franklin, *John Locke and the Theory of Sovereignty*, pp. 92–93, 110–11; Ashcraft, *Revolutionary Politics*, p. 236.

6. For a different view see Tuck, *Natural Rights Theories*, p. 171.

7. Tyrrell, *Brief Disquisition of the Law of Nature*.

8. Locke, *Two Treatises of Government*, First Treatise, para. 5. All subsequent citations are given parenthetically in the text. See Ashcraft, *Locke's Two Treatises of Government*, chap. 3 for an extended discussion of Locke's critique of Filmer.

9. Tully, *Discourse on Property*, pp. 124–28.

10. Rashdall, "Philosophical Theory of Property," p. 52.

11. Pufendorf, *Of the Law of Nature and Nations*, p. 386.

12. See Waldron, "Enough and as Good Left for Others," pp. 319–28.

13. Locke, *Essays on the Law of Nature*, ed. von Leyden, p. 213. All subsequent citations, abbreviated as *ELN*, are given parenthetically in the text.

14. Wood, *John Locke and Agrarian Capitalism*, p. 55.

15. Ashcraft, *Revolutionary Politics*, p. 251.

16. See Wood, *John Locke and Agrarian Capitalism*, chap. 3; Ashcraft, *Locke's Two Treatises*, chap. 6.

17. See Tully, *Discourse on Property*, pp. 133–35.

18. For a rebuttal to the argument that titles to property in civil society are

completely conventional see Waldron, "Locke, Tully, and the Regulation of Property."

19. Wood, *John Locke and Agrarian Capitalism*, p. 33. Also see Vaughn, *John Locke*, pp. 121–22.

20. See Dunn, "Consent in the Political Theory of John Locke," and Ashcraft, *Locke's Two Treatises*, chap. 7.

21. Ashcraft, *Revolutionary Politics*, p. 322.

22. Fox-Bourne, *Life of John Locke*, 2:378–90.

23. Dunn has attached the "Venditio" to the end of his article "Justice and the Interpretation of Locke's Political Theory," pp. 68–87.

24. Conniff, "Reason and History in Early Whig Thought."

25. Scott, *Algernon Sidney*, p. 19.

26. Sidney, *Discourses Concerning Government, Works*, p. 42. All subsequent citations are given parenthetically in the text.

27. Scott, *Algernon Sidney*, p. 20.

28. Citations to Barbeyrac's notes in Grotius, *The Rights of War and Peace*, will use the abbreviation *RWP* and those to Pufendorf, *The Law of Nature and Nations*, will use the abbreviation *LNN*.

Chapter Three

1. Smout, "Famine and Famine-relief in Scotland."

2. Phillipson, "Culture and Society in the 18th Century Province," pp. 407–36.

3. See Moore and Silverthorne, "Gershom Carmichael and the Natural Jurisprudence Tradition," pp. 81–83.

4. Moore and Silverthorne, "Political Writings of Gershom Carmichael," p. 4. All subsequent citations are given parenthetically in the text.

5. Dalrymple (Lord Stair), *Institutions of the Law of Scotland*, and Erskine, *An Institute of the Law of Scotland*.

6. Stein, "Law and Society in Eighteenth-Century Scottish Thought," p. 152.

7. Robbins, "When It Is That Colonies May Turn Independent," and Campbell, "Francis Hutcheson." Also see Teichgraeber, *Free Trade and Moral Philosophy*, and Sher, *Church and University*.

8. Hutcheson, *System of Moral Philosophy*, 2:75–76, 93, 113–14; Hutcheson, *Short Introduction to Moral Philosophy*, pp. 220–21. All subsequent citations, abbreviated as *System* 1 or 2 and *SI*, are given in the text.

9. Hutcheson, *Considerations on Patronages*, pp. 15–16. All subsequent citations are given parenthetically in the text.

10. Moore, "The Two Systems of Francis Hutcheson."

11. Hutcheson, *An Inquiry Concerning the Original of Our Ideas of Virtue or Moral Good*, p. 164. All subsequent citations, abbreviated as *Inquiry*, are given parenthetically in the text. Also see Winch, *Adam Smith's Politics*, pp. 49–50, and Moore, "Locke and the Scottish Jurists."

12. Fletcher, *Selected Political Writings and Speeches*, pp. 46–58.

13. Teichgraeber, *Free Trade and Moral Philosophy*, pp. 53–54.

14. Fordyce, *Dialogues Concerning Education* and "The Elements of Moral Philosophy." All subsequent citations are to these editions, abbreviated as *Dialogues* 1 or 2 and "Elements," and are given in the text.

15. Robbins, "When It Is That Colonies May Turn Independent," p. 237.

16. Jones, "The Polite Academy and the Presbyterians, 1720–1770," in *New Perspectives on the Politics and Culture of Early Modern Scotland*, ed. Dwyer, Mason, and Murdoch, p. 165.

17. Forbes, *Hume's Philosophical Politics*, esp. chap. 2. Also see Teichgraeber, *Free Trade and Moral Philosophy*, chap. 3; and Haakonssen, *Science of a Legislator*, chap. 3.

18. Greig, ed., *Letters of David Hume*, 1:33.

19. Hume, *Treatise of Human Nature*, p. 484. All subsequent citations, abbreviated as *Treatise*, are given parenthetically in the text.

20. Hume, *An Inquiry Concerning the Principles of Morals* in *Philosophical Works of David Hume*, ed. Green and Grose, 4:275. All subsequent citations, abbreviated as *PW*, are given parenthetically in the text.

21. Hume, *A Letter from a Gentleman to His Friend in Edinburgh*, p. 32.

22. Forbes, "Natural Law and the Scottish Enlightenment," p. 198.

23. Sher, *Church and University*, p. 187.

24. See, for example, Miller, *Philosophy and Ideology in Hume's Political Thought*, p. 107.

25. See Haakonssen, *Science of a Legislator*, pp. 27–28, and Hayek, *Law, Legislation, and Liberty*, Vol. 2: *The Mirage of Social Justice*, pp. 16–17.

26. Haakonssen, *Science of a Legislator*, p. 27.

27. See Moore, "Hume's Theory of Justice and Property," pp. 114–15.

28. Balfour, *A Delineation of the Nature and Obligation of Morality*, p. 54. All subsequent citations are given parenthetically in the text.

29. Reid, *Philosophical Works*, ed. Hamilton, 2:643–45. All subsequent citations are given parenthetically in the text.

30. Moore, "Hume's Theory of Justice and Property," pp. 117–18.

31. Home (Lord Kames), *Essays on the Principles of Morality and Natural Religion*, p. 103. All subsequent citations, abbreviated as *Essays*, are given parenthetically in the text. See Ross, *Lord Kames and the Scotland of His Day*, chap. 6.

32. Lehman, *Henry Home, Lord Kames, and the Scottish Enlightenment*, chap. 6.

33. Ibid., p. 88.

34. Home (Lord Kames), *Sketches of the History of Man*, 1:401. All subsequent citations, abbreviated as *Sketches*, are given parenthetically in the text.

35. Home (Lord Kames), *Principles of Equity*, pp. 34–35. See MacCormick, "Law and Enlightenment," pp. 157–58.

36. Home (Lord Kames), *Historical Law Tracts*, p. 80. All subsequent citations, abbreviated as *HLT*, are given parenthetically in the text.

37. Home (Lord Kames), "Considerations upon the State of Scotland with Respect to Entails," in Lehman, *Henry Home, Lord Kames, and the Scottish Enlightenment*, p. 330.

38. For the history and development of the Scottish Poor Law see Mitchison,

"The Making of the Old Scottish Poor Law." Also see her "Scottish Landowners and Communal Responsibility in the 18th Century."

39. Smith, *An Inquiry into the Nature and Causes of the Wealth of Nations*, 1:423. All subsequent citations, abbreviated as *WN*, are given parenthetically in the text.

40. Smith, *Lectures on Jurisprudence*, pp. 333, 487. All subsequent citations, abbreviated as *LJ*, are given parenthetically in the text.

41. Smith, *The Theory of Moral Sentiments*, p. 158. All subsequent citations, abbreviated as *TMS*, are given parenthetically in the text.

42. Haakonssen, *Science of a Legislator*, pp. 126–27.

43. Teichgraeber, *Free Trade and Moral Philosophy*, p. 147.

44. Winch, *Adam Smith's Politics*, pp. 139–40.

45. See Teichgraeber, *Free Trade and Moral Philosophy*, pp. 160–62 and Hont and Ignatief, "Needs and Justice in the *Wealth of Nations*." For an example of an economist contemporary to Smith who urged the use of public granaries see James Steuart, "A Dissertation on the Policy of Grain."

46. Stewart, *Account of the Life and Writings of Adam Smith, LL.D*, p. 54.

47. Like Kames, though, Smith seems to have become somewhat pessimistic about the consequences of commercial development as he grew older. For more on this theme see Winch, *Adam Smith's Politics*, pp. 80–102, and Dickey, "Historicizing the 'Adam Smith Problem.' "

Chapter Four

1. Roberts, *Paternalism in Early Victorian England*, and Poynter, *Society and Pauperism*.

2. Rutherforth, *Institutes of Natural Law*, p. 21. All subsequent citations are given parenthetically in the text.

3. Blackstone, *Commentaries on the Laws of England*, 1:7. All subsequent citations are given parenthetically in the text.

4. Porter, *English Society in the Eighteenth Century*, p. 226.

5. Blum, "English Parliamentary Enclosure," p. 485. Also see Yelling, *Common Field and Enclosure in England*, and Turner, *English Parliamentary Enclosure*.

6. Atiyah, *Rise and Fall of Freedom of Contract*, p. 90. If Christie is correct in his *Stress and Stability in Late 18th Century Britain*, p. 116, the Poor Law did play an important role in maintaining stability during the early years of the industrial revolution.

7. Woodward, *An Argument in Support of the Right of the Poor*, pp. 26, 65–70. All subsequent citations are given parenthetically in the text.

8. Woodward, *An Address to the Public on the Expediency of a Regular Plan for the Maintenance and Government of the Poor*, p. 28.

9. Sherer, *Remarks upon the Present State of the Poor*, p. 10. All subsequent citations are given parenthetically in the text.

10. Ruggles, *History of the Poor*, 1:xix–xx. All subsequent citations are given parenthetically in the text.

11. Haddow, *Political Science in American Colleges and Universities, 1636–1900*, p. 67.

12. Halevy, *Growth of Philosophical Radicalism* p. 23.

13. Meadley, *Memoirs of William Paley*, p. 117. His conservatism, which reached its zenith during the French Revolution, can be seen in *Reasons for Contentment* (1792).

14. Sidgwick, *Outlines of the History of Ethics*, p. 237.

15. Paley, *Principles of Moral and Political Philosophy*, 1:83. All subsequent citations are given parenthetically in the text.

16. The argument that a utilitarian philosophy such as Paley's is unable to provide good reasons for continuing to act by a rule when breaking the rule would increase pleasure or happiness is found in Gisborne, *Principles of Moral Philosophy*, pp. 39–40. Also see Smart and Williams, *Utilitarianism*, pp. 118–22.

Chapter Five

1. For a recent account of the debates over the Poor Law in early nineteenth-century England see Himmelfarb, *Idea of Poverty*.

2. Blum, "English Parliamentary Enclosure," p. 499.

3. Priestley, *An Essay on the First Principles of Government*, p. 17. All subsequent citations are given parenthetically in the text. For Priestley's utilitarian critique of government aid to the poor see his *Lectures on History and General Policy*, pp. 229–36.

4. Price, *A Review of the Principal Questions in Morals*, pp. 14–15. All subsequent citations are given parenthetically in the text.

5. Price, *Observations on the Nature of Civil Liberty*, pp. 6–7. All subsequent citations are given parenthetically in the text.

6. See Long, *Bentham on Liberty*, p. 51.

7. Lind, *An Englishman's Answer to the Declaration of the American Congress*, p. 4. All subsequent citations are given parenthetically in the text.

8. Lind, *Remarks on the Principal Acts of the 13th Parliament of Great Britain*, pp. 58–59.

9. Lind, *Three Letters to Dr. Price*, pp. 21–24.

10. Bowring, *Works of Jeremy Bentham*, 1:268. All subsequent citations are given parenthetically in the text.

11. Long, *Bentham on Liberty*, p. 21.

12. Hart, *Of Laws in General*, p. 253. All subsequent citations are given parenthetically in the text.

13. See Mack, *Jeremy Bentham*, p. 53.

14. See Ryan, *Property and Political Theory*, p. 99.

15. Stark, *Jeremy Bentham's Economic Writings*, 1:335–36.

16. Ibid., 1:117.

17. Parekh, *Bentham's Political Thought*, pp. 197–98.

18. Roberts, "Bentham's Poor Law Proposals," p. 31.

19. For his recommendation for corn granaries and price controls see his

Manual of Political Economy in Stark, ed., *Jeremy Bentham's Economic Writings*, 1:267, and his *Defense of a Maximum*, ibid., 3:296.

20. Bahmueller, *National Charity Company*, pp. 210, 213.

21. Colquhoun, *Treatise on Indigence*, p. 18.

22. Burke, *Reflections on the Revolution in France*, p. 136. All subsequent citations are given parenthetically in the text.

23. Edmund Burke, "Thoughts and Details on Scarcity," in *Works of the Right Honourable Edmund Burke*, 7:404. All subsequent citations are given parenthetically in the text.

24. Eden, *State of the Poor*, 1:411–12, 424. All subsequent citations are given parenthetically in the text.

25. Malthus, *An Essay on the Principle of Population, as It Affects the Future Improvement of Society*, p. 137.

26. Malthus, *An Essay on the Principles of Population; or a View of Its Past and Present Effects on Human Happiness*, 2:198. All subsequent citations are given parenthetically in the text.

27. Winch, *Malthus*, pp. 16–18, 44–48.

28. Hilton, *Age of Atonement*, p. 4.

29. Malthus, *Principles of Political Economy*, p. 379. Also see Winch, *Malthus*, p. 47; and O'Brien, *Classical Economists*, p. 230.

30. Malthus, *A Summary of the Principle of Population*, p. 269.

31. Hilton, *Age of Atonement*, p. 65.

32. Soloway, *Prelates and People*, p. 104.

33. Sumner, *A Treatise on the Records of the Creation and on the Moral Attributes of the Creator*, 2:32, 35. All subsequent citations are given parenthetically in the text.

34. Sumner, "Poor Laws," p. 295. All subsequent citations are given parenthetically in the text.

35. Chalmers, *On Political Economy*, p. iv. All subsequent citations are given parenthetically in the text.

36. Malthus, *Principles of Political Economy*, pp. 379–82.

37. Hilton, *Age of Atonement*, p. 80.

38. Ricardo, *The Principles of Political Economy and Taxation*, p. 61. All subsequent citations are given parenthetically in the text.

39. Mill, *An Essay on Government*, p. 47. All subsequent citations are given parenthetically in the text.

40. Higgs, *Palgrave's Dictionary of Political Economy*, p. 634.

41. Mill, "Beggar," p. 240.

42. Hilton, *Age of Atonement*, p. 80.

43. McCulloch, "Political Economy," pp. 237–38. All subsequent citations are given parenthetically in the text. For more on McCulloch see O'Brien, *J. R. McCulloch*.

44. O'Brien, *Classical Economists*, p. 272.

45. Webb, *Harriet Martineau*, pp. 99–100.

46. Marcet, *Conversations on Political Economy*, pp. 35–36. All subsequent citations are given parenthetically in the text.

47. Pichanick, *Harriet Martineau*, pp. 80–81.

48. Martineau, *Decamera. A Tale*, p. 18. All subsequent citations are given parenthetically in the text.

49. Martineau, *Cousin Marshall*, p. 34. All subsequent citations are given parenthetically in the text.

50. Gilbert, "The Morning Chronicle, Poor Laws, and Political Economy," p. 507.

51. Ibid., pp. 515, 517.

52. Ibid., p. 518.

53. McCulloch, "Poor Laws," p. 315. All subsequent citations are given parenthetically in the text.

54. Senior, *Two Lectures on Population*, p. 51.

55. Senior, *Industrial Efficiency and Social Economy*, 2:307.

56. See Bowley, *Nassau Senior and Classical Economics*, and Paul, *Moral Revolution and Economic Science*.

57. Senior, *Industrial Efficiency and Social Economy*, 2:316.

58. Senior, *Historical and Philosophical Essays*, 2:46.

59. Bowley, *Nassau Senior and Classical Economics*, p. 293.

60. Ibid., pp. 294–95.

61. Senior, *Industrial Efficiency and Social Economy*, 2:312–13.

62. Lloyd, *Four Lectures on Poor Laws*, pp. 55–56. All subsequent citations are given parenthetically in the text.

63. Lloyd, *Two Lectures on the Justice of the Poor Laws*, p. 10. All subsequent citations are given parenthetically in the text.

64. Read, *An Inquiry into the Natural Grounds of Right to Vendible Property or Wealth*, p. 87. All subsequent citations are given parenthetically in the text.

65. Scrope, "*Political Economy* by Thomas Chalmers," p. 66.

66. Scrope, "*Illustrations of Political Economy* by Harriet Martineau," p. 136.

67. Scrope, *Principles of Political Economy*, p. 305. All subsequent citations are given parenthetically in the text.

68. Scrope, "Report by the Commissioners," p. 241.

69. Black, *Economic Writings of Mountiford Longfield*, p. 169. All subsequent citations are given parenthetically in the text.

70. Black, "Introduction," ibid., p. 25.

Chapter Six

1. Wollstonecraft, *Vindication of the Rights of Man*, p. 8. All subsequent citations are given parenthetically in the text. Also see her *Vindication of the Rights of Women*, chap. 9.

2. Powell, *Tom Paine*, pp. 198–99.

3. Foner, *Complete Writings of Thomas Paine*, 1:426. All subsequent citations are given parenthetically in the text.

4. For a recent discussion of Paine's theory of welfare rights see Seaman, "Thomas Paine."

5. For more on *Agrarian Justice* see Foner, *Tom Paine and Revolutionary America*, pp. 249–52.

6. Barlow, *Advice to the Privileged Orders in the Several States of Europe*, pp. 96–97. All subsequent citations are given parenthetically in the text.

7. Oswald, *Review of the Constitution of Great Britain*, pp. 22–23.

8. Dyer, *Complaints of the Poor People of England*, pp. 20–21.

9. Thompson, *Making of the English Working Class*, p. 157.

10. Thelwall, *Rights of Nature*, p. 34. All subsequent citations are given parenthetically in the text; page references to Thelwall's *Rights of Nature, Part the Second*, are preceded by 2.

11. See Dickinson, *Liberty and Property*, pp. 257–69.

12. See the "Biographical Notes" appended to Ogilvie, *An Essay on the Right of Property in Land*, p. 243. All subsequent citations are given parenthetically in the text.

13. Spence, *Pig's Meat; or, Lessons for the Swinish Multitude*, 2:168.

14. For more on Spence's life see Rudkin, *Thomas Spence and His Connections*.

15. Knox, "Thomas Spence," p. 75.

16. Ibid., p. 85.

17. Spence, *Real Rights of Man*, pp. 5–6. All subsequent citations are given parenthetically in the text.

18. Spence, *The Important Trial of Thomas Spence*, p. vi.

19. Spence, *The Rights of Infants*, p. 21.

20. Spence, *Restorer of Society to Its Natural State*. All subsequent citations are given parenthetically in the text.

21. Knox, "Thomas Spence," pp. 95–96.

22. Evans, *Christian Policy, the Salvation of the Empire*, p. 27. See Parssinen, "The Revolutionary Party in London."

23. Spence, *Rights of Infants*, pp. 3, 12.

24. See Hadfield, *Chartist Land Company*, and MacAskill, "Chartist Land Plan," pp. 304–41.

25. The most complete and recent discussion of Skidmore and the politics out of which he emerged is in Wilencz, *Chants Democratic*. See Blatchly, *An Essay on Common Wealths*, p. 3.

26. Byllesby, *Observations on the Sources and Effects of Unequal Wealth*, pp. 26–27.

27. Skidmore, *Rights of Man to Property*, pp. 58–62. All subsequent citations are given parenthetically in the text.

28. See Zahler, *Eastern Workingmen and National Land Policy*.

29. *Radical* 1 (January 1841): 2.

30. Johnson and Porter, eds., *National Party Platforms*, p. 19.

31. Pessen, *Most Uncommon Jacksonians*, pp. 149–50.

32. *Republican* 4 (November 1820). All subsequent citations are given parenthetically in the text.

33. Thompson, *Making of the English Working Class*, p. 746.

34. *Cobbett's Weekly Political Register* 34 (October 1818).

35. Spencer, *Social Statics*, p. 279.

36. Cobbett, *A History of the Protestant Reformation*, vol. 1, paragraph 37. All subsequent citations are given parenthetically in the text.

37. Cobbett, *Poor Man's Friend*, paragraph 73. All subsequent citations are given parenthetically in the text.

38. See Hobsbawm and Rudé, *Captain Swing*.

39. Hollis, *Pauper Press*, p. 218. The best recent discussion of these authors is in Thompson, *People's Science*.

40. See Menger, *The Right to the Whole Produce of Labour*.

41. Dinwiddy, "Charles Hall, Early English Socialist."

42. Claeys, "Four Letters between Thomas Spence and Charles Hall," pp. 317.

43. Hall, *The Effects of Civilization*, pp. 83, 216, 256–57. All subsequent citations are given parenthetically in the text.

44. Thomas Hodgskin, *The Natural and Artificial Right of Property Contrasted*, p. 21. All subsequent citations are given parenthetically in the text.

45. Hodgskin, *Popular Political Economy*, p. 241. All subsequent citations are given parenthetically in the text.

46. Thompson, *An Inquiry into the Principles of the Distribution of Wealth*, p. 1. All subsequent citations are given parenthetically in the text. For more on Thompson see Pankhurst, *William Thompson*.

47. Gray, *A Lecture on Human Happiness*, p. 8. All subsequent citations are given parenthetically in the text.

48. Thompson, *Making of the English Working Class*, p. 812, and Plummer, *Bronterre*, p. 45.

49. Plummer, *Bronterre*, p. 55.

50. *Poor Man's Guardian*, no. 94, March 23, 1833. All subsequent citations are given parenthetically in the text.

Conclusion

1. Smith, *Lectures on Jurisprudence*, p. 468.

2. For more on the new liberalism see Freeden, *New Liberalism*; Collini, *Liberalism and Sociology*; Emy, *Liberals, Radicals, and Social Politics*; and Clarke, *Liberals and Social Democrats*.

3. Mill, *Principles of Political Economy*, p. 233. All subsequent citations are given parenthetically in the text.

4. Green, *Principles of Political Obligation*, pp. 226–29 and Hobhouse, *Liberalism*, pp. 52–53. All subsequent citations are given parenthetically in the text.

5. Spencer, *Social Statics*, p. 103.

Primary Sources

Newspapers

Black Dwarf. 1817–20.
British Magazine. 1832.
Cobbett's Weekly Political Register. 1818–20.
Gorgon. 1818–19.
Poor Man's Guardian. 1831–35.
Radical. 1841.
Republican. 1820–24.

Books and Articles

Balfour, James. *A Delineation of the Nature and Obligation of Morality.* Edinburgh, 1763.
Barlow, Joel. *Advice to the Priviledged Orders in the Several States of Europe* (Part 1, 1792; Part 2, 1795). Ithaca, N.Y.: Cornell University Press, 1956.
Black, R. D. Collison, ed. *The Economic Writings of Mountifort Longfield.* New York: Augustus M. Kelley, 1971.
Blackstone, William. *Commentaries on the Laws of England.* 4 vols. Oxford, 1765–69.
Blatchly, Cornelius. *An Essay on Common Wealths.* New York, 1822.
Bowring, John, ed. *The Works of Jeremy Bentham.* 11 vols. Edinburgh, 1838–43.
Burke, Edmund. *Reflections on the Revolution in France* (1790). Edited and with an Introduction by J. G. A. Pocock. Indianapolis: Hackett, 1987.
———. *The Works of the Right Honourable Edmund Burke.* Vol. 7. London, 1808.
Burn, Richard. *The History of the Poor Laws.* London, 1764.
Byllesby, Langton. *Observations on the Sources and Effects of Unequal Wealth.* New York, 1826.
Chalmers, Thomas. *On Political Economy.* Glasgow, 1832.
Cobbett, William. *A History of the Protestant Reformation.* 2 vols. London, 1829.
———. *Legacy to Labourers.* London, 1834.
———. *The Poor Man's Friend.* London, 1829.
Colquhoun, Patrick. *The State of Indigence.* London, 1799.

_____. *A Treatise on Indigence*. London, 1806.

Cumberland, Richard. *A Treatise of the Laws of Nature*. Translated by John Maxwell. London, 1727.

Dalrymple, James (Lord Stair). *The Institutions of the Law of Scotland*. Edinburgh, 1681.

Dyer, George. *The Complaints of the Poor People of England*. London, 1793.

Eaton, Daniel Isaac. *The Trial of Daniel Isaac Eaton*. New York, 1794.

Eden, Frederick Morton. *The State of the Poor*. 3 vols. London, 1796.

Erskine, John. *An Institute of the Law of Scotland*. Edinburgh, 1773.

Evans, Thomas. *Christian Policy, the Salvation of the Empire*. London, 1816.

Ferguson, Adam. *An Essay on the History of Civil Society* (1767). New Brunswick: Transaction Books, 1980.

_____. *Institutes of Moral Philosophy*. Edinburgh, 1773.

_____. *Principles of Moral and Political Science*. Edinburgh, 1792.

Filmer, Robert. *Patriarcha and Other Political Works*. Edited by Peter Laslett. Oxford: Basil Blackwell, 1949.

Fletcher, Andrew. *Selected Political Writings and Speeches*. Edited by David Daiches. Edinburgh: John Donald, 1979.

Foner, Philip A., ed. *The Complete Writings of Thomas Paine*. 2 vols. New York: Citadel Press, 1945.

Fordyce, David. *Dialogues Concerning Education*. 2 vols. London, 1748.

_____. "The Elements of Moral Philosophy." In *The Preceptor*. Edited by Robert Dodsley. London, 1769.

Gisborne, Thomas. *The Principles of Moral Philosophy*. London, 1795.

Gray, John. *A Lecture on Human Happiness* (1825). Philadelphia, 1826.

Green, T. H. *The Principles of Political Obligation* (1880). Ann Arbor: University of Michigan Press, 1967.

Greig, J. Y. T., ed. *The Letters of David Hume*. 2 vols. Oxford: Oxford University Press, 1932.

Grotius, Hugo. *The Rights of War and Peace*. To which are added all the large notes of Jean Barbeyrac. London, 1738.

Hall, Charles. *The Effects of Civilization on the People in European States*. London, 1805.

Hart, H. L. A., ed. *Of Laws in General*. London: Athlone Press, 1970.

Hobbes, Thomas. *De Cive or The Citizen* (1642). Edited by Sterling Lamprecht. New York: Appleton-Century-Crofts, 1949.

_____. *The Elements of Law* (1642). In *Body, Man, and Citizen*. Edited by Richard Peters. New York: Collier Books, 1962.

_____. *Leviathan* (1651). Edited and with an introduction by C. B. Macpherson. Middlesex, Eng.: Penguin Books, 1968.

Hobhouse, L. T. *Liberalism* (1911). New York: Oxford University Press, 1974.

Hodgeskin, Thomas. *Labour Defended*. London, 1825.

_____. *The Natural and Artificial Right of Property Contrasted*. London, 1832.

_____. *Popular Political Economy*. London, 1827.

Home, Henry (Lord Kames). *Essays on the Principles of Morality and Natural Religion*. Edinburgh, 1751.

————. *Historical Law Tracts.* 2d ed. Edinburgh, 1761.

————. *Principles of Equity.* Edinburgh, 1825.

————. *Sketches of the History of Man.* 4 vols. Edinburgh, 1778.

Hume, David. *A Letter from a Gentleman to His Friend in Edinburgh.* Edinburgh, 1745.

————. *The Philosophical Works of David Hume.* 4 vols. Edited by T. H. Green and T. H. Grose. London, 1882.

————. *A Treatise of Human Nature* (1740). Edited by L. A. Selby-Bigge. New York: Oxford University Press, 1978.

Hutcheson, Francis. *Considerations on Patronages Addressed to the Gentlemen of England.* Edinburgh, 1773.

————. *An Inquiry Concerning the Original of Our Ideas of Virtue or Moral Good* (1725). In *British Moralists.* Edited by L. A. Selby-Bigge. New York: Dover Publications, 1965.

————. *A Short Introduction to Moral Philosophy.* Glasgow, 1747.

————. *A System of Moral Philosophy.* 2 vols. London, 1755.

Lind, John. *An Englishman's Answer to the Declaration of the American Congress.* New York, 1775.

————. *Remarks on the Principal Acts of the 13th Parliament of Great Britain.* London, 1775.

————. *Three Letters to Dr. Price.* London, 1776.

Lloyd, William Forster. *Four Lectures on Poor Laws.* London, 1835.

————. *Two Lectures on the Justice of the Poor Laws.* London, 1837.

Locke, John. *Essays on the Law of Nature.* Edited and with an Introduction by W. von Leyden. Oxford: Oxford University Press, 1965.

————. *A Letter Concerning Toleration* (1689). New York: Bobbs-Merrill, 1955.

————. *Two Treatises of Government* (1690). Edited and with an Introduction by Peter Laslett. New York: Mentor, 1960.

Longfield, Mountifort. *The Economic Writings of Mountifort Longfield.* Edited and with an Introduction by R. D. Collison Black. New York: Augustus M. Kelley, 1971.

McCulloch, J. R. "Political Economy." In *Supplement to the Fourth, Fifth, and Sixth Editions of the Encyclopaedia Britannica,* Vol. 6. Edinburgh, 1824.

————. "Poor Laws." *Edinburgh Review* 47 (1828): 303–30.

————. *The Principles of Political Economy* (1825). Edinburgh, 1864.

Malthus, Thomas. *An Essay on the Principle of Population, as It Affects the Future Improvement of Society* (1798). Middlesex, Eng.: Penguin, 1970.

————. *An Essay on the Principles of Population; or a View of Its Past and Present Effects on Human Happiness* (1803). New York: Dutton, 1933.

————. *Principles of Political Economy* (1820). 2d ed. London, 1836.

Marcet, Jane. *Conversations on Political Economy.* London, 1824.

Martineau, Harriet. *Cousin Marshall.* In *Illustrations of Political Economy,* Vol. 3. London, 1834.

————. *Decamera. A Tale.* In *Illustrations of Political Economy,* Vol. 1. London, 1832.

Meadley, George Wilson. *Memoirs of William Paley.* London, 1809.

Mill, James. "Beggar." In *Supplement to the Fourth, Fifth, and Sixth Editions of the Encyclopaedia Britannica*, Vol. 2, pp. 231–48. Edinburgh, 1824.

————. *An Essay on Government* (1824). Indianapolis: Bobbs-Merrill, 1955.

Mill, John Stuart. *The Principles of Political Economy* (1848). Edited and with an Introduction by W. J. Ashley. London, 1909.

More, Henry. *Enchiridion Ethicum* (1666). Translated by Edward Southwell. New York: Facsimile Text Society, 1930.

Nasmith, J. *The Duty of Overseers of the Poor*. London, 1799.

Ogilvie, William. *An Essay on the Right of Property in Land* (1782). Edited and with Biographical Notes by D. C. MacDonald. London, 1891.

Oswald, James. *Review of the Constitution of Great Britain*. Paris, 1792.

Paley, William. *The Principles of Moral and Political Philosophy*. 2 vols. 14th ed. London, 1803.

————. *Reasons for Contentment*. London, 1792.

Parekh, Bhikhu, ed. *Bentham's Political Thought*. New York: Barnes and Noble, 1973.

Price, Richard. *Additional Observations on the Nature and Value of Civil Liberty*. London, 1776.

————. *Observations on the Nature of Civil Liberty*. 8th ed. London, 1778.

————. *A Review of the Principal Questions in Morals*. 2d ed. London, 1769.

Priestley, Joseph. *An Essay on the First Principles of Government*. London, 1768.

————. *Lectures on History and General Policy*. London, 1788.

Pufendorf, Samuel. *Of the Law of Nature and Nations*. 2d ed. Carefully corrected, and compared with Mr. Barbeyrac's French Translations; with the edition of his notes. Translated by Basil Kennett. London, 1710.

Read, Samuel. *An Inquiry into the Natural Grounds of Right to Vendible Property or Wealth*. Edinburgh, 1829.

Reid, Thomas. *The Philosophical Works of Thomas Reid*. 2 vols. Edited by Sir William Hamilton. London: Longmans, Green, and Company, 1895.

Ricardo, David. *The Principles of Political Economy and Taxation* (1817). London: J. M. Dent, 1973.

Rotwein, David, ed. *David Hume: Writings on Economics*. Madison: University of Wisconsin Press, 1970.

Ruggles, Thomas. *History of the Poor*. 2 vols. London, 1793.

Rutherforth, Thomas. *Institutes of Natural Law; being the substance of a course of lectures on Grotius' De Jure Belli Ac Pacis*. Baltimore, 1832.

Scrope, George Poulett. "*Illustrations of Political Economy* by Harriet Martineau." *Quarterly Review* 49 (1833): 136–52.

————. "*Political Economy* by Thomas Chalmers." *Quarterly Review* 48 (1832): 39–69.

————. "Poor Law." *Quarterly Review* 44 (1831): 511–54.

————. *Principles of Political Economy*. London, 1833.

————. "Report by the Commissioners." *Quarterly Review* 52 (1834): 233–61.

Selden, John. *Of the Dominion, or, Ownership of the Sea*. Translated by Marchamont Nedham. London, 1652.

————. *Table-Talk*. London, 1884.

Senior, Nassau W. *Historical and Philosophical Essays.* 2 vols. London, 1865.
———. *Industrial Efficiency and Social Economy.* 2 vols. Edited by S. Leon Levy. New York: Henry Holt, 1928.
———. *Two Lectures on Population.* London, 1829.
Sherer, J. G. *Remarks upon the Present State of the Poor.* Southampton, 1796.
Sidney, Algernon. *The Works of Algernon Sidney.* London, 1772.
Skidmore, Thomas. *The Rights of Man to Property.* New York, 1829.
Smith, Adam. *An Inquiry into the Nature and Causes of the Wealth of Nations* (1776). 2 vols. Edited by R. H. Campbell, A. S. Skinner, and W. B. Todd. Oxford: Oxford University Press, 1976.
———. *Lectures on Jurisprudence.* Edited by R. L. Meek, D. D. Raphael, and P. G. Stein. New York: Oxford University Press, 1978.
———. *The Theory of Moral Sentiments.* Indianapolis: Liberty Press, 1969.
Spence, Thomas. *The Important Trial of Thomas Spence.* London, 1803.
———. *Pig's Meat; or, Lessons for the Swinish Multitude.* 2 vols. London: 1793–96.
———. *The Real Rights of Man* (1775). In *The Pioneers of Land Reform.* Edited by Max Beer. New York: Knopf, 1920.
———. *Restorer of Society to Its Natural State.* London, 1799.
———. *The Rights of Infants.* London, 1797.
Spencer, Herbert. *Social Statics* (1850). New York: Robert Schalkenbach Foundation, 1954.
Stark, W., ed. *Jeremy Bentham's Economic Writings.* 3 vols. London: George Allen & Unwin, 1952.
Stein, Peter. *Legal Evolution.* Cambridge: Cambridge University Press, 1980.
Steuart, James. "A Dissertation on the Policy of Grain." In *Works, Political Metaphysical, and Chronological,* Vol. 5. London, 1805.
Stewart, Dugald. *An Account of the Life and Writings of Adam Smith, LL.D.* In *The Collected Works of Dugald Stewart,* Vol. 10. Edited by Sir William Hamilton. Edinburgh, 1858.
Sumner, John Bird. "Poor-Laws." In *Supplement to the Fourth, Fifth, and Sixth Editions of the Encyclopaedia Britannica,* Vol. 6. Edinburgh, 1824.
———. *A Treatise on the Records of the Creation and on the Moral Attributes of the Creator.* 2 vols. London, 1833.
Thelwall, John. *The Rights of Nature.* London, 1796.
———. *The Rights of Nature. Part the Second.* London, 1796.
Thompson, William. *An Inquiry into the Principles of the Distribution of Wealth Most Conducive to Human Happiness.* London, 1824.
———. *Labour Rewarded.* London, 1827.
Townsend, Joseph. *A Dissertation on the Poor Laws.* 1786.
———. *Observations on Various Plans Offered to the Public for the Relief of the Poor.* 1788.
Tyrrell, James. *A Brief Disquisition of the Law of Nature.* London, 1692.
———. *Patriarcha Non Monarcha.* London, 1681.
Whately, Richard. *Introductory Lectures on Political Economy.* London, 1832.
Wolfe, Don, ed. *Leveller Manifestoes of the Puritan Revolution.* New York: Knopf, 1967.

Wollstonecraft, Mary. *A Vindication of the Rights of Man.* 2d ed. London, 1790.

———. *A Vindication of the Rights of Women* (1792). New York: Norton, 1975.

Woodhouse, A. S. P., ed. *Puritanism and Liberty.* London: J. M. Dent, 1938.

Woodward, Richard. *An Address to the Public on the Expediency of a Regular Plan for the Maintenance and Government of the Poor.* Dublin, 1775.

———. *An Argument in Support of the Right of the Poor.* Dublin, 1768.

Secondary Sources

Books

Appleby, Joyce Oldham. *Economic Thought and Ideology in Seventeenth-Century England.* Princeton: Princeton University Press, 1978.

Ashcraft, Richard. *Locke's Two Treatises of Government.* London: Basil Blackwell, 1988.

———. *Revolutionary Politics and Locke's Two Treatises of Government.* Princeton: Princeton University Press, 1986.

Atiyah, P. S. *The Rise and Fall of Freedom of Contract.* London: Oxford University Press, 1979.

Bahmueller, Charles. *The National Charity Company.* Berkeley and Los Angeles: University of California Press, 1981.

Becker, Lawrence. *Property Rights.* London: Routledge & Kegan Paul, 1977.

Black, R. D. Collison. *Economic Thought and the Irish Question, 1817–1820.* Cambridge: Cambridge University Press, 1960.

Bowley, Marion. *Nassau Senior and Classical Economics.* London: Allen & Unwin, 1937.

Burkitt, Brian. *Radical Political Economy.* New York: New York University Press, 1984.

Campbell, R. H., and A. S. Skinner, eds. *The Origins and Nature of the Scottish Enlightenment.* Edinburgh: John Donald, 1982.

Christie, Ian. *Stress and Stability in Late 18th Century Britain.* New York: Oxford University Press, 1984.

Clark, M. L. *Paley.* Toronto: University of Toronto Press, 1974.

Clarke, Peter. *Liberals and Social Democrats.* New York: Cambridge University Press, 1978.

Coats, A. W., ed. *The Classical Economists and Economic Policy.* London: Methuen, 1971.

Collini, Stefan. *Liberalism and Sociology.* New York: Cambridge University Press, 1979.

Cowherd, Raymond. *Political Economists and the English Poor Law.* Athens: Ohio University Press, 1977.

Cranston, Maurice. *John Locke, a Biography.* London: Longmans, Green, 1957.

Cullen, L. M., and T. C. Smout, eds. *Comparative Aspects of Scottish and Irish Economic and Social History, 1600–1900*. Edinburgh: John Donald, 1985.

Derry, John W. *The Radical Tradition*. London: St. Martin's Press, 1967.

Dickinson, H. T. *Liberty and Property: Political Ideology in Eighteenth-Century Britain*. New York: Holmes and Meier, 1977.

Dow, F. D. *Radicalism in the English Revolution, 1640–1660*. New York: Basil Blackwell, 1985.

Dumbauld, Edward. *The Life and Legal Writings of Hugo Grotius*. Norman: University of Oklahoma Press, 1969.

Dunn, John. *The Political Thought of John Locke*. Cambridge: Cambridge University Press, 1969.

Dwyer, J., R. A. Mason, and A. Murdoch. *New Perspectives on the Politics and Culture of Early Modern Scotland*. Edinburgh: John Donald, 1982.

Emy, H. V. *Liberals, Radicals, and Social Politics, 1892–1914*. London: Cambridge University Press, 1973.

Foner, Eric. *Tom Paine and Revolutionary America*. New York: Oxford University Press, 1976.

Forbes, Duncan. *Hume's Philosophical Politics*. Cambridge: Cambridge University Press, 1975.

Fox-Bourne, H. R. *The Life of John Locke*. 2 vols. New York: Harper and Brothers, 1876.

Franklin, Julian. *John Locke and the Theory of Sovereignty*. Cambridge: Cambridge University Press, 1978.

Freeden, Michael. *The New Liberalism*. Oxford: Oxford University Press, 1978.

Gierke, Otto von. *Natural Law and the Theory of Society*. Translated by Ernest Barker. Boston: Beacon Press, 1957.

Gore, Charles, ed. *Property: Its Duties and Rights*. London: Macmillan, 1915.

Gray, John. *Liberalism*. Minneapolis: University of Minnesota Press, 1986.

Grunebaum, James O. *Private Ownership*. London: Routledge & Kegan Paul, 1986.

Haakonssen, Knud. *The Science of a Legislator*. Cambridge: Cambridge University Press, 1981.

Haddow, Anna. *Political Science in American Colleges and Universities, 1636–1900*. New York: Appleton-Century, 1939.

Hadfield, Alice Mary. *The Chartist Land Company*. Devon, Eng.: David & Charles, 1970.

Halevy, Elie. *The Growth of Philosophical Radicalism*. London: Faber and Faber, 1952.

Hayek, Frederick. *Law, Legislation, and Morality*. Vol. 2: *The Mirage of Social Justice*. Chicago: University of Chicago Press, 1976.

Higgs, Henry, ed. *Palgrave's Dictionary of Political Economy*. London: Macmillan, 1926.

Hilton, Boyd. *The Age of Atonement*. London: Oxford University Press, 1988.

Himmelfarb, Gertrude. *The Idea of Poverty*. New York: Knopf, 1984.

Hobhouse, L. T. *Liberalism*. New York: Oxford University Press, 1964.

Hobsbawm, Eric, and George Rudé. *Captain Swing*. New York: Norton, 1968.

Hollis, Patricia. *The Pauper Press*. London: Oxford University Press, 1970.

Hont, Istvan, and Michael Ignatieff, eds. *Wealth and Virtue: The Shaping of Political Economy in the Scottish Enlightenment*. Cambridge: Cambridge University Press, 1983.

Hope, Vincent, ed. *Philosophers of the Scottish Enlightenment*. Edinburgh: Edinburgh University Press, 1984.

Hugins, Walter. *Jacksonian Democracy and the Working Class*. Stanford: Stanford University Press, 1960.

Johnson, Donald B., and Kirk H. Porter, eds. *National Party Platforms, 1840–1972*. Chicago: University of Illinois Press, 1975.

Jordan, W. K. *Philanthropy in England*. London: George Allen & Unwin, 1959.

Kenyon, J. P. *Revolution Principles*. Cambridge: Cambridge University Press, 1977.

Knight, W. S. M. *The Life and Works of Hugo Grotius*. London: Sweet and Maxwell, 1925.

Krieger, Leonard. *The Politics of Discretion*. Chicago: University of Chicago Press, 1965.

Larkin, Pascal. *Property in the 18th Century*. Dublin: Cork University Press, 1930.

Lehman, William C. *Henry Home, Lord Kames, and the Scottish Enlightenment*. The Hague: Martinus Nijhoff, 1971.

Leites, Edmund, ed. *Conscience and Casuistry in Early Modern Europe*. New York: Cambridge University Press, 1988.

Long, Douglas G. *Bentham on Liberty*. Toronto: University of Toronto Press, 1977.

Lyons, David. *In the Interest of the Governed*. Oxford: Oxford University Press, 1973.

Mack, M. P. *Jeremy Bentham: An Odyssey of His Ideas*. New York: Columbia University Press, 1963.

Macpherson, C. B. *Burke*. New York: Hill and Wang, 1980.

――――. *The Political Theory of Possessive Individualism*. Oxford: Oxford University Press, 1962.

Meek, Ronald. *Economics and Ideology and Other Essays*. London: Chapman and Hall, 1967.

――――. *Social Science and the Ignoble Savage*. Cambridge: Cambridge University Press, 1976.

Menger, Anton. *The Right to the Whole Produce of Labor*. London, 1899.

Miller, David. *Philosophy and Ideology in Hume's Political Thought*. Oxford: Oxford University Press, 1981.

Mitchison, Rosalind, and Nicholas Phillipson, eds. *Scotland in the Age of Improvement*. Edinburgh: John Donald, 1970.

Moore, James, and Michael Silverthorne. "The Political Writings of Gershom Carmichael." Unpublished.

Murphy, Antoin E., ed. *Economists and the Irish Economy from the Eighteenth Century to the Present Day*. Dublin: Irish Academic Press, 1984.

O'Brien, David P. *The Classical Economists*. Oxford: Oxford University Press, 1975.

――――. *J. R. McCulloch*. London: George Allen & Unwin, 1970.

Pagden, Anthony, ed. *The Languages of Political Theory in Early Modern Europe.* New York: Cambridge University Press, 1988.

Pankhurst, Richard K. P. *William Thompson.* London: Watts and Company, 1954.

Parel, Anthony, and Thomas Flanagan. *Theories of Property.* Calgary: Wilfred Lauren University Press, 1979.

Parry, Geraint. *John Locke.* London: George Allen & Unwin, 1978.

Paul, Ellen Frankel. *Moral Revolution and Economic Science.* Westport, Conn: Greenwood Press, 1979.

Pessen, Edward. *Most Uncommon Jacksonians.* Albany: State University of New York Press, 1967.

Pichanick, Valerie Kossew. *Harriet Martineau.* Ann Arbor: University of Michigan Press, 1980.

Plummer, Alfred. *Bronterre.* London: George Allen & Unwin, 1971.

Pocock, J. G. A. *Virtue, Commerce, and History.* New York: Cambridge University Press, 1985.

Pocock, J. G. A., and Richard Ashcraft. *John Locke.* Berkeley and Los Angeles: University of California Press, 1980.

Polanyi, Karl. *The Great Transformation.* Boston: Beacon Press, 1944.

Porter, Roy. *English Society in the Eighteenth Century.* Middlesex, Eng.: Penguin, 1982.

Powell, David. *Tom Paine, the Greatest Exile.* New York: St. Martin's Press, 1980.

Poynter, J. R. *Society and Pauperism.* London: Routledge & Kegan Paul, 1969.

Prothero, I. J. *Artisans and Politics in Early Nineteenth-Century London.* London: Dawson, 1979.

Reeve, Andrew. *Property.* London: Macmillan, 1986.

Roberts, David. *Paternalism in Early Victorian England.* New Brunswick, N.J.: Rutgers University Press, 1979.

Rose, Michael E., ed. *The English Poor Law.* London: David and Charles: Newton Abbot, 1971.

Ross, Ian Simpson. *Lord Kames and the Scotland of His Day.* London: Oxford University Press, 1972.

Rudkin, Olive. *Thomas Spence and His Connections.* New York: Augustus M. Kelley, 1966.

Ryan, Alan. *Property.* London: Open University Press, 1987.

———. *Property and Political Theory.* Oxford: Basil Blackwell, 1984.

Schenk, William. *The Concern for Social Justice in the Puritan Revolution.* London: Longmans, Green, 1948.

Schlatter, Richard. *Private Property.* New Brunswick, N.J.: Rutgers University Press, 1951.

Schochet, Gordon. *Patriarchalism in Political Thought.* Oxford: Basil Blackwell, 1975.

Schumpeter, Joseph A. *History of Economic Analysis.* Oxford: Oxford University Press, 1954.

Scott, Jonathan. *Algernon Sidney and the English Republic, 1623–1677.* Cambridge: Cambridge University Press, 1988.

Sher, Richard. *Church and University in the Scottish Enlightenment.* Princeton: Princeton University Press, 1985.

Sidgwick, Henry. *Outlines of the History of Ethics.* Boston: Beacon Press, 1960.

Smart, J. J. C., and Bernard Williams. *Utilitarianism: For and Against.* Cambridge: Cambridge University Press, 1973.

Soloway, R. A. *Prelates and People.* London: Routledge & Kegan Paul, 1969.

Spater, George. *William Cobbett the Poor Man's Friend.* Cambridge: Cambridge University Press, 1982.

Teichgraeber, Richard F., III. *Free Trade and Moral Philosophy.* Durham, N.C.: Duke University Press, 1986.

Thompson, E. P. *The Making of the English Working Class.* New York: Random House, 1963.

Thompson, Noel W. *The People's Science.* Cambridge: Cambridge University Press, 1984.

Tuck, Richard. *Natural Rights Theories.* Cambridge: Cambridge University Press, 1979.

Tucker, Robert, ed. *The Marx-Engels Reader.* New York: Norton, 1978.

Tully, James. *A Discourse on Property.* Cambridge: Cambridge University Press, 1980.

Turner, Michael. *English Parliamentary Enclosure.* Hamden, Eng.: Archon Books, 1980.

Vaughn, Karen. *John Locke, Economist and Social Scientist.* Chicago: University of Chicago Press, 1980.

Vollenhoven, C. Van. *The Framework of Grotius' Book De Iure Belli Ac Pacis.* Amsterdam: Martinus Nijoff, 1932.

Webb, Robert K. *Harriet Martineau, a Radical Victorian.* New York: Columbia University Press, 1960.

Wellman, Carl. *Welfare Rights.* Totowa, N.J.: Rowman & Allanheld, 1980.

Wilencz, Sean. *Chants Democratic: New York City and the Rise of the American Working Class, 1788–1850.* New York: Oxford University Press, 1984.

Williams, Raymond. *Cobbett.* Oxford: Oxford University Press, 1983.

Winch, Donald. *Adam Smith's Politics.* Cambridge: Cambridge University Press, 1978.

―――. *Malthus.* New York: Oxford University Press, 1987.

Wood, Neal. *John Locke and Agrarian Capitalism.* Berkeley and Los Angeles: University of California Press, 1986.

Yelling, J. A. *Common Field and Enclosure in England, 1450–1850.* Hamden, Eng.: Archon Books, 1977.

Zahler, Helene Sara. *Eastern Workingmen and National Land Policy, 1829–1862.* New York: Columbia University Press, 1941.

Articles and Chapters

Ashcraft, Richard. "Political Theory and Political Reform: John Locke's Essay on Virginia." *Western Political Quarterly* 22 (1969): 742–58.

Ashcraft, Richard, and M. M. Goldsmith. "Locke, Revolution Principles, and the Formation of Whig Ideology." *Historical Journal* 26 (1983): 773–800.

Aylmer, G. E. "The Meaning and Definition of Property in Seventeenth-Century England." *Past and Present* 86 (1980): 87–96.

Blaug, Mark. "The Myth of the Old Poor Law and the Making of the New." In Blaug, *Economic History and the History of Economics*, pp. 3–35. New York: New York University Press, 1986.

————. "The Poor Law Report Re-examined." In Blaug *Economic History and the History of Economics*, pp. 36–50. New York: New York University Press, 1986.

Blum, Jerome. "English Parliamentary Enclosure." *Journal of Modern History* 53 (1981): 477–504.

Briggs, Asa. "The Language of 'Class' in Early Nineteenth-Century England." In *The Collected Essays of Asa Briggs*, pp. 3–33. London: Harvester Press, 1986.

Campbell, R. H. "Francis Hutcheson: Father of the Scottish Enlightenment." In *The Origins and Nature of the Scottish Enlightenment*, edited by R. H. Campbell and A. S. Skinner, pp. 167–85. Edinburgh: John Donald, 1982.

Claeys, Gregory. "Four Letters between Thomas Spence and Charles Hall." *Notes and Queries* 28 (1981): 317–21.

Conniff, James. "Reason and History in Early Whig Thought: The Case of Algernon Sidney." *Journal of the History of Ideas* 43 (1982): 397–416.

Dickey, Lawrence. "Historicizing the Adam Smith Problem: Conceptual, Historiographical, and Textual Issues." *Journal of Modern History* 58 (1986): 579–609.

Dinwiddy, J. R. "Charles Hall, Early English Socialist." *International Review of Social History* 21 (1976): 256–76.

Dunn, John. "Consent in the Political Theory of John Locke." *Historical Journal* 10 (1967): 153–82.

————. "Justice and the Interpretation of Locke's Political Theory." *Political Studies* 16 (1968): 50–87.

Farr, James, and Clayton Roberts. "John Locke on the Glorious Revolution: A Rediscovered Document." *Historical Journal* 28 (1985): 385–98.

Forbes, Duncan. "Natural Law and the Scottish Enlightenment." In *The Origins and Nature of the Scottish Enlightenment*, edited by R. H. Campbell and A. S. Skinner, pp. 186–204. Edinburgh: John Donald, 1982.

Gates, Paul W. "The Homestead Act: Free Land Policy in Operation, 1862–1935." In *Land Use Policy and Problems in the United States*, edited by Howard W. Ottoson, pp. 28–46. Lincoln: University of Nebraska Press, 1963.

Gilbert, Geoffrey. "The Morning Chronicle, Poor Laws, and Political Economy." *History of Political Economy* 17 (1985): 507–21.

Goldie, Mark. "John Locke and Anglican Royalism." *Political Studies* 31 (1983): 86–102.

Gough, J. W. "James Tyrrell, Whig Historian and Friend of John Locke." *Historical Journal* 19 (1976): 581–610.

Haakonssen, Knud. "Hugo Grotius and the History of Political Thought." *Political Theory* 13 (1985): 239–65.

Hampsher-Monk, Iain. "John Thelwall and the Radical Critique of the British Constitution." Unpublished essay.

Hont, Istvan. "The Language of Sociability and Commerce." In *The Languages of Political Theory in Early Modern Europe*, edited by Anthony Pagden, pp. 20–43. New York: Cambridge University Press, 1988.

Hont, Istvan, and Michael Ignatieff. "Needs and Justice in the *Wealth of Nations*." In *Wealth and Virtue: The Shaping of Political Economy in the Scottish Enlightenment*, edited by Istvan Hont and Michael Ignatieff, pp. 1–44. Cambridge: Cambridge University Press, 1983.

Hundert, Edward J. "The Making of Homo Faber: John Locke between Ideology and History." *Journal of the History of Ideas* 33 (1972): 33–44.

Knox, Thomas R. "Thomas Spence: The Trumpet of Jubilee." *Past and Present* 76 (1977): 74–98.

Kramnick, Isaac. "The Left and Edmund Burke." *Political Theory* 11 (1983): 189–214.

———. "Religion and Radicalism in English Political Theory in the Age of Revolution." *Political Theory* 5 (1977): 505–34.

MacAskill, Joy. "The Chartist Land Plan." In *Chartist Studies*, edited by Asa Briggs, pp. 304–41. London: Macmillan, 1959.

MacCormick, Neil. "Law and Enlightenment." In *The Origins and Nature of the Scottish Enlightenment*, edited by R. H. Campbell and A. S. Skinner. Edinburgh: John Donald, 1982.

Mitchison, Rosalind. "The Making of the Old Scottish Poor Law." *Past and Present* 63 (1974): 58–93.

———. "Scottish Landowners and Communal Responsibility in the 18th Century." *British Journal for 18th Century Studies* 1 (1978): 41–45.

Moore, James. "The Half Philosophers of the Nation: Hume's Critique of Locke and the Scottish Theories of the Original Contract." Paper presented at the Tenth Hume Conference, Trinity College, Dublin, August 25–28, 1981.

———. "Hume's Theory of Justice and Property." *Political Studies* 24 (1976): 103–19.

———. "Locke and the Scottish Jurists." Paper presented at the Conference for the Study of Political Thought, Folger Shakespeare Library, Washington, D.C., 1980.

———. "The Two Systems of Francis Hutcheson: Between Civic Moralism and Natural Jurisprudence." Paper presented at the conference on British Political Thought in the Age of Walpole, Folger Shakespeare Library, Washington, D.C., December 1986.

Moore, James, and Michael Silverthorne. "Gershom Carmichael and the Natural Jurisprudence Tradition in Eighteenth-Century Scotland." In *Wealth and Virtue: The Shaping of Political Economy in the Scottish Enlightenment*, edited by Istvan Hont and Michael Ignatieff, pp. 73–88. Cambridge: Cambridge University Press, 1983.

Norton, David Fate. "Hume and His Scottish Critics" In *McGill Hume Studies*, edited by David F. Norton, Nicholas Capaldi, and W. Robison, pp. 309–24. San Diego: Austin Hill Press, 1979.

Olivecrona, Karl. "Appropriation in the State of Nature: Locke on the Origin of Property." *Journal of the History of Ideas* 35 (1974): 211–30.

Parssinen, T. M. "The Revolutionary Party in London, 1816–1820." *Bulletin of the Institute of Historical Research* 45 (1972): 266–82.

———. "Thomas Spence and the Origins of English Land Naturalization."
Journal of the History of Ideas 34 (1973): 135–41.

Pessen, Edward. "Thomas Skidmore, Agrarian Reformer in the Early American Labor Movement." *New York History* 22 (1954): 280–96.

Phillipson, Nicholas. "Culture and Society in the 18th Century Province." In *The University in Society*, vol. 2, edited by Lawrence Stone, pp. 407–48. Princeton: Princeton University Press, 1974.

Rashdall, Hastings. "The Philosophical Theory of Property." In *Property: Its Duties and Rights*, edited by Charles Gore, pp. 33–64. London: Macmillan, 1915.

Rashid, Salim. "The Policy of Laissez-Faire during Scarcities." *Economic Journal* 90 (1980): 492–503.

Robbins, Caroline. "When It Is That Colonies May Turn Independent: An Analysis of the Environment and Politics of Francis Hutcheson." *William and Mary Quarterly* 11 (1954): 214–51.

Roberts, Warren. "Bentham's Poor Law Proposals." *Bentham Newsletter* 3 (1979): 28–45.

Seaman, John W. "Thomas Paine: Ransom, Civil Peace, and the Natural Right to Welfare." *Political Theory* 16 (1988): 120–42.

Smout, T. C. "Famine and Famine-relief in Scotland." In *Comparative Aspects of Scottish and Irish Economic and Social History, 1600–1900*, edited by L. M. Cullen and T. C. Smout, pp. 21–31. Edinburgh: John Donald, 1985.

Sommerville, J. P. "John Selden, the Law of Nature, and the Origins of Government." *Historical Journal* 27 (1984): 437–47.

Stein, Peter. "Adam Smith's Jurisprudence—between Morality and Economics." *Cornell Law Review* 64 (1979): 621–38.

———. "From Pufendorf to Adam Smith: The Natural Law Tradition in Scotland." In *Festschrift fur Helmut Coing zum 70 Gebutstrag*, edited by N. Horn, K. Luig, and A. Sollner, pp. 667–79. Munich: Beck, 1982.

———. "Law and Society in Eighteenth-Century Scottish Thought." In *Scotland in the Age of Improvement*, edited by Rosalind Mitchison and Nicholas Phillipson. Edinburgh: John Donald, 1970.

Tarlton, Charles. "The Rulers Now on Earth: Locke's *Two Treatises* and the Revolution of 1688." *Historical Journal* 28 (1985): 279–98.

Teichgraeber, Richard F. III. " 'Less Abused Than I Had Reason to Expect': The Reception of Adam Smith's *The Wealth of Nations* in Britain, 1776–1790." *Historical Journal* 30 (1987): 337–66.

Thomas, Keith. "Social Origins of Hobbes' Political Thought." In *Hobbes Studies*, edited by Keith Brown, pp. 185–236. Cambridge, Mass.: Harvard University Press, 1965.

Thompson, Martyn P. "The Reception of Locke's *Two Treatises of Government*, 1690–1705." *Political Studies* 24 (1976): 184–91.

Tuck, Richard. "Grotius, Canneades and Hobbes." *Grotiana* 4 (1983): 43–62.

———. "The Modern Theory of Natural Law." In *The Languages of Political Theory in Early Modern Europe*, edited by Anthony Pagden, pp. 99–119. New York: Cambridge University Press, 1988.

Waldron, Jeremy. "Enough and as Good Left for Others." *Philosophical Quarterly* 29 (1979): 319–28.

———. "Locke, Tully, and the Regulation of Property." *Political Studies* 32 (1984): 98–106.

Waterman, A. M. C. "The Ideological Alliance of Political Economy and Christian Theology, 1798–1833." *Journal of Ecclesiastical History* 34 (1983): 231–44.

Winch, Donald. "The Burke-Smith Problem and Late Eighteenth-Century Political and Economic Thought." *Historical Journal* 28 (1985): 231–48.

81, 87–88, 104, 105, 144, 176; and property inequality, 46, 83, 160, 191; and laws, 66–67; property rights and, 79–80, 84, 86, 96, 100, 110–11, 129, 145–46, 182, 185–86
Pufendorf, Samuel, 10, 28, 32–33, 37–39, 42, 56, 68, 69, 71, 73–74, 88, 93–94, 151, 254; and Grotius, 11, 33–34, 38; and contracts, 14, 35–36, 48, 50–51, 92, 129, 231; and poor relief, 20, 36–37; and negative community, 34–35, 45, 124; and right of necessity, 36–37, 75, 130, 233; criticisms of, 78, 81

Quarterly Review, 196

Radical, 226
Radicalism, 204, 209, 211, 216, 221, 223, 227, 233, 247
Rainborough, Thomas, 23
Read, Samuel, 193–95, 197, 199, 200, 242
Real Rights of Man, The (Spence), 219, 221, 226
Rebellion, 149, 150; justified, 70, 71, 85–86, 120, 253
Reflections on the Revolution in France (Burke), 160, 163, 164, 202
Reform Act (1832), 246
Reformation, 230, 231, 249
Regicide Peace (Burke), 202, 212
Reid, Thomas, 75, 99–101, 103–4, 122, 216, 217
Religion, evangelical, 143
Religion, freedom of, 144, 206
Religious social theory, 175
Remarks on the Principal Acts of the 13th Parliament of Great Britain (Lind), 147
Remarks upon the Present State of the Poor (Sherer), 133
Representative institutions, 205; and property rights, 23–24, 67–68, 71, 99, 108–9, 122; right to, 61–63, 85–86, 146–47, 148, 206; com-

prised of the wealthy, 132
Republican, 227
Restorer of Society to Its Natural State (Spence), 219, 221–22
Review of the Constitution of Great Britain (Oswald), 211
Review of the Principal Questions in Morals, A (Price), 145
Revolution, 160, 168, 205, 230
Ricardian Socialists, 201, 234
Ricardo, David, 171, 175–76, 193–94, 196
Rights of Infants, The (Spence), 219, 221, 223
Rights of Man (Paine), 134, 168, 203, 204–5, 207, 210
Rights of Man to Property (Skidmore), 224
Rights of Nature, The (Thelwall), 212
Rights of Property in Land, The (Ogilvie), 217
Rights of War and Peace, The (Grotius), 10, 11, 18, 65
Right to the Whole Produce of Labor, The (Menger), 242
Roman law, 94, 95, 96, 114–15
Rotten boroughs, 134
Rousseau, Jean-Jacques, 116
Ruggles, Thomas, 133–34
Rutherforth, Thomas, 123–26, 127, 131, 217

Saint Simonians, 238
Savings, 241–42
Say, J. B., 179, 198
Scotland, 72, 74, 87–88, 101, 108; union with England, 73; gentry in, 112
Scottish Enlightenment, 55, 72, 73, 101, 102, 106, 113, 121–22, 173
Scriptural law, 32–33
Scrope, G. Poulet, 196–97, 199, 200, 242
Seizure, 13–14, 25, 49, 254. *See also* Possession

DATE DUE

			Printed in USA

HIGHSMITH #45230